THE GRIND

THE NEW HANDBOOK FOR SUCCESS

THE GRIND

ERIC THOMAS

TATE PUBLISHING
AND ENTERPRISES, LLC

The Grind
Copyright © 2015 by Eric Thomas. All rights reserved.

No part of this publication may be reproduced, stored in a retrieval system or transmitted in any way by any means, electronic, mechanical, photocopy, recording or otherwise without the prior permission of the author except as provided by USA copyright law.

This book is designed to provide accurate and authoritative information with regard to the subject matter covered. This information is given with the understanding that neither the author nor Tate Publishing, LLC is engaged in rendering legal, professional advice. Since the details of your situation are fact dependent, you should additionally seek the services of a competent professional.

The opinions expressed by the author are not necessarily those of Tate Publishing, LLC.

Published by Tate Publishing & Enterprises, LLC
127 E. Trade Center Terrace | Mustang, Oklahoma 73064 USA
1.888.361.9473 | www.tatepublishing.com

Tate Publishing is committed to excellence in the publishing industry. The company reflects the philosophy established by the founders, based on Psalm 68:11,
"The Lord gave the word and great was the company of those who published it."

Book design copyright © 2015 by Tate Publishing, LLC. All rights reserved.
Cover design by Joana Quilantang
Interior design by Jake Muelle

Published in the United States of America

ISBN: 978-1-68118-848-5
Self-Help / Personal Growth / Success
15.10.08

First and foremost, this book is dedicated to God from whom all things are possible. This book is also dedicated to my Mother and Father, who sacrificed so much of their lives to give me opportunity and always showed me, by example, the true meaning of hard work.

Contents

Introduction 9
Start Grinding 23
Examples of the Grind 41
Compete on a Higher Level 67
Never Give Up 131
Doing What Others Won't....................... 159
Grind Work Ethic 181
Improving Your Professional Self 203
Habits.. 233
Matters of the Mind........................... 247
Performance 269
Excellence.................................... 325

Criticism.	345
Mood	367
Grinding with Others.	381
Don't Dos of the Grind	395
Strategies to Keep You On the Grind.	423
Bibliography	443

Introduction

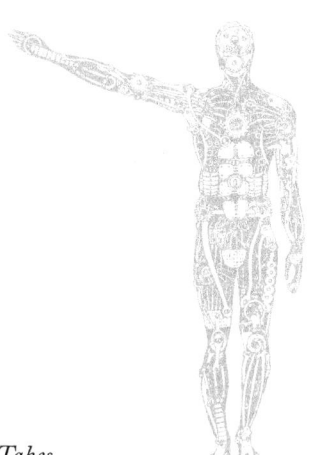

Whatever It Takes
—Author Unknown

*Effort only fully releases its reward
after a person refuses to quit.*
—Napoleon Hill

*There are no secrets to success. It is the result of
preparation, hard work, and learning from failure.*
—Colin Powell

The Grind. Over the years my definition of the term has evolved to incorporate a list of requirements to succeed in business and almost all lifelong endeavors. In my life, I remember the term being used by members of the workforce, from corporate to self employed alike; often used to describe their efforts for success in the careers they chose to pursue. The terms' multidimensional meaning also encompassed the often-dreaded work that could ensue from the "the daily grind." However, the ones who understood that the Grind was an integral part of success and utilized it effectively were the same ones who would set the pace for the members of their respective fields of employment.

As I write this I can recall an instance where this term had manifested itself in a simple real life situation. I had just walked into the post office to deliver packages to fulfill orders for my website online store. As usual the lines in the post office were long and people were waiting for their turn to submit their packages. Of course the postal workers had become irate from the steady influx of customers who added more activity than the anticipated "stamp and mail" routine the clerks had wished for. Three young men in their early twenties walked in carrying shoulder bags and various products including picture frames, hair clippers, and toys. The postal worker, obviously recognizing them from earlier exploits in the station and former attempts to solicit, announced that they were to leave and that "selling" products in the facility was not permitted. Two of them, in efforts of avoiding potential embarrassment and rejection, proceeded to the exit door.

Without hesitation, one of the salesmen said, "I'm not selling these things, I'm giving them away for free." Immediately, everyone in the room turned around and looked at the salesman who had just mentioned their favorite word. The salesman then said, "I can't give all these things away, but I'll throw in a few of these items for free with the purchase of some of my other products," all the while keeping their attention by showing his products.

In the end, he was able to quickly sell a couple items to some people in line as the postal workers gave in to the interest from their customers. He did not take no for an answer and anticipated the situation to keep doors open for success at his intended task. He took what was negative attention, which was the postal worker reprimanding him, and used it as a way to gain attention from potential customers. His progressive actions distinguished him from the other two individuals who had accompanied him into the post office that day.

The Grind should involve more than just going to work and earning a paycheck, but instead appreciated as a level of effort which determines the outcome for success. The emphasis on the details is what makes the outcome favorable. It's the attention to detail like Sam Walton of Walmart and the practice of greeting his customers and directing them to the appropriate product aisles making the shopping experience effortless, or Michael Dell involving himself in all the functions of Dell Computers from customer service to product development to gain a thorough understanding of all aspects of his company in order to create synergy within all the different departments of the company. No matter what forum it's included in, the Grind is significant to all genres of business.

* * *

In a series of studies by Angela L. Duckworth, Michael D. Matthews, Dennis R. Kelly, and Christopher Peterson of the University of Pennsylvania, the subject of grit brought about many interesting findings. "We define grit as perseverance and passion for long-term goals. Grit entails working strenuously toward challenges, maintaining effort and interest over years despite failure, adversity, and plateaus in progress." The purpose of the study was to find the relation that the trait of grit had upon success.

A Grit Scale consisting of a self-report questionnaire was developed to study factors related to higher achieving individuals. These studies dictated that grit was a valid factor toward achievement and may be just as significant as a person's intelligence, in pursuit of success. During interviews of professionals in fields as diverse as medicine to journalism, interviewees attributed their success to grit or one of its similar terms such as perseverance, persistence, will, or drive, in equivalent frequency to talent. In six of the studies conducted, Duckworth found that subjects with grit maintained higher grade point averages, remained longer at programs with intense regimen, obtained higher levels of education, and had fewer career changes.

The relevancy at hand is that very few factors may contribute to making a person smarter, but the possibilities of cultivating grit and higher levels of effort may be a significant option for success. A person may choose to develop this trait and implement it in greater intensity with practice of its methods. This is one of the significant characteristics of the Grind; the continued practice of unyielding effort.

* * *

A personal trainer once told me that the true benefits of lifting weights came in the final repetitions in a training set when a burning feeling is felt in the muscles. Those last repetitions, when fatigue has taken over and the temptation is felt to put the weights down, are when your action matters most and when you get the most results. This is when the trainee should focus his energy and use his remaining resources to continue with additional repetitions. That "burn" is tearing of the muscle which then heals and produces a larger one in its place, adding bulk to the body. If the trainee stops short and does not achieve this additional effort, all his previous actions are in vain and very little results are achieved.

This scenario is very similar to most people's efforts in the workplace. They accommodate the initial workload which gets them by but fall short of the necessary actions that will bring them ultimate success. The stages when the potential gain is usually realized becomes the time when they prematurely cease action or change the focus of their efforts. Most of the time all that is required is the addition of a little more persistence and exploration of options to get past the current hardship.

That "burn" which you may also feel in your professional career can serve as an indication that you are truly benefiting from your diligence. Welcome this stage as it is an opportunity and an indication of progress. How many times have we seen this situation transpire in past business models? Howard Schultz, the CEO and Chairman of Starbucks Corporation, was not the original founder of Starbucks. He joined the company in its early stages and helped shape the company for its future success. Without his ideas of turning Starbucks into a coffee bar retail chain and expanding into the international marketplace, the company may very well still be contained to the Seattle region. He took a promising entity which he believed in and provided the extra action which resulted in the "burn" stages the company needed to grow.

Also, let's examine Ray Kroc's involvement in the building of the McDonald's empire. His conveyer belt theory of making burgers provided McDonald's outlets the ability to produce quality burgers which tasted the same no matter which store you visited. He also did not start McDonald's but provided the insight and vision to produce a company with international notoriety. He took the initial idea and added his own formula to produce the "burn" stage for the company to grow to its current status. The aforementioned term, *burn*, can be thought of as a synonym of the Grind and embodies the very essence of its characteristics.

* * *

The grind is a multifaceted approach which can help anyone accomplish the goals they choose to commit to. Its characteristics are practiced by some of the most successful and accomplished individuals and companies in today's world of business. They are grounded in traditional business practice and can be found in countless examples of those who have succeeded. The practitioner may implement its features to create a habit for high achievement and efficiency. This habitualization can become a new individual standard that becomes common practice in daily operation. It provides a guide to differentiate yourself from the level of efforts which has become commonplace in today's workplace. The user utilizes their own abilities to increase any thresholds present and establishes their own standards of peak achievement.

As previously mentioned, the Grind provides the "burn" stages to take the results of your labor to higher stages of success and help you reach levels most never attain. Top performance is encouraged and becomes the average for the desired outcome of excellence. It is the act of working with a purpose in mind and turning your profession into more than an entity for financial gain. It is a cause which brings meaning to your work and inspires on a personal level of involvement. Hopefully, it will not only benefit yourself, but others who work around you.

The grind focuses on direction of actions with tasks specifically targeted for an intended outcome. Time is of the essence and there is no time to waste in today's fast-paced world. It is inspired and driven by your passion and requires for you to find love in what you decide to engage in. It is an outlet for creativity which allows the individual to express their own true unique strengths and abilities. The unyielding will and drive to achieve all the things you dream of and the perception to make them a reality. The realization that every act is one of significance that can change your reality. It is the inner need for you to exceed all expectations and do all things with perfection.

* * *

The process of natural selection favors any species best adapted for its environment. In nature we see that dominance has its requirements, as coined by the phrase "survival of the fittest." Whether they are quicker, smarter, stronger, or possess any other advantages, those that are superior in any species will outlast their counterparts. With human beings, it is no different. You may not be able to change features such as some physical attributes, but it is possible to develop certain skills that can help you in life.

In business this is certainly the case and the workplace has its own process of selection. Success is reserved for those who are willing to work and acquire the skills to put them in the position of prosperity. Most prefer to take the direction of ease and this constitutes the thinking of the average person in the workplace. In order to include yourself in the company of the "fittest," you must be willing to do more than most people will do. Just like in nature, we must position ourselves for professional survival and this often means hardships in the process. The fittest are justified by being challenged in their environment and earning their place. This process weeds out the unqualified. It is the same with animals in nature that are weaker and are not able to adapt to their environments, struggling with their existence. It is a harsh reality similar to those in the business world reduced to barely getting by or living paycheck to paycheck.

Why should you make the effort? Because if you don't someone else will take the initiative to raise the standards in your field and you may soon find yourself obsolete. It is business nature that all situations will evolve due to the competitive nature of success. Make no mistake that the current level of competition requires you to push yourself to higher levels. With a growing population, globalization, and technological advancements, today's professional must adapt to the quickly changing environment.

The Grind seeks to give the practitioner the edge to earn one's place amongst the successful in any field. It embodies the characteristics for business survival. Don't expect to be comforted with falsehood that there is an easy formula you can follow for success that you will find in this book. I will tell you right now that competing at higher standards is not an easy process but is one which is necessary.

Contemplate the rewards which can be a result of your hard work and the opportunities available to better the conditions in your life. Fortune truly favors those who position themselves according to its requirements. Better to embrace it with proper preparation than to have any upcoming obstacles dictate you an unfavorable conclusion. We have the option of choices only until the reality of the situation starts making its own demands. Control what you can today so that you will continue to have choices available tomorrow. Don't just conform to regular standards but make the effort to place yourself amongst the fittest.

* * *

One of the purposes of this book is to enable you to perform at your absolute highest levels of performance. To do so you must accentuate your current strengths and abilities, as well as improve and develop others, which can add to your resources. You may already possess some of the characteristics mentioned in this book. Some characteristics are also more relevant in some fields than others and you must use your own discretion to formulate a system that works for your own particular situation.

Bruce Lee combined his own ideas with other classical martial arts he learned throughout the years with different masters to form his own style called Jeet Kune Do. He took the best of all the arts including his modified version of Wing Chun combined with western boxing technique and fencing. His perspective of training was wide enough to cover training in Epee, Judo, Praying Mantis, Hsing-I, Jujitsu, and others. He also drew upon the significance of proper nutrition and formulated his diet to give him the proper supplements to perform at his best. Weight training and exercise was all part of his rigorous regimen and he focused on all areas which may help in the improvement of his art and profession.

A business personality is the characteristics that you display when you are in your professional environment. They are your strengths and abilities and the way you exert yourself in your field of work. When seeking to establish your business personality and your own definition of the Grind, you may choose to do so in the same manner Bruce Lee created his style. There is no conclusive, correct formula for engaging in business. We would all be successful if someone had all the answers for guaranteed success. Factors surrounding every situation are different and complicated with variables such as field of employment, timing, ability, competition, circumstance, and many others.

If you were to question a number of prominent businessmen as to their reasons for success, their answers would vary in many regards. Does that mean that their practices are not valid? No, it just goes to show that there are a variety of different approaches to conducting business in their respective fields. Sometimes it is the unorthodox practices that yield great success. Innovation and creativity can bring about new breakthroughs of progress. Business, just like everything else, is always changing and keeping current must be constant. What has worked for someone else may not work for you and vice versa. Business is as varied as the people who participate in it. You must gain intuition by the experience of actually participating in your desired profession. Trust your own instinct but also know when to listen to the advice of others. There is a fine line between success and failure and sometimes it rests upon the smallest of conditions.

In this book, there may appear to be loose ends or a lack of advice as to the exact course of action. The truth is that each situation is unique and distinct with every person. I try to give a broad range of examples from the success of others and suggestions that may be considered. Your responsibility lies in establishing your own formula for success in your own unique situation. At the beginning stages of your career, be fully receptive to information and knowledge that will help you discern between future decisions. When you are in the position to take your own direction, do so with full faith in yourself with all the things that you have learned. Included in this book are other business practices that must accompany the Grind. These are necessities which will make success of its practice more effective. These supplement the Grind and help further its effectiveness. As previously mentioned, some are grounded in business tradition and therefore I detail them in this book as they must be acknowledged.

Take the fundamental characteristics, such as hard work, determination, perseverance, knowledge, and commitment, which have worked for those who have found success, and combine them with others you will need to achieve your goals. These characteristics can span over a myriad of different fields but may be applied to your own distinguished career. Study what has worked for others in varying fields and do not limit your search. Use your strengths and abilities as the basis of your business personality, but add the needed elements to supplement your professional assets.

Start Grinding

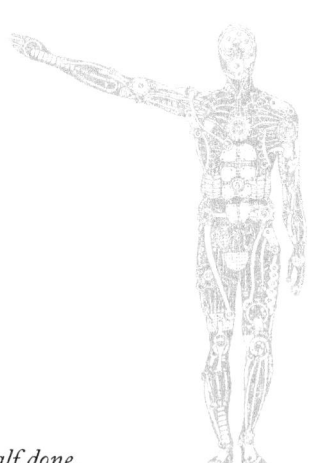

Well begun is half done.
—Aristotle

*I'd rather regret the things I've done
than regret the things I haven't done.*
—Lucille Ball

*The way to get started is to quit talking
and begin doing.*
—Walt Disney

Sometimes all it takes is one moment to change your reality, so make sure you are at all times receptive to these opportunities. According to the conclusion of scientists, the earth has been in existence for over four and a half billion years. In comparison, our lives seem like just one small moment in time. When I think of life in these terms, this makes me realize how little time we really have to make our mark, showing the significance of our existence. Every passing minute seems to be that more elusive. Make sure you value every minute as an opportunity to get you where you would like to be in the future.

If I told you many years ago that I was going to create a fantasy based land where cartoons and animations would come to life and make up its surroundings, you would probably think I was crazy. This is exactly what Walt Disney was able to visualize and make a reality with Disneyland. If I were to tell you that a town in America was built based on the theme of chocolate, with related street names and chocolate kiss shaped street lights, you would probably think this could only exist in a story book. Hershey is an actual town in Pennsylvania, complete with schools, museums, and public transportation, thanks to the efforts of Milton Hershey. If I were to tell you some time ago that there was going to be a brand of coffee shop with locations all over the world, on almost every street corner in the US, and would be one of the world's most profitable companies, you would probably think I was delusional. Starbucks, thanks to the efforts of Howard Schultz, maintains this presence and has started a whole new culture of coffee enthusiasts.

The things we view as impossible or farfetched have already taken shape in the minds of many who have new ideas to offer the world. The only limitation is whether that individual takes action. In doing so, the person can risk so much. Failure, spent finances, wasted time, and energy may all be the sacrifices in pursuit of a dream. But as the examples mentioned previously prove to us, nothing is impossible and some of the greatest ideas have been based on absurd, almost unfathomable levels of imagination and effort in making them a reality.

In show business, it is often said that you are your own worst critic. I believe that the same is true in any pursuit and we must first come to grips with our own self doubt. Sometimes our ideas have the potential to change the world, as many others have done in the past, so the risk may just be worth the reward. The true risk may just be in the fact that we don't enable ourselves to make our dreams and goals a reality. It is a true shame if we never pursue the very thing that we were put on this earth to accomplish. However, imagination is not enough to turn our ideas into substantiated accomplishment. The desire to turn our goals into a reality has to be strong enough for us to initiate action.

It is always the start that requires the greatest effort.
—James Cash Penney

Many examples of great achievement have started with very modest beginnings. Some started with an individual simply discovering a discrepancy in a field and filling the demand. There were others who chose to pursue something that they had a passion for. These individuals saw an opportunity and simply initiated action. They didn't necessarily plan that their efforts would end up on a grand scale or achieve the elaborate success that they eventually went on to accomplish. In fact, many of their beginnings were far from efforts of extensive planning and forecasting and they were eventually even surprised by the amount of success that was generated. They started the very thing that they found interest in and let their passion lead the way.

Daymond John, founder of clothing line FUBU and judge of TV show *Shark Tank*, was watching music videos and saw some of the musicians wearing wool hats that had their tops cut off and tied with a string. He wanted one of the hats but could not find one at a good price, so he used the sewing skills he learned from his mom to make his own. He found that they were popular and were being sold for $20, a price he thought was too much. He sewed eighty of these hats at home with his next door neighbor. They then went out and sold these hats at a lower price of $10 in front of the New York Coliseum and made $800 in a single day. This was one of the early experiences that led to the start of his company, FUBU, a clothing brand that is now recognized around the world and has gained much success with sales of several billion dollars worldwide.

When childhood friends Ben Cohen and Jerry Greenfield decided they wanted to open their own ice cream parlor, the two split the cost of a $5 correspondence course on ice cream making at Penn State University. They then began churning out their own concoctions of wild flavors inspired by experiments Cohen used to make as a kid, mixing ice cream, candy, and cookies. Ben & Jerry's Ice Cream caught on immediately, and customers flocked to enjoy flavors such as Cherry Garcia, Chubby Hubby, and Milli Vanilla which mixed fresh Vermont milk and cream with all their favorite chunks of fruit, nuts, cookies, and other fun ingredients. Even though neither one of them knew anything about starting a business, they invested their life savings and a small loan totaling $12,000 to open their first location in a renovated gas station. From there they managed to build their business into a global chain with over a quarter of a billion dollars in sales.

Zhu Yuanzhang is one of the great people in history whose example of taking action and initiative changed the course of history. Zhu came from extreme poverty and humble beginnings. Founder of the Ming Dynasty, he became the emperor of China during the thirteenth century. Zhu's parents died when he was young. As the youngest of four brothers, the conditions were so bad and food supply so short that his other siblings were given away. Left alone to fend for himself, he begged for food and found shelter in a Buddhist monastery. It was there that he learned to read and write at the late age of twenty-four. The monastery was eventually destroyed by the Mongol Army, and Zhu joined a local rebel group to seek revenge. His natural leadership traits quickly earned him the position as the head of the rebel group. When they soon joined the Red Turban movement, he became their leader as well. He went on to conquer and take control of the cities in China and eventually became its emperor. He is proof that starting and initiating action can lead to endless possibilities! No matter the obstacles, success is surmountable if we are willing to begin the process.

> *The secret of getting ahead is getting started.*
> —Mark Twain

I am a firm believer that every person has the ability to create their own opportunities in life and there is nothing that is unattainable with the presence of passion, creativity, and tenacity. Some may just start with less and have to implement more effort, which in turn makes the success that much more gratifying. However, it takes great sacrifice to be the exception. Unfortunately, it is the standard to perform on an average basis. Most will do just enough to get by and keep their jobs or businesses afloat. They compare themselves to others in their fields and compete at just the level to try to stay competitive. They do not explore all options and find a way to exceed the average and they quit prematurely when results are not immediate. Self evaluation is not practiced to assess true potential; therefore, no breakthroughs are made into professional prominence. Hatred of the job or career is commonplace and a distraction from excellence. It is a shame these individuals do not even realize they are the very reason they cannot get ahead.

If you aspire for more or do not currently feel that you are exercising your full potential, initiate change and get started. Take note of the many others who have defied all odds in the past and have created a better reality for themselves. It may even be your manager or a coworker you come in contact with on a daily basis. It is not impossible to accomplish any of your desires but it first takes your commitment in doing so. Commitment is made up of your dedication and the willingness to compete through blood, sweat, and tears to accomplish your goals. It is really your choice whether or not you will put yourself in the right position to succeed.

* * *

Every great person has been required to start at the initial stages and prove their abilities, just like everyone else. There is no exclusion from the requirements to test our worthiness in any given profession. The most prominent in any field neglects their fears and objections and initiates action toward the success they desire. No matter the obstacles that lay ahead, they enter the forum embracing the opportunity to prove their worth. Many conclude that great success is not available to every person. They use excuses such as not having enough capital, ability, or opportunity as reasons for shortcomings. This is simply just an excuse.

Ely Callaway, founder of Callaway Golf, started the company when he was sixty years old. Most would not have the courage to initiate such an undertaking at this age. He did not use his age as an excuse and turned the company into one of the premier manufacturers of products for the game of golf. He had the vision of creating quality, innovative golf clubs superior to the rival companies which at the time mostly produced mediocre, industry conforming products. Back then, golf clubs had very few distinguishable features and consumers were left with limited features for personalization. The company's most famous club, the "Big Bertha," has now become the most popular club product sold to golfers and the company sells more golf clubs than any of the rival manufacturing firms. The company has forever changed the game of golf, and had it not been for Ely's determination to defy the odds, this success would not have been possible.

> *It is better to offer no excuse than a bad one.*
> —George Washington

Most people will find excuses that will enable them to justify that they don't have all that is required to make a start. Whether the excuse is that they do not have the finances, knowledge, time, or any other reason, they will find some justification to limit their own progress. However, anything that you really want can be attained as long as you are willing to commit to the effort required.

Marc Cuban, owner of the Dallas Mavericks and judge of TV show *Shark Tank*," wasn't knowledgeable about the tech field and didn't know a thing about computers when he first started out but took the initiative of spending many late nights learning about the subject by reading manuals, books, magazines, and anything else he could get his hands on. He went on to use this knowledge to make his first millions selling the company he created, Microsystems, which was a reseller of local-area network and connectivity products.

Many people maintain the belief that in order to make money, you have to have a great deal of money to start with. "It takes money to make money" is a common phrase stated in relation to this assumption. It is definitely true that there are more opportunities available when you start with a budget, but it is not the only way to achieve success. There have been countless examples of individuals who have started with very little and amassed great fortunes.

When you think of the name Wrigley, you automatically think of gum. The William Wrigley Jr. Company is the biggest gum manufacturer in the world with its products in 180 countries and thirty separate languages around the globe. The company maintains 140 factories in various countries, and produces different flavors to cater to each region's taste. By the time of his death in 1932, the company reached revenues of $75 million, which increased to over $5 billion worldwide by 2008. Wrigley proved that you don't have to start with a lot of money to succeed, and when he moved from Philadelphia to Chicago to start his business, he only had $32 in his pocket. Wrigley may not have had much money to start with, but he made up for it by his perseverance and by paying attention to what his customers wanted. He emphasized quality and was quoted as saying, "Even in a little thing like a stick of gum, quality is important."

Gela Nash-Taylor and Pam Skaist-Levy launched Juicy Couture with a mere $200 each of their own money and a revolving credit line. The two began modestly, starting their operations out of a one-bedroom apartment in Los Angeles. They didn't pay themselves for the first two years, opting to reinvest earnings directly back into the business. They created the brand based off clothing they would want in their own closets and the Juicy line caught on, quickly selling $1 million worth of their products in the first year. The line is stocked at department stores such as Bloomingdale's, Saks Fifth Avenue, and Nordstrom, and the company has since opened their own Juicy Couture retail stores in locations nationwide. They have also expanded the brand throughout the years, adding men's and kid's lines, accessories, handbags, shoes, fragrances, sunglasses, swimwear, and watches. Juicy received great notoriety when their signature velour track suits were photographed on the likes of celebrities such as Madonna, Gwen Stefani, Kate Moss, and many others. By 2002, the company achieved sales of $47 million. A year later, Liz Claiborne, Inc. bought Juicy Couture in a deal rumored to be about $90 million. The company has been growing and expanding ever since with estimated sales of well over $200 million annually.

There are countless examples of individuals who have started with limited resources and were able to achieve success. What all these individuals had in common is that they were not afraid to initiate the process and get started in pursuing their success. They did not talk themselves out of acting by finding excuses not to do so. Of course, there were many obstacles along the way but all of them were eventually able to find a way to persevere. Too often our actions are stuck in the procrastination stages and we won't even get far enough to give up. You must plan thoroughly and gain as much knowledge of the field that you would like to get involved with as possible. This preparation will increase the willingness to initiate the process, the step in which most of us never advance from. The truth is that we are usually our own biggest obstacle in success and our own preconceived notions often make the situation more difficult than it has to be.

> *If you have the courage to begin, you
> have the courage to succeed.*
>
> —David Viscott

The initiation of one action usually begets the ease of additional actions. We stretch so we can warm up to jog. We may jog to pace ourselves to sprint. We sprint and gradually gain our ideal speed. Action follows a flow which results in momentum being established. It is very similar to the process of a snow avalanche. Small movement, vibration or sound vibrations cause movement of particles of soil, ice, branches, etc. This collection of materials begins to move down a slope and once more particles collect, the mass begins to grow. As it makes its way down the mountain, the speed, mass, and collection of more objects increases its effect. It turns into a great force. All it takes is a small trigger and this little movement turns into a great natural force.

It is the same in business, and you will find that after you make a start your momentum will add various resources which will help you finish. With small accomplishments comes inspiration to continue on to larger pursuits. As we gain more experience in our profession, the knowledge we begin to accumulate makes our responsibilities more manageable. We gain other resources along the way such as additional financial support, more connections to others and their help, and increased confidence which also makes our forward progression stronger. Therefore, we must find any way that we can initiate action, even if the movement is subtle at the beginning. Its value is of great worth.

* * *

It is a challenge to figure where to start as this will determine the course of action for our goals. Following the wrong course may leave you distracted and misdirected. You don't want to work on something just to later realize that your efforts were worthless toward the achievement of that particular goal. Planning is itself an action and is the best way to get started. If you don't know where to start then begin by planning and preparing a blueprint for your actions. Don't get stuck in the planning stages or get into the habit of over thinking the details. Some people exhaust themselves planning and never even begin the action. Difficult conditions are mostly just situations which we have not been previously exposed to or been forced to adapt to. If you expose yourself to these situations you will find that they are manageable and surmountable so long as you have a desire or necessity to do so.

People often view goal setting and execution as a routine effort universally deemed necessary by "business tradition" or educational requirements learned earlier in life and end up highly underestimating its necessities and benefits. Unfortunately, New Year's Resolutions are examples of ways people usually set up and accommodate their goals. It is such a common practice that it is rare that these goals are actually carried out to completion. For many, these resolutions lose priority after just a few weeks and the tasks are postponed to a later time once we acknowledge again their significance. We know that we want a desired outcome but the process is more difficult when applied to real life situations. Once things become difficult to execute, we give up.

Then the following year it's the same ritual once again, as if our minds were conditioned to follow this common practice. For many, this example can be a model of their goal setting and execution. We can also draw examples from the college level, where it is common to find the absence of planning and concise goal setting. There are many who go to college for a specific degree and end up working in an entirely different field they focused their academics on. Ineffective planning and noncommitted decision making, free from long-term consideration, is usually the reason. Many also choose to change majors and jump from one to the other as their thinking changes with more experiences. This is the same thing which often happens in the workplace.

It should be stressed to always set realistic and attainable goals when you plan. Be as detailed as possible and plan for ways to execute each task including variations which may occur. None of your goals should conflict with each other and ultimate goals and subgoals should work in unison with one another. Subgoals should directly compliment and lead up to the completion of your ultimate goals. Try to set the least amount of goals possible for you to achieve your desires and finish your initial goals before establishing more. The goals should be able to be visualized in proximity and a time of accomplishment should be within grasp. Setting them beyond your reach will make them seem unattainable or less of a priority as time passes by. Knowing your potential is very important when setting goals as they should not be set with levels of difficulty which will deter you from pursuit or accomplishment. Another key factor when creating your goals is to consider how they will be carried out. Your goals should be established in conjunction with a detailed plan of action which guides you through every step toward completion. Making these action plans more thorough bring greater chances for success and leave less room for abandonment or error. Preferably, these actions should be in line with your potential strengths and abilities or attainable by delegation within your resources. Plan for the variations that can result and give yourself realistic solutions to the problems you will encounter.

> *Twenty years from now you will be more disappointed by the things that you didn't do than by the ones you did do, so throw off the bowlines, sail away from safe harbor, catch the trade winds in your sails. Explore, Dream, Discover.*
>
> —Mark Twain

One day someone asked if I remembered my great, great, great grandfather. I answered no. Then he proceeded to ask if I remembered my great, great grandfather. Again my answer was no. He continued to ask me this same question about other previous family members. I gave him the same answer. He then told me, "Do you know why? It's because they never did anything in their lives worth remembering." As harsh as this may seem, I realized it was the truth.

If you are not content with your current situation then it is time to take action in changing your reality. Delaying a start and not considering the limitations of time may run the risk of an opportunity passing you by. Time is a commodity that none of us can afford. As a result we should value it as such. Be honest, and consider whether your reason for not doing something warrants legitimate reasoning or is just a list of excuses.

Most people are afraid of the unknown even if it sometimes leads to success or growth. It is comfortable to remain in familiar surroundings. If you conclude that your goal may be attainable and your desires may allow you to commit, then there is no time to delay. The worst thing is wasted potential. The Grind is only relevant if you begin its process. I have been fortunate to talk to many people in higher age brackets who have lived their share of life's experiences. Their experiences give insight into real life events and the wisdom gained through lessons learned throughout a lifetime. It is of great value to be provided an outlet to learn through their mistakes.

One of the most common things that come up in conversation is the longing for another chance to take a missed opportunity that had passed by. Comments made such as, "I wish I had…," "If I could do it all again I would…," or "If I was your age again I would…" are indications of regret. I realize from these conversations that the time they are speaking of is my present time. I am in the position to never utter those words when I get to be their age. I want to spend my golden years content in how I lived my life, not the regrets of passed opportunity.

Some form of action, even if it results in short term failure equals progression toward a goal. Better to have tried than to regret your inactiveness thus remaining in a miserable situation. By doing nothing you are simply ensuring that no progress or change will apply to your current situation. For me, the simple action toward an intended goal provides momentum toward additional actions of progression. It serves our competitive nature to instigate action and put ourselves in a forum where we can display our strengths and abilities. Remember, without a start we never really place ourselves in the position to succeed.

Examples of the Grind

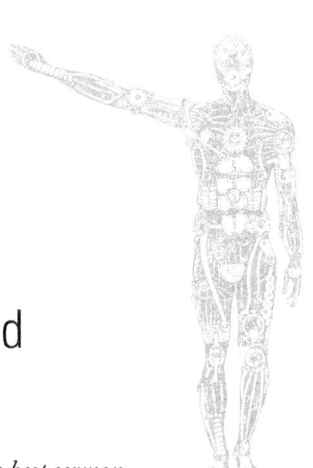

A good example is the best sermon.
—Thomas Fuller

Example has more followers than reason. We unconsciously imitate what pleases us, and approximate to the characters we most admire.
—Christian Nevell Bovee

Setting an example is not the main means of influencing another, it is the only means.
—Albert Einstein

The following chapter contains examples of a number of accomplished individuals whose pursuit of success have been achieved by implementing the characteristics of the Grind. These individuals come from all walks of life and their own particular situations are as diverse as life may possibly encompass. Take the time to analyze the following examples and notice the details which have contributed to their success. Acknowledge the level of effort that was required for these people to attain their success. Compare this to your own situation and determine whether you are employing the same amount of dedication in your own situation. None of these people have been blessed with a level of ability which cannot be matched by anyone else if they so desired. Some may possess extraordinary talent or ability but it is no different than the potential we may possess for our own specific areas of interest. We just have to take the time to identify what it is our own individual strengths are, and exploit them to fit our own situation. Everyone has their own gifts, it just requires the assertiveness to put ourselves in the right position to succeed. Some of these individuals have gained great notoriety and others are people who we may come across in our daily lives. They come from various background, social classes, and time periods. This is proof that there are no set requirements to become successful, and achievement is available to anyone who is willing to put forth the work.

* * *

Julia Stewart is the quintessential example of the rewards of hard work and determination, a person who started at the ground floor of a company only to work through the ranks to become its CEO. Stewart's ambition was apparent at a young age, starting at fourteen years old when she sold Hoover vacuums over the phone and later worked at a retail store selling waterbeds. At sixteen, she was waiting tables as a waitress at IHOP, a company she would later run. After decades of employment at restaurant chains such as Burger King, Carl's Jr., Taco Bell, Black Angus, and Applebees, she rejoined IHOP in 2001. By 2002, she was CEO of IHOP, using her years of experiences in the restaurant business to breathe new life in the restaurant chain's operations.

She increased the company's cash flow by selling IHOP restaurants to franchisees. In efforts to keep the tired chain up to date, she pushed franchisees to remodel their restaurants every few years, and update all tables, carpet, and lighting. Stewart improved the menu, such as selling fresh-squeezed orange juice and adding better quality coffee. She added new menu items like cream cheese-stuffed French toast and other interesting items which enhanced the old menu. As a result of her efforts, IHOP reported a $45 million profit and its stock prices doubled in 2006. She was able to lead IHOP through eighteen consecutive quarters of growth by implementing her franchise business model.

DineEquity was formed in 2007, when Stewart was responsible for leading IHOP in a takeover of Applebee's for about $2 billion. DineEquity, where Stewart serves as chairman and CEO, formed by the merger of IHOP and Applebee's, franchises and operates over 3,500 restaurants globally in eighteen countries with a workforce of over 175,000 employees. The food she supervises is consumed by nearly two million people a day. In 2007, Stewart was ranked forty-ninth on *Forbes Magazine*'s list of the Fifty Most Powerful Women.

People who know her describe her as a tough boss, a perfectionist who demands results. She is known for constantly visiting the restaurants in her chains to make sure that they are performing at optimum level. Some say her attention to detail can be excruciating. For example, one of her visits to one of her franchised restaurant involved her checking to make sure all menu items are up to her exacting standards, down to the detail of each chicken nugget and strip being made to a specific size and receiving the correct mixture of coatings and seasonings. She moves very fast and has little patience for those who place blame on factors such as the economy, competition or other excuses. Her drive is attributed to her love of the restaurant business and she has stated, "I fell in love with the restaurant business. I love the constant feedback. I love the interaction with the guests. I love the ability to make a difference in someone's life in thirty-five minutes or forty minutes, from the day I went in the restaurant and put on the uniform and felt proud to be a part of IHOP."

* * *

Dr. Dre is one of hip hop's most iconic music producers, a Grammy winner who has achieved great success with a career which has endured the span of over thirty years. Few are able to achieve high levels of success in both the creative and corporate forums, and Dre has been able to conquer both, doubling as a business man who occupies the second position on the Forbes Hip Hop's Wealthiest Artists List for 2014, with a net worth of $550 million. Perhaps most recognized to the mass public for his company which produces the hugely profitable line of headphones, Beats by Dr. Dre, he has created a brand whose value is quickly soaring toward $2 billion. Dre stays busy with a variety of endeavors including his own brand of cognac, endorsement deals with Hewlett-Packard, Dr. Pepper, Chrysler, and Coors Light, and a number of music releases he executive produces on his label, Aftermath Entertainment. He has fathered the careers of many music greats, providing productions and direction for many artists including Snoop Dogg, Eminem, 50 Cent, Tupac, and a number of others. Dealt a bad hand in his dealings in the music business early in his career, he was often the victim of record labels who would exploit his talents making huge profits for themselves, only to leave him with the lowest levels of compensation for his work. At one point, he had to walk away from a record label he built, Death Row Records, reportedly with very little financial gain. But as a testament that hard work, determination, and love for what you do contributes greatly toward success, he continued onward and in 2012 was acknowledged by Forbes as the world's highest paid musician. Almost every artist who has had the privilege of working with Dre has stated that he is a perfectionist with extremely high standards. This can be the very reason why *Detox*, an album the producer has claimed will be his last solo album, has been in the works for over thirteen years, and still has no release date established as of yet. It is rumored by those who have worked on the project with him that he has already recorded over four hundred songs with various artists, but is unwilling to release the record until he deems the project "perfect" according to his standards. In an interview with an artist who recorded a song in the studio with Dre, it was mentioned that the super producer required that he deliver his lyrics over thirty times in efforts to conform to the producer's exacting standards. In addition to his own personal standards, he has been known to demand the same level of output from the artists he works with, often "pressuring" them to give flawless performances. He simply does not settle for any mediocrity. There is no doubt that this dedication to perfection has paid off, as his productions and performances have generated revenues of over a billion dollars. His work ethic is exceptional as he regularly keeps long hours in the studio, despite his financial status, still working every day to perfect his craft. He revealed in an interview that he has set a personal record of seventy-nine nonstop hours recording in the studio. Dre's career is littered with the implementation of many of the characteristics of the Grind, including his unyielding pursuit for perfection, intense work ethic, perseverance and making the decision to do things that other's would not have done, and all these have been contributing factors to his success. He is as good an example as any, for a person who loves what they do and someone who embodies the very essence of the Grind.

* * *

Milton Hershey "The Chocolate King" was born in Derry Church, Pennsylvania. His parents moved the family around frequently and Milton ended up attending six different schools before the fourth grade. Although they were poor, his parents instilled in him the value of hard work. Education was not a strong point in his life and Milton never got past the fourth grade leaving him essentially illiterate, although he never stopped learning the skills of the trade he would eventually devote his life to.

He began his career in candy with an apprenticeship with Joseph Royer, a Lancaster confectioner, and by the time he was eighteen years old he started his own candy shop in Philadelphia. His aunt funded the venture with $150 of seed money to get him started. Despite his hard work, making the candy at night and selling it throughout the day, the business failed after six years. He then moved to Denver, Colorado, to take on a job for a caramel maker. He ended up working there for about a year and then moved to Chicago but found that there was too much competition out there in the candy business. He moved and tried to establish his candy business in New Orleans, then in New York, but found no success in either area. He then acquired equipment to start a cough drop business but this eventually led to his fifth failed attempt.

Undaunted with his past failures and unwilling to give up, he tried again moving to Lancaster to produce caramels. At this point his family declined to loan him any further money to support his ventures and he entered into a partnership with William Henry Lebkicher, a man he had hired in Philadelphia. The two formed the Lancaster Caramel Company, producing "Crystal A Caramels" which finally bought him the success he had been pursuing, making him a millionaire after selling the company.

Hershey had become interested in making chocolate which at the time was a luxury not afforded to everyone. His idea was to make it enjoyable to all and used the money he made from the sale of his business to start a new venture. He built a factory back home in Derry Church, in the middle of the neighboring dairy farms. This gave him the outlet of fresh milk, an ingredient he used to produce his milk chocolate. He revolutionized the chocolate business which became recognized for products like the "Hershey Bar" and "Hershey's Kisses."

With the success of the chocolate factory, Milton bought prosperity to the community. With a part of the earnings, Milton built affordable houses, parks, public transportation, and schools to enrich the lives of his employees and the people of the community. The town was named after him and the streetlights in the town were even shaped like the chocolate kisses his company produced. He gave selflessly and built the Milton Hershey School, which provided education for orphans enrolled from all over the United States. His Hershey School Trust was established to help administer his and his wife's fortune to the thousands he has helped over the years. He ended up donating his entire fortune to the trust after his wife's death, a living legacy that continues giving to this very day.

Even with the number of failures throughout the years, Hershey remained persistent with his goals, never leaving the candy business. He exposed himself to great risk, and was not afraid of moving to new areas and establishing new businesses. His family refused to loan him any further money after a few of the failures, which must have been very discouraging. However, he remained determined and eventually persevered creating one of the most successful candy companies in history. In the end, he was able to create a town which signified his life's work and became a legacy to carry on his cause of helping others.

* * *

Screenwriter, director, actor, and producer, Quentin Tarantino is no stranger to persistence and patience. One of the most distinctive and impactful talents of modern filmmaking, he is credited with movies such as *Pulp Fiction*, *Kill Bill*, *Reservoir Dogs*, *Inglorious Basterds*, and many others. His untraditional schooling consisted of a job as a clerk at a video store, viewing countless movies and writing scripts during his tenure. Known as a master crafter of clever and elaborate dialogue-driven scenes, his diligence in screenwriting often takes years of revisiting and rewriting to finalize his projects.

Such was the case of his movie, *Inglorious Basterds*, which was written over a span of over a decade. The story takes place in Nazi occupied France, where a group of Jewish

American soldiers, called the "Basterds," seek retribution through acts of violence and scalping of the heads of their enemies. Shosanna, who witnesses the murder of her family in the opening scenes of the movie, also seeks her own revenge on the Nazis. Both parties' plans eventually coincide during a gathering of the leaders of the Third Reich at a cinema in Paris that Shosanna owns and operates. The movies climax features the "Basterds" and Shosanna carrying out their plans for the Nazi's demise, simultaneously in the movie theatre. The movie stars Brad Pitt, as Lieutenant Aldo Rain, as the leader of the "Basterds." The film blends real and fictional characters creating an alternate reality carried out in true Tarantino style.

In the film's production notes, producer Lawrence Bender recounts viewing early scripts of the screenplay over ten years ago and thinking, "We've got to make this." But he would have to wait, as Tarantino went to work on other projects and would continue developing "Basterds" throughout the years. Eli Roth, an actor playing the role of Donny Donowitz in the film, says he first heard Tarantino read him the script in December of 2004. Years later, Roth said that Tarantino would call him and tell him he had written additional scenes for the movie. For over a decade there were numerous rewrites and revisions of the plots and various scenes and the final draft was eventually finalized in July of 2008.

Opening in 2009, the movie surpassed almost all expectations, resulting in making *Inglorious Basterds* Tarantino's highest grossing movie at the time worldwide. The calculated dialogue and intricate storylines in the movie are testament to the work that transpired in the creation of the film. Since its opening, the movie has earned hundreds of millions of dollars worldwide and has been received with much critical acclaim. The patience in perfecting the film paid off for Tarantino and audiences, and shows that great work sometimes takes time in creation. Who knows what would have transpired if he rushed the film out prematurely, and casted the actors at a different time period?

* * *

When Pope Julius II requested that Michelangelo paint the Sistine Chapel, the artist was initially hesitant and a bit reluctant. A self proclaimed sculptor, his preferred method of creating was with marble, and at the time had not been painting regularly. Pope Julius was adamant that the work was done by Michelangelo as he felt that no one else could match his genius. From the results of the final painting, it appears that he was correct.

The enormous feat was a painting that covered well over five thousand square feet and depicted various scenes of the Bible. The frescoes included the creation in the book of Genesis, portraits of the prophets, and hundreds of biblical figures. The scene displaying man reaching for the hand of God was perhaps one of the most familiar works of art history.

Michelangelo did not have ample experience painting on this medium and the curved surface of the ceiling, and had to learn and master the process during the painting. There were many setbacks such as mold and damp weather, and it eventually took over four years to complete. To paint on the ceiling he had to build special scaffolding curved to match the shape of the ceiling and he often had to bend backward and paint over his head for long periods of time. The pain that he felt from the task over the four-year period must have been great. It was said by the sculptor himself that his vision was compromised from the effort and for a time it hurt him to look downward to read letters. He even wrote a poem detailing the misery of pain he endured from the painting and was said to have complained often about not wanting to do the job.

Originally, the work commissioned was to be a simple painting, but Michelangelo's penchant for perfection made it an elaborate effort. Pope Julius and others grew impatient over the delays in progress and finalization, and would complain and rush the artist. In the end, all would agree that it was worth the wait. The painting eventually became one of the more recognized and acknowledged accomplishments in the body of works by the artist.

The Grind involves situations when you have to do things that you really don't want to do. Great people do so pursuing excellence in any case, and Michelangelo ended up producing one of history's greatest paintings. Even though he was not commissioned for such an elaborate production, he still committed four years and his physical health to his high standards. Thirty years after the completion of the ceiling, Michelangelo was brought back to paint "The Last Judgment" on the alter wall. Even to this very day, when one views the painting, there is no question as to Michelangelo's dedication to his work.

* * *

The Ultimate Fighting Championship is a company which promotes and organizes mixed martial arts events. Fighters showcase their skill in the "octagon," the ring in which the matches are held. Most of the time a mixture of more than one martial arts style is displayed by each fighter, including Judo, Muay Thai, Jiujitsu, Karate, Wrestling, Grappling, Sumo, and many others.

Dana White, a former sports manager with boxing experience, found out that the company was having problems and was up for sale. He urged childhood friends, casino moguls Lorenzo Fertitta and Frank Fertitta III, to invest in the company. They formed a company called Zuffa LLC, and acquired the company in 2001 when the original parent company was experiencing financial problems. At the time, Dana White served as the president of the struggling company.

The company's previous owner, The Semaphore Entertainment Group, originally promoted the events as a brutal and bloody sport, and according to some critics similar to a human cockfight. After some experience and interaction with the fighters, White found that many were well educated and great athletes. He changed the company's marketing to reflect the amazing combat sport and highlighted the ability of the athletes. The company experienced its share of struggles and after some time it became $44 million dollars in debt. On at least one occasion the owners considered selling the company to cut any further loses. They even solicited an amount for which the company could be sold but finally decided to persevere.

One event, UFC 32, took place in the Meadowlands in New Jersey. The UFC had just moved arenas from the Taj Mahal to the Meadowlands and expected large crowds. They placed billboards all over New York and New Jersey, and invited various press outlets. Although there was a great turnout and it gained awareness for the sport, the event ended losing $2.4 million dollars. Under the new ownership of Zuffa, the UFC worked hard to organize the combat sport and expose it to audiences internationally. A major breakthrough was made when Spike TV picked up *The Ultimate Fighter*, a UFC reality show which showcased two opposing teams coached by two of the sport's prominent figures. Members from the opposing teams would fight at the end of the episode and the loser would go home. The contestants who would remain would be competing for the ultimate prize of the show, a contract with the UFC.

Audiences eventually caught on and the UFC is now highly successful with viewers internationally. In 2006, the company's events grossed more annual pay-per-view earnings than any other promotion in history. You can find the events on DVD or watch *The Ultimate Fighter* or *Fight Night* on Spike TV. The company has even expanded and bought out competitors such as WEC and Pride. A UFC event in Montreal, Canada, drew an audience of over 21,000 people, the largest draw of any mixed martial arts event in North America.

The UFC's story is a great example of persistence, remaining dedicated to their goal despite being in a situation of potential failure. With that much debt looming, it can be hard to see any positive outcome that can come about. Even amongst this pressure, under the leadership of Dana White, they pushed on and took the necessary steps to expose their events. Sometimes it just takes the right outlets for people to catch on and a major breakthrough was made with "The Ultimate Fighter" show. Key ingredients such as redefining the combat sport from a brutal, bloody slugfest to a skill-oriented sport gave audiences and fans a greater respect for the events. More people are now able to accept the sport and it is no longer regarded as mindless violence. The company has been a major force in influencing many to practice mixed martial arts and the popularity of the sport has reached great heights.

* * *

I recently took a vacation to Thailand, where my aunt currently resides. My aunt has lived her life there as a nun for many years. She has selflessly devoted her life to God, helping people who live their lives in great poverty. Her efforts are unyielding and she works continuously to help others better their own situation.

She currently takes care of about forty children from neighboring hill tribes who have had no formal education and live a very humble existence. Over the years, she has maintained the responsibility of taking care of up to sixty children at a time. Besides giving them a formal education, she teaches them how to raise livestock, produce clean water, and maintain basic modern life functions. They live with her in housing provided for her by the church. She has helped them established sales outlets to sell eggs and produce that they are able to grow themselves. She helps raise funds for them to gain an education and also teaches them how to conduct themselves within society away from their remote environment. After years of teaching in various schools, she also tutors these children.

She has been performing these types of duties for over forty-five years and has helped thousands with her contributions. When she first devoted her life to her current vocation, the requirements were very strict. It was viewed as total sacrifice and submitting yourself fully to the teachings of God. They endured harsh conditions and had a number of responsibilities to adhere to in their committed lives. They were not even allowed to go to their parent's funerals if it would conflict with their duties. There was no tolerance for variations of their teachings and practices so anyone who seeks this life would have to do so with full dedication. Their lives are filled with self sacrifice. Often shelter consisted of poor conditions with no air conditioning, no television, and exposure to the many pests that Thailand has to offer. Food was often bland or not a luxury one could expect. It is not the life for the weak at heart. These conditions were expected if you chose that life, and the perception of their commitment was viewed as strict devotion. As a result anyone who made the decision to do so expected complete hardship.

Nowadays, the conditions are different. I stayed at a convent hotel during my last visit to Thailand and the accommodations rivaled some of the average hotels out there. The church has grown and they now enjoy a better financial situation. Their schools produce income and the contributions of their clergy members have provided more positive outlets. All these developments have come about due to the hard work and selfless contributions of people like my aunt who have dedicated many years to this cause.

When I last visited Thailand I saw the direct results of her sacrifice. I went into a hospital and was introduced to several nurses who were raised by my aunt and have gone on to a promising career. In their original background, they would not have been provided an education which led to their current professions. They are able to sustain an ample lifestyle and send money back home to their families, providing more opportunity outlets to a whole new generation of children. As a result of her hard work and devotion, she has now gained the help from many people that have come to know her and her actions over the years. These people have donated cars, cell phones, lodging, funds and many other items to help her cause. They have gotten behind her cause and this has greatly benefited the people she helps.

In one instance, she was talking with one of her friends and was describing the conditions of the power lines in the area. The lines were exposed and in very bad condition. The friends' husband happened to maintain a prominent position in the electric company and sent laborers to fix all the lines and poles in the area. They did this because they wanted to help in any way possible. Another time, she was speaking to one of her friends she went to school with and mentioned these people from the hill tribes were in need of medical attention. A week later, a bus full of doctors arrived providing free medical services to all who needed help.

The Grind is not only reserved to people who have high incomes and work in an orthodox profession. Some of the most accomplished people give of themselves without the benefits of financial gain. These people are truly great individuals with immeasurable levels of high achievement even without the motivation of income.

Reputation, like the one my aunt has built throughout the years, and the things that you put your full heart behind, lead to others getting behind your convictions. As a result, your cause is magnified to others who discover your vision and follow your examples. It took decades for people to realize her convictions and as a result many people now have a better quality of life. Many maintain that one person can not change the world but this is a clear example of how one person can help others make a growing change. I had to pry a lot to gain the information regarding her past as she is never one who toots her own horn. I believe she prefers to let her actions and results speak for her. She may not be known or exposed to a large group outside her own areas but it is surely enough to help a large number of people who need her help. Great actions often take many years of efforts, and in this case it is a cause that keeps on giving to others through kindness and sacrifice.

* * *

Daniel Day Lewis is an actor who is a great example of a person who exemplifies great commitment to his profession. He has been regarded by critics and peers as one of the greats who will stop at almost nothing to bring the characters which he portrays to life. As a youth, Lewis was shy and introverted which resulted in the development of the fantasy aspects of his character which later helped him in his craft. Some of the films that he has participated in include *The Last of the Mohicans*, *The Crucible*, *The Age of Innocence*, *Gangs of New York*, *There Will Be Blood*, *Nine*, and *The Ballad of Jack and Rose*. He is a very accomplished actor whose talents have been recognized with awards such as Oscars, Golden Globe Awards, Academy Awards, SAG Awards, and others.

What makes him so great at what he does is the amount of attention to detail that he contributes to his craft to display these epic performances. This includes his superior commitment to the preparation of the roles he chooses. He is very meticulous in his selection of roles and decisions are made to purely serve artistic fulfillment. According to one of his costars in the movie *Gangs of New York*, he rarely ever got out of character when playing the role. Lewis would talk in a New York accent the whole day and could be seen sharpening his knives during lunch, which were all characteristics of actions of the character roles he was playing for the movie. He got sick during the shooting because he would wear a threadbare coat which he refused to replace with a warmer coat. This was because the coat was not part of the fashion of the time period which the movie took place. He was said to have listened to musician Eminem, as this helped to get him in an angry self righteous frame of mind for his role as Bill the Butcher in *Gangs of New York*. In the movie *The Ballad of Jack and Rose*, which his wife Rebecca Miller directed, he moved out and lived alone in a hut on the beach away from her and his children. This was in order to keep with his tradition of keeping in character while he was shooting a film. During work on the Last of the Mohicans he built a canoe, learnt to track and skin animals, perfected the use of a gun that he used in the film and carried it everywhere even to a Christmas dinner he attended. For his role in the movie *My Left Foot*, he confined himself to a wheelchair for months during filming.

One of his quotes included, "If I weren't allowed this outlet, there wouldn't be a place for me in society." The importance that he places on his profession directly attributes to his caliber as an actor. Lewis' dedication and commitment to his trade comes across as a result of the effort that he exerts for each role, and has made him very prominent in what he does. He practices measures that few others would dedicate to their work, and if you ever view one of his films you can see the results of this hard work. There is no question as to why some are so great at what they do.

* * *

Whole Foods Market was conceived when John Mackey and Rene Lawson Hardy merged their business, Safer Way Natural Foods, with Clarksville Natural Grocery, owned by Craig Weller and Mark Skiles. This merger resulted in a 10,500 square foot store employing a staff of only nineteen people. Located in Austin, Texas, the store opened its doors in September of 1980.

Safer Way Natural Foods was a small natural food store in Austin started up by twenty-five-year-old John Mackey and his then girlfriend, twenty-one-year-old Rene Lawson

Hardy with seed money from family and friends. Like all humble startups, the couple went through their own adversity. They were kicked out of their apartment for storing food there, and were eventually forced to live in the store. They were even forced to take showers from an attached hose from their dishwasher since the store had no shower stalls. Mackey was not the everyday entrepreneur, as he never took a business class or worked for any other companies, and eventually even dropped out of college.

Combined with their new partners from Clarksville Natural Grocery, the first Whole Foods Market was an instant success. The store quickly became a hotspot in the community. However, about a year after the opening in 1981, Austin was hit with the worst flood the city had seen in seventy years. The store's inventory was destroyed and most of their equipment was rendered useless. What was worse was that the store had no insurance and losses amounted to about $400,000. Fortunately, the city's customers and neighbors helped the staff clean and get the store back in order. Investors, creditors, and vendors all provided leniency and allowed them the chance to get past this trying time. After this major setback, Mackey emerged as the company's leader and was instrumental to guiding the company through the troubled times and onto success. The company began to grow quickly accomplished by mergers and acquisitions with other companies in the natural foods business sector which helped them break into new markets.

One standout attribute, implemented under the leadership of Mackey, is the team-oriented atmosphere at Whole Foods and its emphasis on tending to their employee needs. His philosophy, labeled "conscious capitalism," is grounded in the belief that business should have a greater purpose and the company shall provide value to all members and people involved with the company. The management and staff positions are set up in a way as to work together to best serve the company's goals. The variation in management and staff position salaries is very minimal in comparison to other companies. Executive salaries are capped at nineteen times the average employee's salary, compared to rival Fortune 500 companies who commonly draw three hundred times the average employees' wages. To date, the company has placed in the "Fortune 100 Best Companies to Work For" every year since 1998. Even part-time employees enjoy the benefits of health insurance. Employees enjoy many other employment benefits such as rewards in the form of discounts on store products in efforts to improve their health. Health and retirement benefits are generous and superior to many of the rival companies. Mackey leads by example and foregoes the usual benefits most people in his position enjoy or exploit. He has established his salary at just one dollar per year, and has forgone bonuses and stock incentives, citing that he already has enough money. He has created an employment atmosphere which values its members and when the company enjoys success, so do all the members. This stimulates those who work for the company to do the best not only for themselves but for the good of the company.

This example of Whole Foods is consistent with many characteristics of the Grind. John Mackey and the founders of the company made sacrifices early on, went through adversity such as recovering from the flood, and never stopped their efforts. Their employee focused environment is unique and unlike any of their other rivals. They have identified a discrepancy in the demand of the natural foods market and were bold in expanding the company through mergers and acquisitions. Today, Whole Foods is the world's largest natural foods retail chain.

Compete on a Higher Level

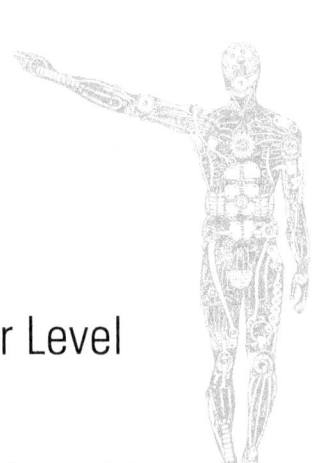

It always seems impossible until it's done.
—Nelson Mandela

One of the main goals of this book is to motivate you to perform at the highest personal level possible. It is a shame that most of us never push ourselves to this point. The ideal situation would be for you to realize that you possess all the potential you need to make almost anything possible in your future. It is a personal choice and no one else can cause you to commit to these higher standards. It is through practice and pushing yourself to realize these goals that you will acquire these standards.

It's always been fascinating to me to experience and meet people in my life who are so driven it seems like they operate with a different consciousness than the average. It almost seems like they are addicted to the process of accomplishment. They have worked to possess characteristics that give them a superior edge over the rest of those in their respective fields. They give of themselves completely and perform at this standard on a consistent basis. They are not wavered by numerous impending obstacles and this does not deter them in the pursuit of goals. They innovate and have foresight to set trends and create their own possibilities others believe may be unreachable. They work fervently to realize any of the needed skills they lack to acquire their personal best. They have the courage to attempt ventures no one else would dare. In short, they compete on a higher level.

What is interesting is that this level often seems to be viewed as the standard to them. You must change your thinking in order to include yourself in this company of individuals, if you do not currently possess this type of drive. The things that society perceives as standard should be omitted from your thoughts. Instead, focus on your personal best, your own situation, and your own goals. The possibilities are endless as long as you strive accordingly.

It is interesting how record breakers in the area of sports change the minds of others on the thinking of what is possible. For a while, there seems to be an unattainable moniker of scoring, speed, or distances, and the record remains intact because most feel that it is unbreakable. One day a competitor breaks the record and raises the bar. Afterward, a number of others do the same because they see it is possible. It seems like once the average mind comprehends that something is possible, then they are able to pursue the goal knowing there is a chance for success. The innovators and industry leaders don't have to wait for these validations, and set their own pace for success. They are confident and find assurance within themselves that their strengths and abilities are ample to accommodate their ambitions. They respect other high level performers in various fields and may draw inspiration, but they do not need to compare themselves to others in order to become motivated in their own situation.

The following paragraphs in this chapter are characteristics that should be practiced by all those who aspire to achieve high standards. You should take inventory of them and work to master each of them for inclusion in your own business personality.

Success is the sum of details.
—Harvey S. Firestone

People who compete on a higher level pay great attention to detail. Every detail of an effort is significant in order to gain overall positive results. The neglect of one part can have an affect on the whole process. Make sure that you are always mindful in practicing quality control for every aspect of your business affairs so you can maintain the high standards that the Grind requires.

Michael Ovitz is an extraordinary person who was described as very meticulous in his professional life. Ovitz founded Creative Artists Agency, a talent agency which represented stars such as Tom Cruise, Sylvester Stallone, Dustin Hoffman, and many others. Ovitz was described to be very calculated or formulated in his actions by Hollywood insiders and those who dealt with him directly. He would control the movements of his body down to the detail of absence of sporadic movement when he walked to show that he had full control of himself at all times. All communication including body language was done with intent. From the tone and volume of his voice to the way things were said or not said; all were delivered with the strictest of purpose. He would use psychological methods of talking in almost a whisper to make the listener lean closer, rendering them off balance. This would give Ovitz a dominant position, giving him the advantage when negotiating or whenever this helped his cause. He was said to have gained great insight into the thoughts and desires of the talent that he represented and was able to anticipate their innermost concerns. He learned to think like an entertainer and gained empathy into the artistic and business elements of their careers. He learned what it was that his clients really wanted and was able to satisfy and gain new clients with this insight. This is a true example of an individual who exceeds what is generally practiced in average performance. The great attention to detail distinguishes him and gives him the advantage over other competitors.

Great people only accept great results. Analyze your professional characteristics and determine the level of quality control you exercise in the judgment of your efforts. Make sure that you are attentive to the details and not just the end results. If you are to truly gain the best results you have to make sure your intolerance for imperfection extends to the smallest of details. It is like a simple cup of coffee. You can scour the whole earth to find the best coffee beans in the world to use, and still not have a good cup of coffee. If you use poor quality water that has not been properly filtered, over brew the coffee, use poor tasting creamer, or lack in any of the other elements; then you would take away from the quality of the beans. Everything has to be perfect, each and every part. Paying attention to detail is a necessity if you plan to gain a competitive edge in business and exercise the standards of the Grind.

Small modifications, made by founder Manoj Bhargava, greatly contributed to the success of the 5-Hour Energy Drink, which made its inception during the advent of the popularity of energy drinks. Brands like Red Bull were just beginning to make their mark on consumers, and were generating a demand in the new highly caffeinated beverage market. The idea of 5-Hour Energy came to Bhargava after he attended a natural products trade show in Anaheim, California, in 2003. He came across a booth with a sales rep promoting a sixteen-ounce beverage which was said to boost productivity for hours. He tried it and found that the product was effective and realized that it was an item he could sell after making a few modifications. Instead of following suit and adding another brand to the energy drink market, founder Manoj Bhargava created his own spin, pioneering the "energy shot" market by offering his product in a smaller two-ounce size. Bhargava realized that not everyone wants to drink a whole twelve- or sixteen-ounce beverage just to get a boost of energy and 5-Hour Energy is a perfect alternative size. If Bhargava did not establish the current two ounce size, 5-Hour Energy Drinks would have had to compete with Red Bull and other energy drink competitors. It would have also had to fight for beverage space and compete with Coke and Mountain Dew and other soft drinks. The smaller red bottles also meant that they can be positioned near the check out counters of retailers, a major reason for success through impulse buys and high visibility. In 2004, health chain GNC was the first to agree to stock 5-Hour Energy in 1,200 of its stores around the nation. Nowadays, it has become very common to find these little red bottles at the counters of many retail outlets, including Walmart, Walgreens, and many others. In a few years, 5-Hour has gone from nothing into $1 billion in retail sales.

As we can see in the example of 5-Hour Energy, even a small modification to a product can make a big difference in its chances for success. This is why even the smallest of details is relevant in business. Although changing the size wasn't the only contributing factor to the company's success, it was definitely relevant. The two-ounce size helped the product establish its own market and avoid competitors, namely Red Bull and other soft drink companies. There are now many new competitors in the "energy shot" market, but since 5-Hour Energy was the first in the market, this enabled them to establish a foothold and enjoy the benefits of being the first of its kind. Its size also helped the placement of the product into high visible areas near check out counters. All the details of an effort add up to determine the quality of the sum result. If you truly wish to perform at your highest levels, then you must make sure every detail of your efforts is conducted with the highest of standards. Always assess all stages of your work, not just your overall effort, so that you can ensure that your best work is being exerted each and every time.

* * *

People who perform at higher standards exhibit their own unique characteristics and display the traits which make them different in their business practices. People are naturally drawn to things that are unique which are not seen on a regular basis. In your business practices, focus on identifying and cultivating your individual abilities that few others may possess. If you can exploit these traits and create a demand you will surely enhance worth in your profession.

The Virgin Group consists of four hundred companies worldwide including Virgin Mobile, Virgin Atlantic Airways, Virgin Megastores, Virgin Records, and many others. Virgin Group founder Richard Branson has been effective in promoting his many companies throughout the years by simply incorporating his personality and life philosophies into the corporate culture of the company. As a result, the company has taken on the culture of adventure, fun and living life to its fullest; all characteristics of how Branson lives his personal life. His many PR campaigns have included flying around the world in hot air balloons, driving tanks down Fifth Avenue to launch Virgin Cola, dressing up in a wedding dress to promote Virgin Brides, and jumping off the Palms Hotel Casino to celebrate the inaugural flight for Virgin American Airways. Many of these are activities Branson would enjoy for fun in his personal life. Some companies are a direct reflection of their leaders and such is the case of Virgin Group. He writes in his book, *Business Stripped Bare*, "Every business…operates according to its own rules. There are many ways to run a successful company."

The Tower of Pisa was designed to stand perfectly vertical despite its current leaning position. Although it is famous for the fact that it leans, it is still considered a remarkable architectural achievement on its own merit. The monument was built to serve as a bell tower for a cathedral site accompanying three other structures making up the Campo Dei Miracoli, which is translated as the Field of Miracles. The Tower is one of the tallest bell towers in Europe and stands eight stories high with over two hundred columns in its construction. Construction of the Tower began in 1173 and continued on and off for a couple hundred years initially halted due to a war with Florence. After the construction of the first three floors, the tower was already discovered to be leaning, so the builders performed various measures to correct the fault throughout the years. The attempts to remedy the disposition were not realized and the tower remained in its current state. Eventually, centuries later, the tower was completed and has become one of Italy's great tourist attractions. Visitors come from all over the world to view the leaning tower. The original intention of its construction was to draw attention to the architectural design and beauty, but it is really the leaning position of the Tower that has increased its appeal.

Uniqueness has undoubtedly an appeal. This is just like the example of the Tower of Pisa, which has become world renowned because of its uniqueness even with the flaws of its construction. People gravitate toward subjects that peak their interest through breaking the monotony of conformity. We are all blessed with our own individuality, and we can use these unique attributes to enhance all our efforts. At your employment, always seek to bring about new levels of performance by exploring different options for creativity. Make it a conscious effort to do things not only better but differently. This will bring attention to your intentions of performing at higher levels of achievement and let others know that your abilities should be valued as unique.

> *A ship is always safe at the shore-but that is not what it is built for.*
> —Albert Einstein

Risk taking has always been one of the great barriers for those who aspire to compete on higher levels. It is also one of the requirements in breaking new ground and realizing success that has not been previously enjoyed by the majority. Because it is of greater ease to pursue the things that do not have high potential for failure, most individuals conform to the safest and quickest methods of doing things. The problem is that these methods often do not allow a person exposure to unfamiliar experiences or rewards. The person never goes outside their familiar comfort areas, and no new opportunities are discovered. Many times this is so because of a fear of the unknown. However, in history many great discoveries and accomplishments were born from individuals who neglected caution and took great risks. Sometimes there is a need to be bold and challenge yourself in ways you haven't done before. There is a time to take risks and put yourself in a position to test your worth. As the saying goes, "The biggest risk of all is not taking one." Risk is present in almost all situations where an individual has accomplished an extraordinary feat.

In the case of Howard Schultz, a job with a sufficient salary of $75,000 a year, a company car, unlimited travel, and an expense account were not strong enough factors for remaining content in the same situation. He had a job he liked and after three years was in a position of comfort. He and his wife had settled into a home which they were able to purchase and were living a great life. They even enjoyed the luxury of renting a summer home in the Hampton's. This was quite a change from his humble beginnings growing up with financial concerns and uncertainty. But in his heart he knew he wanted more and when he made the move to involve himself with Starbuck's, he risked his comfortable situation to pursue something that had no guarantees. His ambition led him to take the chance of leaving his job, moving 3,000 miles across the country to Seattle, and putting himself in financial risk to pursue his mission of bringing Starbucks to the world. He did so against the advice and logic of loved ones. At that time Starbucks was a small operation that had little recognition and had a long way to go to realize the success that it has today.

It is harder to think of a bigger risk than starting a new company during the height of the Great Depression in 1936. It requires more efforts and creative ideas to continue operating in these times of economic decline. That is what Leo and Lillian Goodwin implemented when they had the foresight to start GEICO. The Government Employee Insurance Company, or GEICO, initially served the needs of federal employees and certain categories of enlisted military officers. He targeted good drivers as customers, selecting government employees and members of the military as they were likely to be responsible and maintain a steady income. He didn't enlist the help of insurance agents and salesmen, and this, combined with the pool of good drivers as customers, enabled him to sell policies at a reduced price and still make money. This was vital for the troubled financial times. Goodwin and his wife worked continuously to turn their startup into a success, laboring twelve hours a day, all year long. He even worked on weekends, visiting local military bases to solicit customers. They took the time to hand write responses to complaints and questions. GEICO established a direct mail operation which took the place of a sales force of insurance agents and helped the company save money and keep costs low. By the end of the first year, the company was able to write $104,000 worth of premiums. Goodwin chipped away at losses until six years after their start, when the company finally showed a $15,000 profit. Goodwin did what was needed to stress customer service and on one occasion a large hailstorm severely damaged thousands of cars in the Washington area. During this crisis, he made a deal with repair shops to put in extra operating hours to work on customer's cars for twenty-four hours a day, and also had extra automotive glass shipped in to fill the demand. As a result of these efforts, GEICO customers had their cars repaired far before others who were insured by other insurance companies. It was these efforts in the early days of the company that enabled GEICO to weather the storm and become the success it is today. The company is now the largest auto insurer in New York, Maryland, Hawaii, and other states. They employ 26,000 associates in twelve major locations across the country. In 2012, GEICO maintains over eleven million policyholders with assets of $28 billion.

When taking a risk, the best way to proceed is to try to reduce the chances of failure as much as you possibly can. You can try to give yourself a better chance to succeed by only taking calculated risks. GEICO was able to do so by catering to responsible drivers, taking on customers who were more likely to be good drivers. This meant less payout for loss on behalf of their customer's claims. Both Leo and LIllian also worked very hard, working twelve hour days, even coming into work on the weekends. This also decreased the risk factor of their investment as putting in their own hours meant less expenditures on employee's wages. Saving money by reducing your expenditures is a vital means toward decreasing risks. By doing without salesmen and insurance agents, they were able to sell their policies at a reduced rate. All the creative practices and ideas that Goodwin implemented ensured that they were very competitive. Whenever taking a risk, it is very important to take as many measures that are necessary to give yourself the best chances for success.

The nature of a risk provides no assurances and has to be done with full faith in yourself and your abilities. Make sure you are mentally ready for what may lie ahead. Test yourself with smaller risks first before moving onto bigger things. Understand, that sometimes the only way to achieve high levels of success is by making the decision to let go of something that already seems like an ideal situation. Only you know what your true aspirations are and what your ideal definition of ultimate success is. Consider what you are giving up and if it is a position you can bring yourself back from. Take the calculated risk when you see an opportunity that warrants the change you need in your professional life.

> *If your ship doesn't come in, swim out to meet it!*
> —Jonathan Winters

Those who compete on a higher level possess the ability to act boldly when the situation requires. This is an ability which can help you deal with potential problems by taking extreme action when a normal remedy won't suffice. Sometimes, you have to be aggressive in order to realize progress and the situation requires you to take a bold stance. Not all problems can be solved from solutions derived from the usual ideas and ways of thinking, so being creative and daring may be your only alternative.

Multibillionaire media mogul David Geffen has found success in a wide variety of areas in the entertainment business. He is one of the founding partners who started entertainment company Dreamworks with Jeffrey Katzenberg and Steven Spielberg. He is also the founder of Asylum Records and Geffen Records. With investments that span from art collection to real estate investment, he has become one of the world's most richest and influential people. However, just like most of us, he started with very humble beginnings. When David Gefffen landed a job at the William Morris Agency, he did so keeping with the company tradition of starting out in the mailroom. A college degree was a requirement for the job so Geffen claimed that he graduated from UCLA. Not to let this falsehood cease his employment at the firm, he intercepted a letter from UCLA that had arrived in the mailroom. He steamed the letter open and used the stationary to forge his own proof that he had indeed graduated from the university. His resourcefulness moved him out of the mailroom and eventually into the prestigious agent position he desired, with a salary of about two million dollars per year.

In fact, Geffen is a great example of a person who was never afraid to be bold when needed throughout his illustrious career. On another occasion Geffen was involved with a renegotiation for Geffen Records with Warner Bros. Records' heads Mo Ostin and Steve Ross. A joint venture deal with the two companies was about to expire, and new terms had to be renegotiated. Geffen did not want to deal with Mo Ostin who in the past tended to be a tough deal-maker. He understood the significance of addressing specific detail in the negotiation and established an elaborate strategy to position himself to deal with only Steve Ross. He was reported as telling an associate that he would fail if he would have to deal with Ostin and that it was "essential" that he began a conflict between the two. He began by starting a fight over rock group Van Halen who was signed to Warner Bros. Records. Sammy Hagar, who was signed to Geffen Records, was to replace David Lee Roth as Van Halen's lead singer, and Geffen staged out public opposition that this was an attempt to steal one of his star acts. Mo Ostin, who had been previously been on friendly terms with Geffen, found himself as the sudden recipient of this planned assault. To distance the relationship between the two further, Geffen took Ostin's wife, Evelyn, out to lunch for the next stage in his plan. He began hurling personal insults to a surprised Evelyn, who had shared a past personal friendship with Geffen. The lunch resulted in Evelyn walking out and left Geffen and the Ostins on nonspeaking terms for the next year and a half. With this development, Geffen was able to negotiate the deal and gain favorable terms with Steve Ross, since he and Mo Ostin were not speaking to one another. Geffen has many examples of how calculated he was throughout his career in his dealings and this is undoubtedly one of the factors for his success.

Sometimes, we have to go above and beyond the normal ways of dealing with adversity, and the situation requires us to be bold in our actions. Situations may arise which require us to meet the challenges with extreme intensity and we must come up with solutions we may not normally practice. You have to be confident in these times and think of ways to make a statement. Contemplate what would leave a strong impression with the other party who you are dealing with. Next time you face one of these types of situations that require the use of intense action, just remember, as the old saying goes, "Fortune favors the bold."

* * *

One common factor of people who perform at high levels of effort is that they truly love what they choose to do as a profession. Finding the love and passion in what you choose to do for a living can be a great driving force for success.

I was very fortunate as a music producer to work with recording artist and actor Xzibit on one our projects. To me he exemplified a living example of why people succeed in the music business. The minute he stepped off the plane he was talking about the album he had been working on and its developments. He seemed to be perpetually examining what he could do better and how he could make improvements in his creative efforts. He also talked about other songs and albums which were currently released and I immediately sensed how much he really enjoyed both making and listening to music. Accompanying his love of music, he also conducted himself according to what would make his career successful. In the hotel lobby while checking in, he was going over *Nielson Soundscan Reports*, which indicate release sales numbers and demographic areas where consumers were buying his albums. He asked me to take him to music stores in the area. When we arrived to each retail store, he checked his product positioning and placement. He inquired and conversed with the sales clerks regarding his releases. When we arrived at the studio, he tracked his verse in one take, after rehearsing what he had written once. We took less than seven minutes recording his vocals. The recording process seemed second nature to him and his experience was evident.

Everyone he met was embraced genuinely and people took an immediate liking to his presence. It seemed as though he had an ability to further his own career by his natural character. His love of the music in which he involved himself daily, projected into everything he did and has yielded many accomplishments, including platinum releases, *Pimp My Ride*, a show he hosts on MTV, and various movie roles.

Russell Simmons is a great example of a businessman who has built a stellar career adhering to pursuits that peak his personal motivations. In an interview for businessweek.com, he said, "I've poured my passion into ventures that made me happy before they ever made me a red cent." As a testament to the effectiveness of this formula, his past choices of business ventures he has engaged in has enabled him to build a personal bank account worth over $325 million. With his love of music, he co-founded Def Jam Recordings, the record label that bought the world LL Cool J, Run DMC, Beastie Boys, Method Man and many other prominent music artists. He started Def Jam out of his college dorm room and his passion for music drove him to often work twenty to twenty two hours a day building the label. Simmons stated in his book, *Super Rich: A Guide to Having It All*, that he showed up to work each morning because he was motivated by the fun and happiness of sharing new hip-hop records to the world. Millions of record sales later, he was able to sell his shares of the company to the Universal Music Group in 1999 for $100 million.

Simmons is a proponent of choosing passion over money as an incentive for professional aspirations, one of the fundamentals he suggests to the readers of his books to find the success they desire. He is a businessman who has been able to find success in a variety of various industries including clothing brands, record labels, publishing, films, television shows, websites, soft drinks, financial service businesses and many others. He is one of the original serial entrepreneurs, who have been able to keenly identify discrepancies in the marketplace and fill them with his own ideas for progress. For someone to find success in so many diverse fields of business, there has to be a presence of great motivation and his future ventures were also those which captured his professional interests. In 1991, Simmons began the Def Comedy Tour, a stand-up comedy series, hosted by Martin Lawrence, featuring the comedic talents of Tracy Morgan, Chris Tucker, Chris Rock, Jamie Foxx, Bernie Mac, D.L. Hugley, Cedric The Entertainer and many others. The hit comedy show found great success and ran on HBO for several seasons, providing many of the then-young and up-and-coming comedians a forum to display their talents. Now, those same comedians have moved on to star in a number of television shows and films that have grossed hundreds of millions of dollars. Next he launched the highly successful clothing brand, Phat Farm, which later sold and contributed another $140 million to his personal fortune. His first book, *Do You! 12 Laws to Access the Power in You to Achieve Happiness and Success*, was a New York Times Best Seller and was featured on *The Oprah Winfrey Show*.

By choosing pursuits only for the sole purpose of economic gain, your productivity will be dictated by your level of compensation. The problem is that often in business, the rewards and amounts of pay may not always meet our expectations, and this may negatively affect the outcome. Remember, that the Grind requires the best of you at all times and in order to gain these results, you must be able to draw from any professional resources that can be used to bring out your very best. Therefore, choose the pursuits that get you excited and keep you motivated at every stage of the venture no matter the challenges that may be present.

When someone truly loves what they do, the passion is apparent in all areas of their profession through their actions. Their affection for their craft makes it a natural occurrence to perform at higher levels. Engulf yourself fully in the activities that you love and motivate you, and let nature take its course.

* * *

My uncle once told me that it's not how much money you make, it's what you do with the money afterward that counts. Saving money is a skill in its own right and unfortunately one of the least practiced necessities of the Grind. Saving is such an integral part of performing on a higher level, because so few are willing to exercise this discipline. Your ability to account for every dollar you earn and spend matters. Even if it is one dollar, it all adds up in the end.

Many view spending as one of the main types of enjoyment in life and believe that restricting yourself from these rewards is negative. Some people actually maintain that you are doing something wrong by saving your money, and that by doing so you are depriving yourself of "living life." It's funny because these are the same people who will be complaining about not having enough money or will ask to borrow yours later. People will spend for luxuries in the present time, and then get stressed out later when bills or unexpected expenditures come up. I hear people say all the time that "the money is burning a hole in my pocket," and feel just because they have money at the current time, they have to spend it no matter how frivolous the case.

To be consistent with the Grind, purchases should only be made on something you really need and there has to be a significant reason to do so. You can either sacrifice and save today, or be in the same financial situation tomorrow. When I spend money I often think of what it took me to earn that money. When you think of your salary, think of the hours, stress, efforts, and actions you had to put forth to earn that money. When you think of it in these terms, it's no longer "just a few dollars."

Learn to live with what you have and don't spend money that you don't have. Nowadays with credit cards, lines of credit, and various ways to spend money you don't have; people have a mentality that they will spend first and earn later. When you use a credit card or borrow money, you are not spending your own money but that which has been lent to you pending repayment. Remember you will have to pay back this money at a later date. This is a major problem and reason as to why so many do not have the options to better their financial future. In this case, there is no extra available money saved to invest in options that will earn you money in the future.

Saving money takes time and effort. Maintain a bank account that you contribute a part of your salary to every paycheck. Keep alert for incentives that may exist which can enable you to save. For example, if you keep a certain balance in some banks they will forego check fees, safety deposit fees, or monthly maintenance charges. Transferring credit card balances to other companies who are offering incentives of lower interest rates may allow you to save and pay back balances faster. Find ways to cut corners on your spending and take the necessary steps to save. Coupons may not be glamorous but they will cut your costs. Find ways to save money such as buying in bulk on items that will be needed anyway. Little things like paying your bills online and saving money on stamps all add up in the end. Some people are perfectly content on spending money on late fees, and penalties by paying bills late. Instead, keep a thorough schedule of when payments are due so that you avoid these unnecessary fees.

One strategy I recommend is to carry on your person a notebook or small planner in which you can list all your purchases and expenditures during each day. To be completely accurate, list everything, even those which are less than a dollar. At the end of each day, review how your money was spent. You'll be surprised how even the small purchases can add up to so much. This is the only way to be able to accurately assess the small expenses that become significant when added up. Most of the time these notes will yield interesting findings and detail your spending habits. Determine from these notes how you can decrease your spending.

Learn to delay your pleasures and live according to the rules of balance. Every moment does not have to be one of enjoyment. The truth is the more opportunities you take to enjoy yourself, the less satisfying they become with frequency, so give yourself something to look forward to and space out your rewards.

Saving money can greatly contribute to bettering your chances for success. Save money with the intent to provide yourself more opportunities in the future. Having a goal in mind helps you stick to the task by having a reason that will drive you to save. It can be saving to open your own business or for an education for your desired profession. By saving, you will put away more resources that you can use later to increase your future opportunities. The skill of saving may be difficult to learn and require great sacrifices in the present time, but it may just be the key factor in providing you the long term satisfaction that you aspire for.

* * *

What many great business people have in common is their ability to command respect. Respect must be earned and is completely up to discretion of others. One of the best ways to command respect is to be as authentic as possible with what you choose to pursue. When a person is at the pinnacle of their chosen profession and considered an expert or innovator of their respective field, others believe in their authenticity. They are considered a reliable source in the area which they personally represent.

Tony Hawk, the pro skater, is an individual who commands great respect in the sport of skateboarding. Not only does he produce products for the skate market but is also considered one of the sports all time greats. He has established himself as a pioneer of the sport with years of experience in competitions and demonstration. His business which includes, video games, clothes, skateboards, books and many other products are fueled by the very thing that he has devoted his life to. Hawk is not just another business man trying to sell a product, but a peer able to understand their true needs and wants. There is no doubt as to why his company generates millions of dollars a year and has put him in the Forbes top lists for his genre. When he started his career, skateboarding was not yet mainstream and he eventually was the catalyst which provided its presence for the masses. He stayed active in competitions even after making the transition to the boardroom, and his accolades gained his company additional notoriety through authenticity.

People respect those who respect what they do. Whatever it is that you are involved with make sure that you involve yourself with the culture surrounding the entity. Get to know the details of your business and represent it with true insight. Don't just involve yourself with it professionally but get involved with it personally and this passion will come out in your work. People can always tell when you are just going through the motions.

Respect also comes to those who have respectable characteristics, and demonstrate them in everyday practice. Loyalty, poignancy, honesty, hard working, knowledgeable, understanding, and other traits show others that you respect what you do through actual practice. Showing respect to others helps bring about the mutual feelings another person may display toward you. Many advantages accompany respect. With respect, most people will acknowledge that you have showed your worth in past action and will give you the benefit of any doubts. Once one person has these feelings toward you it is likely that others will feel the same way also. Whether through word of mouth or acknowledged through reputation, respect is contagious. Respect brings you greater opportunities and people will most likely seek out your services, product, advice, or contributions as they feel they have a better chance of positive outcome. People favor associating themselves with those who they admire or look up to. Earn the respect of your peers and you will be able to compete at higher levels.

> *If you say you can or you can't you are right either way.*
> —Henry Ford

Sara Blakely's success came from an idea that resulted from her answering an irritating problem she was experiencing. The panty hose that she was forced to wear at work always stuck out of an open toe sandal or kitten heel. However, the control-top served the purpose of eliminating panty lines and made her body look firm. So she cut the feet off and kept the custom-top, and as a result started her company Spanx. So at twenty-seven years old, she set aside $5,000 in her savings for the business and patented the product herself. She would spend evenings on a friend's computer designing her packaging for the product. At first, manufacturers would send her away and thought the product "made no sense, and would never sell," until one agreed because he had two daughters who liked the idea. Her obsession for comfort resulted in the prototype of the product taking a year to perfect. She kept her day job and stayed up all night filling Spanx orders from Office Depot. She provided her own 24/7 customer service and answered calls form her bed or bathtub. In the early days, Blakely didn't have money to advertise so she would stay in department stores all day, every day, introducing customers to Spanx. She even became notorious for lifting up her pant legs or skirt to every woman walking by to show her product. She would go to great lengths to promote and sell her products, once even sneaking in Spanx packages onto a rack she bought and placing them by the cash register at Neiman Marcus. The staff assumed someone had approved the placement until her plan was foiled, when they caught her on CCTV. One of the greatest life lessons Blakely learned was taught to her by her father at a young age: "Don't be afraid to fail." In fact, she says her dad encouraged her to fail, and would ask her what she failed at that week. If she didn't have anything to mention about failures she recently experienced, he would be disappointed. Spanx Inc. went on to produce more than two hundred types of body-shaping garments, sold in about 10,000 retail stores around the globe. Today it is a multimillion dollar company and has recently made Blakely the youngest female billionaire!

One of the characteristics that stood out when reading Sara Blakely's story, is her incredible resourcefulness. This is a person who definitely made use of all the resources at her disposal to help further her situation. In the beginning stages of her business she took the initiative to learn how to patent the product herself. She then designed the packaging and came up with a number of creative ideas to promote her product to customers. From positioning her own display rack prominently displaying the product near the counter in stores, to spending her days showing potential customers the product she was wearing underneath her clothes one person at a time; she did all she could to promote the items she had for sale. She also maintained her own call center to make sure that she was in touch with her customers. Any time she ran into a roadblock in progress she would come up with her own remedy to the situation. In the early stages of any businesses, we must be able to tend to any problems ourselves in order to save money and make due with the resources we may be limited to. Resourcefulness is a skill that anyone can develop, and we must be willing to have the confidence to fix any problems on our own accord without always relying on others. Any potential chances that you have to learn should be taken to expand your overall knowledge of various subjects. For example, when we are children we may encounter our fathers fixing a plumbing problem. It is our prerogative whether to watch and learn or to ignore the potential lesson. Learning about such plumbing issues may help later in life if you decide to buy real estate, possibly a fixer upper, and save money by improving the house yourself. To perform at a higher level, never be afraid to learn to do things yourself. Just like Blakely learned to attend to various responsibilities of starting and operating the company herself, you can also use your own resourcefulness to learn about a subject and take care of it yourself.

* * *

Competing at higher levels can sometimes bring great stress due to the requirements of maintaining these competitive standards. You must be able to keep your cool under pressure. Anger and other emotions only cloud judgment and make you act out of haste. The way a person handles themselves at a time of crisis is the true gauge of their character. During ideal times a person does not have to make crucial decisions that may have serious repercussions. Therefore, when dealing with this type of challenge, seek to find the solution and do not dwell on anything that will not be productive. Thinking of how much money you lost, bad press, or arguing will not help solve the issue. Step back from the situation and figure out logically how to make the best of the situation. There are always options, put your energy into finding alternatives instead of getting caught up in the moment.

The example of Earvin "Magic" Johnson is very inspirational. In November 1991, Magic held a press conference announcing to the world that he was inflicted with the HIV virus. Many people sympathized that the game of basketball would lose one of its greatest players ever. Not only that, but Earvin Johnson the person was at a risk of losing his life. However, even to this day, Magic is still in the headlines for various successes he has accomplished in business and is still in good health. After his exit from basketball, he formed Magic Johnson Enterprises which owns, franchises, and/or operates companies such as 24 Hour Fitness, T.G.I. Friday's, Starbucks, movie theatres, and many other businesses across the country. The company also includes a private investment arm, with over $1 billion in funds which will help the company expand and also fund various real estate projects. The empire has been estimated to be worth well over $700 million and is expanding rapidly. From the success of Magic Johnson Enterprises to his many other investments, he has proven that even in the mist of life's greatest turmoil, greatness can be accomplished. Some even would conclude that Magic is a better businessman than he was ever a basketball player!

We all face adversity in our lives but this does not have to translate to a dreaded future. Finding potential and success amongst negative ordeal is what makes a great business person. Don't let your immediate emotions dictate your outcome, but make every effort to keep a level head at all times.

* * *

Those who compete on a higher level are willing to make sacrifices and exercise discipline in delaying pleasure and reward for a future time. Sacrifice can be defined as a practice that delays current satisfaction for the potential future greater good of a situation. It is also the faith that working hard today will yield you the success that you desire tomorrow. There are a number of ways to make sacrifices in business including time, energy, money, sleep, and anything else that is valued. Any entrepreneur who has achieved some form of success has had to make the decision of giving up things that are important to them in hopes to benefit from their actions later. For example, a person who is busy trying to build their company may have to sacrifice enjoying some of life's rewards like giving up vacation time, spending time with loved ones, or treating themselves to expensive gifts.

You must exercise discipline and restraint to delay what may be easier to enjoy in the current time. You can either enjoy the fruits of your labor now or postpone this reward for the future. The difference in postponing your rewards is that you have the opportunity to make it greater with time. If you choose to enjoy things now, you may cut off potential resources, which could have later helped multiply your future reward. This is the very essence of sacrifice. Naturally, when we sacrifice anything, we do so with the expectation that it is for good reason and that we will somehow benefit in the future. Sacrificing is a process that is usually not comfortable or pleasant. This creates a barrier between those who are willing to make these compromises and those who are not willing to endure its hardships. No success is without sacrifice and you must be prepared to do all that is required today if you want to get the most out of your future.

Ingvar Kamprad, the founder of IKEA, made key sacrifices early in his life which directly contributed to his current success. Today IKEA is known worldwide as the retailer of innovative and stylish furniture sold at a great price. The company operates over two hundred retail stores globally and maintains a store catalog which employs over 90,000 people. The company brings in revenues of over $10 billion annually and has made founder Ingvar Kamprad one of the top ten richest men in the world.

In its early days, before furniture was introduced in their product line, Ingvar sold a variety of goods including wallets, watches, jewelry, stockings, and any other items that could turn a profit. Starting at the young age of ten, Kamprad found he could buy matches very inexpensively in Stockholm and bring them back to his home town to sell at a profit. He continued to search for new products to retail and reinvested his profits back into his company, expanding the product line continuously. When he turned seventeen years old, his father rewarded him with money for doing well in school. Instead of doing what most adolescent young men tend to do which is to spend it on short-term rewards, he sacrificed and put the money into founding IKEA. Although all other products have since been removed from the items IKEA sells, the early products undoubtedly helped paved the way for the company's success.

The example of Ingvar and IKEA is one of the great stories of the gain and success that can be realized from sacrifice. Delaying the reward of spending the money that his father gave him must have been very difficult for a person who was that young and had not yet had the chance to get spending out of his system. Often with youth, it is common to want to conform to what others their age are enjoying, which is usually spending without much consideration of the future. Having the foresight to save in order to increase opportunities for the future is something that few have the discipline to do.

Sacrifice involves learning the importance of patience and delaying your pleasures of enjoyment for the future ideal time. If you are not willing to ever delay your pleasures, you may solely expose yourself to short term gratification indefinitely. People are generally rewarded with two types of compensation for their work, short term and long term satisfaction.

Short-term satisfaction can be defined as pleasure which gives us gratification for limited amounts of time. We are often left unsatisfied and longing for more fairly quickly. To gain these pleasures some may buy a new wardrobe, go out to a club or event, or eat a good meal. Short term satisfaction provides a temporary intermission from our current workload. Long term satisfaction can be thought of as lasting gratification. It can come in the form of a promotion at work which may give us a lasting feeling of accomplishment and greater future financial reward.

You may either maintain a balance of both types of satisfaction in your life, or pursue one more diligently. The short-term satisfaction can serve to keep you currently motivated. It breaks the monotony of "all work and no play." However, don't let the enjoyment of these short-term pleasures prohibit you from the potential to reach any long term satisfaction you may desire. The more you sacrifice today, the better your chances of achieving long term satisfaction.

People who Grind effectively lean more toward long term satisfaction and are not hesitant to make its required sacrifices. Those who are truly disciplined can forego short term pleasures altogether or keep them at a minimum. Their vision is for the future and they realize that short term outlets fade without any true sustainable satisfaction. Short term satisfaction is viewed as a way to slow down the achievement of their ultimate goals. Every time you think of expending the resources for something in the short term, calculate its pleasure value and its affect on future endeavors. Sometimes one must be sacrificed for the other, so you must make your choice that balances what ultimately makes you happy with what is most beneficial for your future.

> *Listen to many, speak to a few.*
> —William Shakespeare

In *Bowling for Columbine*, Michael Moore's documentary which features the tragic high school shootings, he asked musician Marilyn Manson what he would say to the two shooters. He answered, "I wouldn't say a single word to them. I would listen to what they have to say, and that's what no one did."

In the world, many of our problems could be solved if we only took the time to really listen to other views. When another person speaks we gain the insight to concerns, suggestions, and overall information about what is on their mind. We can process this information to make our relationships with others more cohesive. With communication, we all can express our views and add to the collective of thoughts to improve our surroundings. These thoughts can benefit us by bringing about enjoyment of broader results that more minds have had a chance to contribute to.

In business, we take so much time relaying messages to others through advertisements, sales pitches, promotions, speeches, presentations and a number of other ways. As obvious as it may be, we should not neglect the importance of listening. Sometimes the most obvious and simple things are the things we overlook as they have become so routine. It is said that during conversations, people often hear but do not listen to what is said. While the other person is talking we are busy thinking of the next thing to say. We do this instead of taking in the messages they are trying to relay to us. We diminish the benefits of direction that another person may give us as to what they really want from this communication.

We can also listen with our eyes in the form of body language. Much of what is being communicated can be said by the subtle actions one presents. It is important that we are able to interpret the things that one does not say but makes apparent with their body language as these can give us further insight. In the game of poker, players often study other players for clues that might be presented. From any indicating behavior, one player can gain the advantage of insight on the type of hand others are holding. This can be the deciding factor on the result of the game. When you are conducting business take the time to listen, as it may be the most important part of the communication process.

* * *

Having integrity for what you do shows the value that you place in your profession. It is a sort of discipline that propels you to do your best and never compromise due to your respect of the field you pursue. It is an unwavering stance to continue an action that you believe is moral and righteous. Integrity will keep you mindful of the value system that you maintain and keeps you on course with guidelines that you believe in.

I have a friend named Eddie who I used to talk to about jazz and buy records from. Eddie was a radio disc jockey and successful jazz musician and when I visited his home he would share great stories about some of the greats he had been around when he was touring. He possessed many rare recordings he would play me as we sat in his studio and talked. His knowledge of the early days of jazz was not only thorough but much vaster than information I was able to read about in all the jazz books I came across.

The story that stands out in my mind and still influences me is one he told about Charlie "Bird" Parker at Birdland. Birdland was a place which many of the prominent jazz musicians at the time performed at, named after the nickname of the great Charlie Parker. Charlie Parker was scheduled to perform that night at the venue and drew a crowd. Eddie was in the audience and like all the attendees they were waiting for Charlie Parker to arrive, who was late as usual. After about an hour, he arrives dressed in a tee shirt, despite the snowy weather outside, with two females in each arm. His band was already on stage warming up the crowd without him. He approached the stage and as he was going up the stage stairway, Charlie Parker slips and falls flat on his face, all the while holding his saxophone straight up in the air and never letting it touch the ground! It was truly amazing to me that even at such a vulnerable time, the jazz great had it in his mind to not let his instrument become damaged even at the expense of his pride in front of an audience. It's so rare nowadays for artists to have such integrity in their art form and ultimately respect their craft in this way. Eddie went on to tell me that the night progressed into one of the greatest performances he had seen of Charlie Parker and that this experience would never be forgotten. Unfortunately, the Birds life was plagued with continued drug use that caused him to lose passion for his work as indicated by the many books and literature written about his life, but this was an instance that personified the love that he had for music.

When you have integrity for your work, you are on a path toward excellence. The respect that you have for your craft empowers you to bring out the best from inside yourself. Build a genuine attachment for the things that you are involved with and this will show your commitment to your profession.

* * *

Think of what you would give up to be able to go back in time or time travel. Consider how many people go to palm readers and fortune tellers to somehow cheat time and afford a glimpse into the future. The future is directly attributed to how you use the time you currently have. In the fast paced forum of business, time is of the essence. Sometimes, in order to stay ahead of your competition and perform at higher levels, the rate of speed at which you conduct your business is of great significance. Whether it is quicker turnaround in manufacturing or providing faster services, it can be a factor in giving you a competitive edge. Therefore, if this is relevant in your profession, make sure that you are able to provide a quick turnaround to meet the demands of your customers or those you are working with.

H&M is a worldwide retailer of men, women, and children's clothing operating over 3,100 stores in fifty-three different markets in five regions of the world. They offer fresh-off-the-runway fashion at affordable prices, targeting mostly people eighteen to forty-five. Consumers love H&M's ability to stay on top of new fashions at the best prices, and have shown their appreciation by their patronage. When H&M first opened their store in Manhattan, crowds grew so large they had to restock their merchandise hourly. For the Japan store opening, people stood outside in lines at six AM in the morning waiting for hours before the store opened. These occurrences are not that unusual and every H&M store is busy enough to be restocked daily. A high volume store can receive as many as three truckloads of merchandise a day. Daily customers can find something new every single day as the company introduces new designer lines daily, and no same style of clothing stays in the stores for longer than a month.

What may be their most competitive advantage is the speed of turnaround of their fashions. They have one of the fastest lead times in the business, which means how long it takes for a garment to travel from design table to store floors. A garment can move from the design process to the store racks with a lead time of around three weeks. This enables H&M to add items that weren't in their collections or increase quantities of an item that takes off. For example, if a shirt began to sell well, the company can produce more units to meet the size, color, etc., to be distributed to a number of stores or all stores where the product is in demand. Their lightning fast turnaround process quickly stocks their stores with the adequate numbers, therefore increasing sales while limiting waste. All their merchandise is designed in house by a team of ninety-five designers and manufacturing is outsourced to a network of hundreds of garment shops located in twenty-one countries. The company's speed maximizes the ability to turn out more hot fashions during any given season and their profits reflect this ability. H&M does not sacrifice quality in their attempt to meet their customer time demands and each year, the products in their collection undergo about 500,000 quality tests such as washing to test shrinkage and colorfastness. They also work with eight hundred and fifty independent suppliers, eliminate middlemen, and buy in large volumes to provide the best prices. In 2013 H&M stores sold more than 550 million items with annual sales of over SEK 150 billion.

Understand that time is a commodity that can never be bought or made. Its value is priceless and you must always be sensitive to the time that you require of others. Place any systems in place which will help speed up delivery time of your product or services. If you are in an employment situation make sure that you make the best use of the time that is given. After all you are specifically compensated by how much time you spend at your employment. Many managers and people in prominent positions take into account how you make use of your time and the amount of work you are able to output. Business moves quickly and often if you are not prepared, one of your competitors will be more than obliged to take your place. You have to remember that today is a day of consumers who are used to instant gratification. From pushing one button on the remote control to order a movie on demand, to pressing keys to converse by instant messenger; everyone is catering to a consumer base that is getting more and more accustomed to the speed of service. Make sure that you are receptive to the response times others may require. The prosperity of your business or career can directly hinge upon your ability to meet this criteria. Those who compete on a higher level know when to consider their pace when working and maintain the ability to manage their time efficiently.

The Grind

* * *

There is a saying that goes, "There is nothing new under the sun." I don't really subscribe to this theory, but I do acknowledge that with all our advancements since our existence, we have already covered a great deal of ground. Ideas are limitless, and there will always be breakthroughs that may enhance our lives or change its dimensions. However, there are still those who maintain a preference in adding their individual contributions to ideas which have been widely, previously pursued. Those who compete on a higher level strive to do what others can do, better than anyone else. In business, it is not necessarily mandatory that we come up with the most original profound ideas, but instead make the best out of those which you choose to pursue. There are thousands of pizza shops, and although they make the same product, certain characteristics make some more highly regarded than others. It could be the marketing of the shop, price point, taste, quality, convenience, ingredients, and many other factors that contribute to their success. No matter how common the business or profession you choose to pursue, make sure that it is done better than any other competitors. Examine all the aspects of the field and make sure that you are superior in every way. From service to product, all these aspects must be focused upon. Acknowledge that fields which are common, most likely have the involvement of many others so your level of effort must exceed this competition. The key is to do the same thing better than anyone else. Also, bring out any differences or unique characteristics that may give you an advantage.

A great example comes from the story of Raising Cane's founder, Todd Graves. It started as a business plan written for a college paper which earned Graves the lowest grade in the class. He envisioned a restaurant which serves only the highest quality chicken fingers. The professor found it hard to believe that a restaurant with a menu consisting of mostly chicken fingers would become successful. Along with the professor, the bankers who he presented his plan to in attempts to receive investment funds also did not believe it would work. At that time, the menu contained only four items consisting of chicken fingers and a number of sides. Undaunted, Graves realized that he would have to raise his own capital to open up this business. After working in an oil refinery and as a commercial salmon fisher, he was able to raise his own seed money and opened his first location. After only twelve short years the company has expanded to include eighty locations and has earned the moniker of one of the fastest growing private companies in the US. Graves pursued what many people thought was an oversaturated idea that was not unique, and didn't seem an exciting new prospect. Chicken fingers are not at all hard to find in the US and many restaurants and fast food restaurants offer them on their menus. The difference was what Graves put into the idea that made it successful. First, the actual fingers are always fresh cooked to order, and never frozen. The prices are very competitive. They serve a special sauce that you can't get enough of. The store is decorated like "a college dorm room" with interesting themed decor and the workplace maintains a unique culture. In summary, the food is good, service is great, fast, priced right, and brings a different, more quality focused rendition of how a chicken finger should be.

Therefore, if you feel that you can bring success and superiority to something which is common, you should not be discouraged to pursue the goal. Make sure that you are aware of what is considered the very best in your field, and be certain that you can compete. Ensure that the advantages you feel you have over competitors are strong enough to be considered groundbreaking. Don't feel limited if you love something that seems to be a common profession. There have been plenty of success stories of people who have found success making a product or service many others offer, so don't necessarily base your success off of a new idea.

Strength does not come from physical capacity.
It comes from an indomitable will.

—Mahatma Gandhi

Will power and self-discipline are very significant traits of the Grind and high achieving individuals. Will power is the ability to control or resist harmful or useless habits. It is the inner strength that propels us to take action in situations when we feel lazy or unmotivated. Once we have made a decision, our will power is our ability to persevere through the hardships that are present in a situation. Self-discipline can be described as a pattern of behavior and conduct that reinforces a set of beliefs and ideals. Discipline involves the ability to stay within boundaries and the practice of self control. It is the ability to exercise restraint in the things that you want today in sacrifice for a better future. Will power and self-discipline work hand in hand to aid the practitioners in taking control of their own situation instead of letting outside factors control their actions.

The Stanford Marshmallow Experiment was conducted in 1972 by Professor Walter Mischel at Stanford University. The study consisted of a group of four-year-old children, who were each given one marshmallow to eat. A condition was presented to each child, that if he/she was able to wait for twenty minutes without eating the marshmallow, he/she was given a second one as a reward. It was concluded that most of the children did not have the will power to wait the twenty minutes and gave in to temptation. The findings were of great interest, as the researchers continued studying the developmental progress of each child into their adolescent years. The ones who could wait the twenty minutes, who were able to practice self control and self discipline, turned out to be more successful in life than the other group who could not delay gratification. The kids with the highest will power grew up to do better in school, to have better social skills, and to be better able to handle stress.

By the results of this research, we can see the benefits that the traits of will power and self-discipline can have on our levels of success. Maintaining the discipline of studying and working harder to get good grades to qualify you to attend a respected college. Saving money through will power to later open up your own business. Maintaining discipline by exercising to keep you in good shape to meet any challenging requirements. Working extra hours to gain a promotion or show your dedication to an employer. All these and many more are all goals utilizing will power and self-discipline to accomplish, and these would most likely to be pursued by the children in the study who maintained discipline.

It is in our nature to resist the use of will power and self-discipline as their practice is usually unpleasant. This is because both are traits which cause us to go against our will. Research has shown however, that both are traits which we all can develop through continued practice. In other words, other than the degree of practice of both, no one is endowed with more of these abilities than any other person. Therefore, working on strengthening both characteristics is a surefire way to increase your potential level of performance.

One way to develop these traits is to initiate action in the things that you do not want to do, but know are beneficial in the long run. For example, you may have just come back from work and would like to watch TV and relax. I am referring to a day where you may not be too tired from work and still have energy to perform other activities. Instead of ending your day you may do something that will better your professional future. This could be writing down a plan to complete a goal, research some information for a future project, or the many other options which can contribute to progress. In this example you are working on both traits at once, practicing your will power to avoid watching TV and utilizing your self-discipline to work on an activity which will benefit your employment. Most people know what is right according to their common sense. Most also know that doing these things will be beneficial, but are resistant because of the extra work that it takes. By doing things that you do not like or by working when you feel too tired or lazy, you condition yourself to overcome your initial natural resistances. After continued practice, it becomes easier and easier to go against this resistance and you develop your inner strength to resist. The use of these traits becomes second nature with enough practice and you will find in time that you will be able to tend to these activities with greater ease. There are so many benefits in using these traits and they must be developed and implemented in your business personality in order to meet the high demands of the Grind.

> *Believe you can and you're halfway there.*
> —Theodore Roosevelt

Those who perform at higher levels believe in themselves and are willing to make difficult decisions even at the opposition of others. In these cases, take the time to make sure that your decision is sound and then proceed with confidence. Take the time to do your "due diligence," and after you determine that you have come up with the best option, don't hesitate to make your choice. We often are influenced by others opinions, and will allow our perspective to be distorted by popular consensus. Remember that these opinions are usually from people who are not directly involved in or do not have a complete understanding of the situation. In the end, no one has to answer for the decision that was made but you. Always make your decision on the facts in relation to the subject and not only the opinions or feedback of others, unless they are giving you sound advice from a reliable point of view. One instance that often comes up that requires you to remain confident in your decision is the choice to pursue a career that others may feel is unorthodox or nontraditional. Although it would be great to have the support of others, you have to decide on a career that you truly love or have a passion for. Others may be skeptical of your choice as the field is still new and unproven, so it may seem like a risk. However, there are advantages to pursuing these kinds of professions, as there are still very few competitors and may not have many limitations for growth in place yet. Always take heed to the advice of others, but ultimately make sure that the decision is yours and comes from your heart. Remember, in the end you are the one who is responsible for the decision and it is your time that is committed as a result.

A great example of a person who went against the grain and found success with an unorthodox profession is Guy Lalibete and his company, Cirque Du Soleil. There are few other rags to riches story that evokes as much excitement as that of Guy Laliberte and his entertainment company,

Cirque Du Soleil. Most success stories of today consist of corporate CEOs, real estate moguls, oil tycoons, and inheritance heirs finding success in the usual uneventful sectors of business. Such is not the case of Guy Laliberte, who turned his early experiences of street performing into an international performance phenomenon.

Born to a large middle-class family in Canada, Laliberte left home at age eighteen to hitchhike across Europe working as a street performer *busking*, which is another word for a traveling street performer. He had developed a passion for performance arts at a young age when his parents bought him to a Ringling Brothers and Barnum & Bailey Circus. He even produced his own performance events in high school and learned how to play the accordion and harmonica to enhance his performances. During his travels through Europe he played music and juggled for small amounts of cash, and soon was accepted into a performance troupe that put on street shows featuring fire breathers, sword swallowers, acrobats and stilt walkers. Although the money earned was very little, he became rich with knowledge learning the skills of stilt walking and art of fire breathing. Money eventually became a problem so Laliberte returned to Quebec to accept a full time job at a hydro-electric power plant. Just three days into his new employment the plant workers went on strike and he was fired. He took this as a sign and vowed to devote himself 100 percent to performance arts from then on. He met Gilles Ste-Croix and Daniel Gauthier around this time, who would become his future business partners.

In the early eighties, the three partners organized a summer performance fair in Baie-Saint-Paul, which grew into a moderate success. In 1983, the Canadian government offered a cultural budget for the celebration of the 450th anniversary of Jacques Cartier's discovery of Canada and asked them to develop artistic concepts that could bring the festivities to other areas. Laliberte took charge of the circus project, becoming its producer and was able to obtain a $1.5 million contract from the government after it was said that his partner Gilles Ste-Croix walked fifty-six miles from Baie-Saint-Paul to Quebec City on stilts to impress them! He used the money to create and launch "Le Grand Tour du Cirque Du Soleil," the first version of the Cirque shows. The show was a critical and financial success, earning $40,000 profit, and more importantly it was Cirque's big break and glimpse of what was to come.

For the next number of years Cirque traveled to various areas around the globe performing and continuing to grow as an entity. In 1992, Laliberte secured a deal with casino mogul Steve Wynn who signed Cirque to perform at Las Vegas' Treasure Island Hotel. The first show, "Mystere," went on to sell out every single ticket for 480 shows in its first year and the show is still maintains a permanent residence. Laliberte had no contract restricting him from setting up shows in any other venues in Las Vegas so he was able to expand and include other Cirque shows at various casinos. One only has to attend one of these shows to see why they are so popular. The shows feature awe-inspiring stunts and techniques from traditional circus arts mixed with today's modern theatrical innovations. Each type of Cirque show features visually stunning backdrops and landscapes with characters dressed in elaborate costumes. The Las Vegas shows produce about 60 percent of Cirque's annual revenues. Today, Laliberte still owns 80 percent of the company and maintains full creative control of each of his ten traveling shows and ten permanent shows around the world. Cirque has performed for more than 100 million spectators in 300 cities and employs over 5,000 employees representing 57 nationalities worldwide. They earn $1 billion in annual revenue which has amassed Laliberte a personal fortune of $2.6 billion.

Laliberte has stated in an interview that he is from a middle-class family whose parents dreamed of their children becoming doctors or lawyers. When he originally came back and told his parents he wanted to pursue a career as a creative producer and artist and that he would not go to college, there were lots of tears. It is often difficult to gain the support of your loved ones when you pursue a career that is nontraditional or not yet tested. Most people are not yet informed about these career types and these fields may not have yet been proven enough to indicate the extent of success that is possible. However, the advantage is that there are usually no limitations in place and people who get involved in the field early may establish their own potential opportunities. There is less competition since it will usually be the road less traveled. Believe in yourself and find the subject of work that you love first and your passion will generate income. Whether it is a career choice or other decision which has to be made in your career, always have faith in yourself to make the decisions you feel are best. Whether right or wrong, you have to practice being confident in your career choices as you will not always have someone there to give you encouragement. Sometimes, people will become conditioned to asking for advice before every decision and it becomes a habit. Those who strive to perform at higher levels of effort must possess the characteristics of a leader and be able to make difficult decisions and take full responsibility for their choices.

> *Positive anything is better than negative nothing.*
> —Elbert Hubbard

Those who perform on a higher level maintain a positive outlook even after any failure they experience. They keep steadfast toward their goals and proceed to keep trying no matter the obstacles they must overcome. They maintain a positive outlook for the future and approach any new challenges with a fresh perspective not tainted by any past shortcomings. Any failures are viewed as a learning experience to be used as a lesson in future endeavors that are pursued. Maintaining a positive outlook is imperative to success, and as studies have proven, expectations have a great affect on the end results of a situation. As the Galatea Effect suggests, a person's opinion and self expectation of themselves and their abilities, dictates their performance. So if you choose to remain positive and expect the best, this will have a positive affect on your business performance and motivation.

From the words of David Neeleman: "If I hadn't gotten fired from Southwest, there would never have been a JetBlue. And if I hadn't gotten fired from JetBlue, there wouldn't be an Azul." Neeleman, founder of JetBlue and Azul Airlines, is an example of a person who has taken the negative circumstance of getting fired from a previous job, and turned it into an opportunity to start a new situation. He is the quintessential example of what should be done in situations where we find ourselves starting over after a loss in our career. Instead of quitting, he had enough confidence in himself to try again in a business sector which has been known as the most difficult to succeed in. The first time occurred when he sold his first airline startup, Morris Air to Southwest Airlines. He became a contender to replace CEO Herb Kelleher at Southwest, but Kelleher did not feel the position was a fit for Neeleman and instead ended up firing him. This set stage for him to start Jetblue Airlines, an airline providing luxury flying at discount prices. The airline offers all economy class flights with stylish perks such as leather seats, Direct TV, satellite radio, additional legroom, and assigned seats. He quickly built Jetblue into America's eighth largest airline with revenues of $2.5 billion annually. Then a tragic event changed the course of his success with Jetblue. An ice storm descended on Valentines 2007, and almost all airlines closed down but Jetblue believed the storm would pass and sent planes to the runways. The weather continued and planes could not take off, while other planes landed blocking the gates. More than 130,000 were stranded for about ten hours. Media coverage was extensive and public opinion critical. Three months after, Neeleman found himself replaced as CEO and ousted from the company he started, despite accepting responsibility and efforts to remedy the shortcomings. Getting fired from the company you founded must have been crushing, but Neeleman never allowed this to cease his efforts. In fact, this resulted in his next endeavor which was to establish a new airline in the Brazilian market. Although many believed that starting an airline in Brazil was a risky venture and could not sustain another airline, Neeleman believed in the market. Brazil is Latin America's largest economy, and like China at this time is experiencing a high growth rate in its rising middle class. He also recognized that companies such as Coca Cola, Procter & Gamble, Ford, and others were raising their own stakes in Brazil. So he raised over $200 million, and personally invested $13 million of his own money to start the airline. In the end Neeleman's instincts proved to be sound, and Azul became his fourth successful investment in the airline industry. At Jetblue, it took him ten months and ten days to reach 1 million passengers, but at Azul he was able to accomplish this in eight months. Azul is now the third largest airline in Brazil, and was able to break a record previously set by Jetblue, which was registering 2.2 million passengers in its first twelve months of operation.

* * *

People who compete on a higher level are able to spot trends early and realize the potential of a good idea, even if it is not their own. To do so you must have a genuine interest in the world around you and a desire to keep up with new developments that are emerging in your field. Many of today's success stories are people who didn't necessarily come up with a new groundbreaking idea but were instead able to recognize a good idea and later find success by bringing it to another area. For example, Howard Schultz was able to do exactly this when he recognized that there was a culture surrounding coffee drinkers in Italy and that he could bring this same culture to the US and find success with Starbucks. He found that it was an integral role in the social life of most Italians, and that this could be recreated in the US by initially opening a coffee bar in Seattle.

Rupert Murdoch was said to have a gift in spotting trends. In the 1950s, he wanted his company, News LTD, to break into television. America was at the forefront of this medium and the TV revolution and Murdoch began to travel to the US frequently to learn more. At the time, Australia was several years behind America in the development of TV. Determined to get on the air first and bring TV to Adelaide, he set out to Los Angeles to seek programs that he could acquire for his new station. While he was out there he would travel to other areas such as Las Vegas, seeking out any other ideas that he could bring back to Australia with him. He would pick up magazines and look for new trends in the U.S. Murdoch made contact with the owner of ABC, Lenard Goldenson. The two went out to lunch and Goldenson was said to be so impressed by Murdoch and his drive that he offered to buy shares of News LTD. This was the perfect union as Goldenson had aspirations to spread TV into a worldwide medium and Murdoch needed this resource to benefit his startup in Adelaide. Murdoch wanted to start a weekly television magazine, and felt that the American program, TV Guide, would be the perfect model to follow. He traveled to Philadelphia where TV Guide was published to seek out any ideas that he could use for his own program. He figured the best way to proceed with this venture would be to copy their success and learn the most that he could to bring back with him to Adelaide. When he got back, he started an Australian version of TV Guide, and the station became a hit. The information that he had learned by visiting the U.S. gave him the advantage of getting on the air before the competitor stations could do so. The station made him a great deal of money and enabled him to pursue his ambitions of expanding outside the area of Adelaide, eventually taking his company worldwide.

In Los Angeles where I grew up, there was a Taco Bell fast food restaurant located across the street from where I had lived. For all of my childhood until I left my home for about fifteen years, I had easy access to eat there whenever I chose to do so. I never thought much about it and grew sick of eating there from my frequent visits. I did like that it was cheap, a luxury I could afford back then. I then moved to Massachusetts to live with my uncle. I remember one day I was driving home and the traffic had come to a standstill. There were police directing the traffic and I thought a car accident may have occurred. As I came closer to the cause of the delays, I discovered that the source of the traffic was actually cars waiting to get into a new Taco Bell location that they had just opened in the area. Cars were lined up in the drive thru and in the parking lot as people were waiting their turn to visit the restaurant. I was shocked and it dawned on me that I never had seen one Taco Bell chain restaurant in the area and that this was the first one I had seen since moving from Los Angeles. They had just opened the location and the cause of the traffic was actually a result of their grand opening that very day. There were news crews present and it turned out being a pretty big deal. We all come across ideas every day that may be able to be relocated and established for success. What may be an old, uneventful idea in one area may be an entirely new prospect in another area that has not been exposed to the type of business or idea. Make sure that you keep aware of any of these types of situations and seek to benefit from these possible opportunities.

The Grind

This event taught me one of the important strategies of business, which is to take a business that is successful in one area and bring it to an area where it does not yet exist. It is safer and less of a risk to bring something that has already been tried and tested as a success in one area, to an area which has not yet experienced its potential. Something that works in one area has a much higher potential to work in another area, as long as its success is not due to regional demand.

Those who aspire to perform on higher levels must develop the keen ability to recognize the potential for success in any opportunity that they come across. Remember that success is not always a result of a new original idea. You can experience the same amount of success by recognizing good ideas that have worked for others, which you can further exploit again to realize additional success in your own situation. Our pride may limit us from taking this action, but you have to acknowledge that even when your goals do not involve your own ideas, your abilities are still required to find success. Success is still hinged on your performance and the work that you must put forth. In your efforts, don't only spend your time looking for the next new idea but stay alert for trends which may provide you new opportunities to find the success that you seek.

Never Give Up

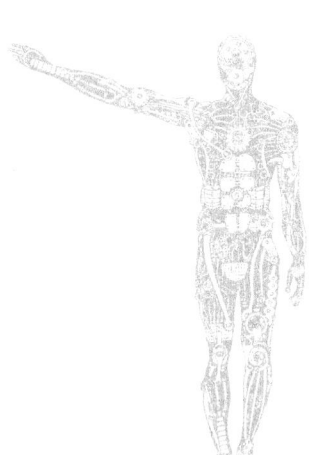

When you have ten to fifteen doors slammed in your face, you still need to be as enthusiastic at door No. 16 as you were at door No. 1.
—John Paul DeJoria

Throughout history we have been given the blueprint of success. All we really have to do is look at the history and biographies of people who have become prominent in their respective fields. Many factors are required from these individuals to achieve success, but the one thing they had in common is that they never gave up despite all adversity. Their tenacity for perseverance is great and the ability to sustain effort consistently over long periods of time toward intended goals are relentless. They have done what their counterparts would not do and their efforts pay off with accolades others could not attain. Affluence, prestige, fulfillment, and accomplishment are indicating markers for their success. Unfortunately, most people do not take heed to these examples or acknowledge them as a reality which may be enjoyed by all people. They neglect their previous work and give up prematurely succumbing to failure and never realizing their full potential.

The story of Joanne K. Rowland, author of the Harry Potter series, is a testament of true perseverance. Around the time she was soliciting a publisher for the first book, her life was unraveling as she was going through a divorce and living in a small flat with a young daughter. She wrote the first drafts in longhand and did not even have enough money for a used typewriter. Enlisting the help of a grant, she finalized the book but was rejected by about twelve different publishers before one accepted. As a result of her persistence, the Harry Potter empire was born, and the first three books of the series eventually occupied the first three slots of the New York Times bestsellers list. The books have been translated into about sixty different languages with sales of over a quarter of a billion copies worldwide. She is now one of he richest female entertainers in the world and considered a phenomenon and inspiration to many.

The Grind is synonymous with words such as will, drive, hunger, vigor, persistence, grit, perseverance, passion, drive and others which are directly associated with your ability to endure adversities in your given profession. The factor which separate successful individuals from most is that they keep trying despite all odds and eventually find their way to success. It's almost as if they possess precognition that their efforts will eventually pay off so short term failure is not viewed as a reason to cease efforts or pursue a different goal. They have a realistic perspective of what it will take to meet the demands set forth each day, and motivation and passion for what they pursue fuels them on. They not only accommodate short term tasks but keep steadfast in maintaining aim despite the number of years required for completion.

> *You might never fail on the scale I did, but it is impossible to live without failing at something, unless you live so cautiously that you might as well not have lived at all-in which case, you fail by default.*
> —J.K. Rowland, speaking to the graduating class of Harvard in June 2008

In most instances of individuals who have been extraordinarily successful in their pursuits; there has been accompaniment of a long string of failures. If you don't have any failure present in your life, chances are you are not really challenging yourself or seeking your full potential. Failure is one of the greatest teachers. Great people embrace failure as an asset, an outlet to gain knowledge for future endeavors. It is not necessarily a bad thing and many greats use it as motivation in their desire for better.

Upon reflection of his career, Michael Jordan, one of the greatest basketball players to ever play the game, said, "I've missed more than nine thousand shots in my career. I've lost almost three hundred games. Twenty-six times, I've been trusted to take the game winning shot and missed. I've failed over and over and over again in my life. And that is why I succeed."

Notice how he takes inventory and is fully mindful that his shortcomings have contributed to his ultimate success? It's almost as if this awareness drives him to pursue greater things. There is no question as to why he has accomplished so much success. His continued effort grants him the opportunity for achievement. Failures provide a sort of checklist, eliminating the many options which may be at hand which distract you from the ultimate favorable outcome. With each failure, you eliminate an option that is no longer a present distraction and a dead end is closed off. Embrace failure as closure to one of many paths on the road to success. The only time you truly fail is when you use it as an excuse to give up.

* * *

Sometimes people will quit before they really even begin the effort. They may get discouraged from someone giving them a negative opinion, feel that it may be too large an undertaking, misunderstand information, or some other reason that makes them not even initiate the process. The advice of never giving up goes for these types of situations also not just situations you have invested large amounts of time into. They can be as equally as important to the goals you wish to pursue and are needed for your success. If you don't even try, you don't even get an idea of what the effort will entail. It can actually be much easier than you expected and the advice you may have received may have been information that did not apply to your particular situation. Every person and their abilities are different from others and you shouldn't compare the two if you do not know the particular details of this specific situation. Make sure that you always make an attempt to explore the situation for yourself before ever giving up something that you truly aspire for. This is especially true if it is something you must complete for a goal that you have set for yourself.

A pivotal moment in the history of the True Religion Jeans came when Jeffrey Lubell wanted to have his products stocked on the shelves of major retailer Fred Segal. However, there was one major problem, Lubell showed the buyer the collection and he hated it. So he did the next logical thing, he went over the person's head to his boss, the Vice President of Menswear buyer and asked her to give him a chance. Then came the next major obstacle, she hated the collection also! So he pleaded back and forth with her telling her that he needed a break and to give him a chance. She said they were not Levi's and said no. He said in an interview about the incident that she kept coming in the room and then going, but he said he would not leave until she placed an order. At one point she was even going to call security, but Lubell said he would just make a scene. In the end, after going back and forth with each other for hours, Lubell wore her out and she agreed to an order of twenty-four pieces. Not taking no for an answer, he ended up staying in her office for two hours! It was not all in vain, however, and the store did eventually end up selling all their products and True Religion took off not long afterward to the success that it is today.

But this was not his only challenge of getting the line into retail stores in his early days, which can often be a tough challenge for a new brand. The second time came when he wanted to include the line at retailer, Barneys NY. Lubell was displaying his brand, True Religion Jeans, in a tradeshow in Italy, when the buyer from Barneys came to his booth. He also said he did not like the jeans, so Lubell said that when he got back to LA, he was going to go to Barney's and give jeans to every single employee and have them call him up. True to his word he gave the entire sales floor at Barney jeans as long as they said they would call the buyer. So he ended up receiving an order for 480 pieces from the men's buyer and a 600-piece order from the women's buyer. A year later at the same tradeshow in Italy, he ran into the women's buyer and she thanked him for making sure that Barney's had carried the line and that it was outselling any other jean collection that they carried.

Many people in Lubell's position would have quit. In doing so, they quit before they even really get anything going and the effort is still in its earliest stages. In these types of situations, doing what Lubell did is the best way to proceed; which is to not accept rejection and attempt to find any alternatives toward making progress. When you first start a task, the motivation to keep going is not yet strong or developed as the effort is still in the early stages and there has not been a lot of time and energy invested yet. Therefore it is easier to walk away from, and some will abandon the effort. However, just remember that you made the decision to pursue the goal for a reason. It may just be a situation where the biggest challenges of the goal came at the initial stages of the effort and may just become easier as things develop. Therefore, keep steadfast to your goals and do not give up. Give the situation some more time to develop so that you can get a better indication of what to expect in the later stages.

> *If you don't have the time to do it right,*
> *when will you have time to do it over?*
>
> —John Wooden

Remember, when you quit a goal that you have set for yourself, you will invariably have to start from the beginning of another. People tend to always think the grass is greener on the other side, and believe switching over to a new goal may be easier. There is a saying that I have heard regarding the previous quote that makes sense to me which is, "The grass may be greener on the other side, but it's only because there is more bullcrap buried there that you don't see from the other side of the fence!" This can be the truth in many instances, and until you are in the other particular situation, you never know what additional obstacles you will have to deal with. Try to stay on course with the initiatives that you have already started and find new alternatives to get you through any obstacles that may come up. Don't just avoid a problem by looking for a whole new goal to start, but instead search for ways in which you can progress by finding new solutions.

A conscious effort must be made to explore the problem and seek options for remedy. Sometimes the requirement calls for exhausting many different options and patience and creativity must be exercised. First, view all your options for any solutions available for your current task and put thought into finding various alternatives. For example, let's say your goal is to obtain a promotion at work and your boss does not seem to notice your efforts. You feel that no matter what you do there is no chance that your actions will be acknowledged so you are thinking of finding a new job. Some available options may be to look carefully into your boss's business personality. Study his or her professional past thoroughly. Who has he or she given promotions to in the past and why? You may want to ask that person what they did to find favor and earn the promotion. How did your boss get into the position he or she is currently in, and what actions led to his or her success? What compliments has he or she given to you or a coworker in the past? What actions does he or she favor and take the most notice of?

Learning the details of a person's business characteristics goes a long way. Don't just leave things up to chance but take control of the situation and control your own fate. Once you get answers to the questions, implement the actions which will give you a better chance to gain your desired outcome. Be very meticulous to better your chances. If all else fails you may even want to approach your boss and ask for advice and guidance making him/her aware of your intentions for advancement. In many instances, inquiry and genuine interest goes a long way. Sometimes, all it takes is one small breakthrough to take your career or business into the success you desire. Finding options opens up the doorway for this possibility. Before you give up, give yourself the potential for success through creating solutions. Realize that giving up is a dead end which produces the inevitable requirement of starting a new pursuit and having to begin the process once again.

* * *

Sometimes progress takes a long time to be realized. There are certain professions which have long standing employment hierarchy, and whose employees have been with the company for a long term, so upward movement is very gradual. Patience is in order in these situations and there is a requirement to remain consistent with your efforts. Don't give up and realize that your actions will have an effect sooner or later. Most people want immediate results but these things are often out of our control. Many people experience frustration when their efforts are not realized by the people in their workplace. Whether it's a manager, partner, or your customers, acknowledgement is not always obtained with every action. Sometimes it may take years. Just realize that whether you are credited for your efforts or not, if you keep persevering someone will take notice.

When I was about ten years old my father took me with him to the airport to pick up a relative coming into town. We got there early anticipating traffic and the plane was delayed. I became bored waiting and began looking around.

I noticed a machine that collected change for carts used to transport luggage to the check-in counters or to parked cars in the parking lot. Patrons were inserting money to obtain the carts and I noticed that it dispensed money as a reward if you returned your cart back to the machine. The reward for the return was about fifty cents. Realizing the potential for profits I went around collecting as many carts as I could find. People would leave the carts behind after they had transported their luggage to their cars or check-in counter, and this was all to my benefit when I returned the carts and collected the reward. At the end of my efforts I ended up earning over thirty dollars before my relative arrived and we left the airport. Proud of myself, I showed my father the money and he smiled but said little else.

Years later, when I was obtaining my college education, my father came into some money after being injured at work. Because of his health he needed someone to administrate his finances and assets. He had a number of options from friends to other family members but he ended up granting me this responsibility. He sat me down and began to explain to me that the reason for his decision was because he had seen what I had done at the airport that day, along with other efforts he seen me perform growing up, which proved to him I would one day be successful at anything I would choose to pursue.

After all this time my father revealed to me that he had acknowledged my efforts that day, something I had not even realized he took notice of. Sometimes in life and work, our actions are not acknowledged for years to come. We may think that the action was in vain but the consequences of our actions can have effect years later. We have to engage in our actions not expecting that each effort will bring us reward but that the sum combined results of our work will put us in a better situation eventually. We should not always expect immediate reinforcement but instead be grateful for the very actions we have taken to better our cause in the future. Every action serves as a piece to the puzzle eventually forming a whole picture others can view and acknowledge.

> *It's always too soon to quit!*
> —Norman Vincent Peale

Even some of the world's most prominent companies have had to experience instances in their history where they were on the brink of failure and had to go through the process of persevering and not giving up their efforts. Even though these companies have achieved such prominence, they are not immune to the challenges that everyone else has to endure. The following examples are instances of those companies and individuals which have had to come back from dire situation to prove why they deserve the position that they currently enjoy. Take into account, the measures which had to be taken to make it through these tough times, and consider whether you can follow their example in your own situation.

When you are flying to Las Vegas to gamble your company's last $5,000 to try to win enough money to pay bills, you know that you are in a pretty bad place. Believe it or not, this was a reality for Frederick W. Smith, founder of FedEx, and despite this grim reality, he still had no plans of quitting. In his book, *Changing How the World Does Business: FedEx's Incredible Journey to Success—The Inside Story*, the author and founding executive who was with Smith in the beginning days, Robert Frock, describes how Smith admitted to him that he actually took the last of their money to Las Vegas to play blackjack. The company was denied a vital business loan, and they were not able to pay for a $24,000 fuel bill. Smith actually won about $27,000 which kept them in business for another week. Even before its inception, legend had it that he received a modest C grade when he decided to first present his idea for an express delivery service for an economics term paper he had written in college. It was a rocky start from the beginning for the shipping giant and even on the company's first night's run they were only able to secure 186 packages; to be delivered on its fourteen Falcon jets routed to twenty-two cities. With continued low volume of customers, the company had lost almost one-third of its startup cash within the first three months of operation. Unexpected increases in aircraft fuel and gas prices resulting from the Arab Oil Embargo of 1973 and high advertising costs hurt the company's profits. They went on to lose about $27 million in the first two years of operation, and were on the verge of bankruptcy. But despite all the adversity, Smith never quit, and thanks to his leadership and perseverance, FedEx rose to the success it is today. In an interview, Frederick Smith responded to the question of whether he ever considered quitting, "No, I never felt that way at all. I was very committed to the people that had signed on with me and if we were going to go down, we were going to go down with a fight. It wasn't going to be because I checked out and didn't finish it out." FedEx today has revenues of $30 billion, and employs more than 250,000 employees, operating a fleet of over six hundred aircrafts and more than 70,000 surface street vehicles.

When Paul De Joria and Paul Mitchell were starting Paul Mitchell Systems in 1980, they originally had an investor who was going to invest $500,000 for 40 percent ownership of the company. But the investor changed his mind, and pulled out of the deal leaving the two remaining partners to start the company with only $700, which was all the two had between them. De Joria had just given all his money to his former wife as things were not working out with the relationship, and moved out, leaving him homeless. While he started the company, De Joria was living in his car in Los Angeles. Even under these conditions of just ending a relationship and losing his place to live, he did not give up, having enough faith to put the last of his money in the venture. The end result was that they started the company with no partner, allowing them to keep all of it to themselves. Had the investor gone through with the deal, he would have been part owner of the Paul Mitchell empire enjoying the hundreds of millions of dollars he would have earned had he invested!

Martha Stewart was regarded as the reigning queen of living and homemaking before the highly publicized stock trading scandal that landed her in prison in 2004. She was accused of insider trading after selling four thousand shares of ImClone shares a day before the firm's stock price plummeted. Although the charges of securities fraud were thrown out, she was convicted of four counts of obstruction of justice and lying to investigators and sentenced to five months of prison, five months of house arrest, and two years of probation. She also had to pay a heavy fine, and had to agree to a ban which restricted her from serving as a director, CEO, CFO, or any other officer role responsible for preparing, auditing, or disclosing financial results of any public company. Stewart's imprisonment took a great toll on her company, Martha Stewart Living Omnimedia, and she estimates that she lost nearly $1 billion during her trial and prison sentence. Her television and radio shows were cancelled, many advertisers abandoned her magazine, MSLO stock prices plummeted, and she stepped down from her position as CEO and chairwoman of her company. In short, the future of her company and ventures was unsure.

Before the scandal, Stewart became a living and domestic mega-brand, building an unstoppable multimedia and merchandise empire. Her magazine, *Martha Stewart Living*, peaked at a circulation of over two million copies per issue, and the companion website received weekly visitors of 925,000 per week. Her television show was estimated to reach 97 percent of the country and her radio show was carried on 260 stations. She is credited as the author of more than sixty-five published books, many of which were bestsellers. She also started a catalogue business, Martha by Mail and a direct to consumer floral business.

But as a testament to her true resilience, Martha Stewart was able to stage a comeback that many who experience her same adversities, never recover from. She did not quit despite the work that was needed to rebound from the losses she took from the public scandal. Years after her prison stint, she has led the recovery of her company, MSLO back into profitability with over 600 people employed at the company. She has added over 7,000 new products to her brand, published her seventy-first book, runs four magazines, and has a number of television shows on the Hallmark Channel. She may have not reached the same prominence as she maintained before her prison term, and has had a few bumps along the road back to success, but the fact that she is still persevering may be her greatest accomplishment up to date.

* * *

Walt Disney's story is a model for why no one should give up on their efforts. What made him unique was not only his extraordinary vision, but also his belief that his dreams were attainable no matter what obstacles he would have to face. Early in his career, he formed a company called Laugh-O-Gram Films, an animation company operating in Kansas City. Unfortunately, studio profits were not able to pay for all debts incurred and the company ended up going bankrupt. Walt was unfazed by this failure, and later began working on a series for a new animated character, Oswald the Lucky Rabbit for Universal Studios. In another stroke of misfortune, the character and many of the key animators were stolen from him during contract disputes. Not to be swayed from his goals, Walt immediately began to doodle on paper what would eventually lead to the creation of his Disney classic character, Mickey Mouse. However, it wasn't smooth sailing from this point on, as audiences were slow to appreciate and understand many of his future works. The first couple of versions of his early Mickey Mouse films did not sell. He eventually added synchronized sound to "Steamboat Willie," and it was picked up.

When Walt, wanted to create an animation that ran the length of a full-feature film, critics deemed the idea and film "Disney's Folly." However, *Snow White and the Seven Dwarfs* ended up being a success even amidst the period of the Depression. It took years and a number of failures to get to the prominence of its current state and Disney is now a household name. The appeal of Disney's characters has crossed many cultural boundaries and is now embraced and adored by people all over the world.

One of his greatest acts of perseverance was during the process of creating the film for the book, *Mary Poppins*. At the urging of his daughter, Disney began the slow process of attempting to interest the book's author, Pamela Travers, on his ideas for releasing the project on film. However, Travers had no interest and did not want her creation involved with Hollywood or an animation company. This obstacle was not easily remedied and Disney would visit Travers when he traveled to England over the next several years to tell her his ideas for the film and interest her in the project. He never gave up and after sixteen years of pitching his idea, she finally agreed to him. The movie ended up being one of Disney's great accomplishments and most successful projects.

Every aspect of an effort is vital and Disney never gave up but instead used the alternatives that were available to make progress. Small adjustments such as adding sound to his pictures changed the course of the effort. Disney's success rested purely on his belief in his ideas and the endurance and unwavering commitment to see his vision into a reality.

> *The temptation to quit will be greatest just before you are about to succeed.*
>
> —Author Unknown

Most of the time you really don't know what action in your attempts will give you a breakthrough toward the success you desire. Sometimes it is one distinguishable contribution and sometimes it's just the sum of the parts. All actions are relevant to the final outcome and even if they don't bring you closer to finalization, they eliminate an option that may otherwise stand in the way as an obstacle.

You must really explore all your options and take every one seriously as you never know the contribution it will make toward finalization. Instead of giving up, concentrate on the alternatives at hand that you may utilize as an option for progression. You can realize success at any time. It could be one more phone call, an additional email, one small action, one idea, or mentioning a simple phrase; to make the breakthrough to success. Wouldn't it be a shame if you were to exert a significant amount of time to a task, only to quit and fall short by one small action.

The truth is you will never know what may be the final contributing factor which can give you the results that you seek. Therefore, keep trying and keep exploring your options. It can seem like you still have a long time to go or a lot more effort that must be put forth, but the truth is that it can be much less of an effort than you anticipated. I was cutting down a tree the other day and this provided me a good example of the importance of continuing your efforts. When you use an axe, you never know when the final stroke will be that finally makes the tree fall. You can tell when you are near but you cannot tell until it starts to fall. Many efforts are similar and you should not try to anticipate how much work needs to be done until you reach finalization. You are setting yourself up for disappointment if you have established a time and cannot meet that time period. This is actually a negative way to conduct a task as every time an additional attempt is made but no success is realized, you become more frustrated and more likely to quit. Instead, you should just keep trying until the task is done, and be prepared for any additional work that needs to be exerted. Therefore always go into any task willing to do what is necessary to finish the job. In other words, expect the best, but prepare for the worst.

One situation that Michael Ovitz pursued may have helped take CAA to the next level in the company's growth plan: management of film stars. Originally, CAA's strength and list of talent were predominantly comprised of television talent. Ovitz had the intuition that if he acquired the resources of a literary agent, he would be able to have an outlet for movie scripts which would help his goals of "packaging" talent. The term "packaging" was used to describe the practice of the talent agencies placing talent they represented which included actors, directors, writers, financiers, etc.; into a number of positions in a film or TV show before any other company could submit their clients. This also gave them the discretion to gain work for talent that may have been having difficulty gaining work as well as an increase in commissions. For example, one scenario could be if the studios wanted a certain director, they were forced to use the services of the actor that the agency wanted to place in the film or TV show. Ovitz specifically targeted a literary agency, Janklow. Initially, Janklow had no interest to sign with a new company with no established credentials. Ovitz would call diligently and eventually, Janklow agreed to give him half an hour of his time for a meeting. So, Ovitz flew to New York, walked in the office, put his watch on the desk, and after his half hour of presentation ended the meeting and walked out. He took no more than one minute extra than he requested showing his respect for the time he was given. He was concise with his request and made an impression with this memorable display of action. He asked to call Janklow on a weekly basis thereafter and did so at 10:30 sharp every Thursday for a month and a half, never calling late or missing a single call. For his extraordinary effort he was able to land the deal.

This lone act did not make the Creative Arts Agency a success but it was definitely a pivotal point for the development of the company. Who knows where the company would be if this business relationship never transpired. Ovitz went above and beyond to show his dedication, calling on time and showing that he would deliver on his responsibilities. People remember these extreme acts of effort as they set the individual apart from the average. Instead of giving up use your creativity to produce alternatives which you may exercise to gain success. Even one small attempt may mean the difference in obtaining your desired goal, so explore your alternatives before you decide to give up.

I was reading an interview by Zappos's former CEO, Tony Hsieh, in which he was discussing an instance in Zappos history where one of the founding partners was attempting to interest Hsieh in the idea of a shoe store online. In 1999, Nick, one of his future partners, sent him a voicemail stating that he had an idea of selling shoes on the internet which Hsieh, at the particular time, felt and described as the "poster child of bad internet ideas." He felt that no one would ever buy shoes online. On first thought, a person may conclude that in order to purchase shoes a customer would only do so if they could try them on and have them in front of them physically to look at. Hsieh even said that he actually almost deleted the voicemail as he initially thought it was a bad idea. As he was going to do so, a part on the voice mail came up where Nick mentioned that footwear in the US was a $40 billion market, and 5 percent of that number, or $2 billion, were sold by paper mail order catalogues. This fact let it be known that customers may in fact buy shoes from online, as mail order purchases and internet sales had the same limitations to the customers and retailers. Hsieh then realized that internet sales had the potential to be just as big. As a result, Hsieh decided to join his partners to make a leap of faith into the online shoe business, and Zappos was born.

It was just the small mention of this little fact that made all the difference in this pitch for Hsieh to join Zappos. As in many other instances, sometimes it takes the smallest of factors, information, actions or statements to change the course of how a situation will proceed. Therefore, it is important to acknowledge this fact and to always consider each option carefully when trying to achieve progress in any venture. This is so because you never know what will be the final contributing factor that will make a situation progress and reach finalization. You must try each and every option as well as not overlook what may be a seemingly irrelevant factor. Make it a point not to give up as it may be just something minute as the fact mentioned in the example above to make all the difference in the situation. Always exhaust all options and research what factors may make the difference to the party or person you are proposing something to. It may just be something minor which makes all the difference to its success.

> *Many of life's failures are men who did not realize how close they were to success when they gave up.*
> —Thomas Edison

None of us are immune to failure. We all experience the highs and lows that life dictates amongst us. The difference is the way in which we deal with these situations and what we learn from them. Dwelling on a negative situation will not correct the past, and it will not allow you to take any steps that will better your future. The only thing that matters is the present, the here and now. It is the only time we have control of the situation. It is reality that we can not change the past or see into the future. We can however place ourselves in the right position to take on future events. Preparing for the future means learning from your past but not tainting yourself with the feelings of past failures. Failures can be looked upon as experience and knowledge that can help guide you on to future pursuits. Great things come from failure, and the more failure is present, the greater the reward.

Examine the example of Colonel Sanders, the founder of the food chain Kentucky Fried Chicken. He would travel by car to different restaurants and would cook his chicken on the spot for the owners. If they liked the recipe, the restaurant would include the chicken on their menu. It is said that he received 1,009 no's before his chicken was finally accepted! Just remember this example when you are discouraged, and realize that anything is possible with hard work. If you fail, dust yourself off and wake up with a new perspective because every moment is a chance to make your future situation better.

Appreciate your situation for what it is, a new opportunity for success. The point that you consider the prospect of giving up is the same moment that you should focus most of your attention on the alternatives that may be present. This is the point that usually separates success from failure. Remember, life is what you make it! I can honestly say that the best way that I have found to get over any of the pain that life has to offer is to find purpose and stay busy trying to achieve the goals that I have set. To focus on current pursuits and accomplishments to fill my void. By finding purpose by engaging in pursuits to achieve my goals, past failure seems that much easier to deal with.

A positive outlook to maintain is viewing failure as a form of progression. In almost all situations, failure is a precursor to success. Ironically failure is a direct result of taking action, which is also the same ingredient for success. Accepting the possible consequences of failure, but still proceeding, shows that the person is ambitious and maintains the desire for greater prospects. It is proof that the person is willing to compete in a forum that presents a worthy challenge and accepts the possibility of loss. Remember that individual failure of one aspect of your efforts should not cause you to cease all your initiatives altogether. Before you even think about the prospect of quitting, make sure you have exercised all the alternatives which may be present. If I don't have failure or something wrong going on in my life, then I know that I am not challenging myself. I am most likely just pursuing goals within my comfort zone. Only when we challenge ourselves in ways that we have not previously done, do new opportunities to gain present themselves.

Failure results in fear and pacifies us. Just like any fear we must learn to overcome it by going through it. Challenges increase the skill level of the participant and refines abilities. Accepting failure is a way to prove to others that you will exercise perseverance and will keep striving even amongst the presence of setbacks. This in turn generates trust from others and the benefits that this confidence can bring. It shows that a person wants more out of themselves.

An amateur runner who competes in a long distance marathon is a consistent example of the value of efforts. Although the person may not come in first place, even finishing the marathon is an accomplishment. It is a substantial effort that is appreciated even without the prestige of placement in the race. It may be considered a failure from some perspectives, but the only sure way of such failure in this situation is giving up. However, the attempt alone merits praise and is an effort not everyone can accomplish. Even if you do not place in this race, the conditioning and experience can be used as a benefit for future marathons. The more energy and sacrifice is required of you in the process of achieving, the more value that the goal possesses once success is realized. Let's say that the runner attempts to place in the race and success is finally realized after five years of the marathon taking place. The accomplishment is of greater worth than if the runner achieved this accolade on the first year attempted.

The hard work that is exercised to achieve ultimate success becomes the worth for the particular task. The amount of work also alienates others from pursuing the same goals. In fact, you should learn to derive pleasure from the work itself. There should be a sense of joy present in all your pursuits as this is another opportunity to find success. This is especially true if you love what it is that you choose to do. I have always structured the pursuit of my goals in relation to my childhood memories of carnival games. The main initiative to play any of the games is to attain the prize of a stuffed animal or other reward. However, even when I did not receive the prize that I was trying to win, the process of playing the game provided entertainment and enjoyment in itself. The prize was desired, but fun was present in the actual activity leading up to the goal. Tasks should be thought of in the same way and the process should be enjoyed as much as the desired goal.

Doing What Others Won't

> *The difference between successful people and
> unsuccessful people is that successful people do a lot
> of the things that unsuccessful people don't want to
> do…Like when the door is slammed in your face ten
> times. You go to door number 11 with just as much
> enthusiasm.*
>
> —John Paul De Joria

Doing what others won't. It sounds like such a simple concept, but you will find that the ones that are most relevant usually are. The true challenge lies in the practice of these words, not the quote. Most people never end up practicing this simple concept because as it may sound simple, it is actually difficult to put into practice. It is surely one of the most effective characteristics of the Grind. People who practice the Grind actually look for these opportunities to separate themselves from others who are not willing to take on these challenges. This gives them a clear competitive edge and separates them from the average. The average person usually does just enough to get by but when you aspire to achieve high standards, you want to ensure your success with whatever it takes. In your profession, look for these opportunities to take on the challenges that others will not attempt as a way for advancement of your career.

In the examples of many successful individuals and businesses, we can find the efforts that high achieving individuals have conducted, that others are not willing to do to find success. Most of the times these consisted of very small and seemingly simple actions, but the effects were of great significance. Each of these efforts has contributed to their success in some way, and has given the practitioner an advantage of offering something that their competitors would not. In your own situation, try to find any ways that you can to separate yourself from your competitors by challenging yourself to do what others are not willing to. The following examples show various examples of ways that people have chosen to do things that others would not do to find their own success.

David Neeleman of Jetblue, would implement his own personal touches like boarding flights just so that he could talk to passengers and the crew about ideas that he could use to improve the airlines. Jet Blue has been consistent in maintaining his founding standards and has enforced other creative ways to improve their customer service commitment by offering incentives such as "People Officers" who attend random flights. If you fly Jet Blue you may just run into one of these employees who stands up mid-flight and plays trivia games with the passengers. The people who know the answers receive free tickets to anywhere that the airline flies. These "People Officers" also ask the passengers for suggestions and concerns to improve Jet Blue's services and answer questions and interact with passengers. It's just another small touch that Jet Blue is willing to include in their services that makes them different from their competitors. After all, it's hard to ever forget an experience like running into a "People Officer" and receiving free tickets, with no strings attached.

In a great display of faith in himself, Paul De Joria chose to sacrifice the last $350 he had to start Paul Mitchell Systems, even though he was homeless and was living out of his car. He thought of the long term and his future instead of the immediate necessities, and chose to make the great sacrifice of putting all his money he had left in the world into the Paul Mitchell brand. His gamble has obviously paid off, as he has built Paul Mitchell into a billion-dollar company. Doing things that others will not also includes taking the risks that others won't in order to position yourself for success.

In 2000, Howard Schultz decided to move on, and step down from his CEO position after building Starbucks into one of the world's most recognizable and successful brands. But by 2008, Starbucks had suffered from the rough economy and many strategic mishaps, compelling the return of the company's iconic leader. Schultz returned to a company that was in crisis and in desperate need of a turnaround. He took these responsibilities with nothing less than total commitment, putting in thirteen-hour days and even continuing to work from home after leaving the office. Since his return he gets in the office by six in the morning and stays until seven in the evening. He also goes in the office on Saturdays and Sundays. His actions have shown that he has committed himself to bring back the original prominence of the company, expending the efforts that few in his position would consider.

Jim Koch of Samuel Adams has built a career doing what others would not do. First, he left a job at the prestigious Boston Consulting Group, which earned him an annual income of about $250,000 to follow his dream of owning a brewery. He did so even though those around him told him he was stupid and asinine for doing so. When no distributors would take on Sam Adams beer in the early days, he went from bar to bar getting people to taste his beer. Few people have experienced the amount of success that Jim Koch and his company Sam Adams have had, and still have a hand in ensuring the quality of his product and company functions. To this day he still tastes a sample from every batch of his Boston Lager and personally meets every Sam Adams employee. From the products to the people who work for the company, he makes sure that the quality is up to the standards of when he started the company. He does what few founders of their company will do, and is still involved in the company's day to day operations ensuring that Sam Adams will continue to have success for many more years to come.

Tennis greats Venus and Serena Williams routinely woke up to practice hitting tennis balls at six AM from the time they were seven and eight years old, while most children their age were still playing with toys. The Williams sisters, who have dominated women's tennis for many years, spent every chance they could on the court practicing their craft. Few their age would dedicate so much of their time practicing and their lives were described as, "get up, 6 o'clock in the morning, go to the tennis court, before school. Afterschool, go to tennis." Their total commitment to the game of tennis has kept them in the top-ranked positions for years and has made them two of the best to ever play the sport.

Sean Combs is a self-made multimillionaire who runs a number of business interests under his umbrella company, Bad Boy Entertainment Worldwide. He stays busy taking on his many roles as entrepreneur, actor, television producer, fashion designer, restaurant operator, recording artist, music producer, record label executive, Broadway performer, and others. With the success of the company's he owns and operates like Bad Boy Records, Sean John Clothing and Revolt TV, he has amassed a net worth of $700 million securing the top spot on the Forbes Hip Hop's Wealthiest Artists List for 2014. Combs is quickly approaching the feat of becoming Hip Hop's first billionaire. Known through the years by various stage names like "Puff Daddy," "Puffy," "P Diddy," and others, his long career is endowed with stories of his exceptional work ethic and willingness to do all that is necessary to achieve success. When Combs was only twelve years old his family moved to Mount Vernon, New York. He saw an opportunity to make some money managing a newspaper route but was stifled by restrictions requiring him to be a year older in order to benefit from these early aspirations. Not willing to let age and unfitting circumstances become a hindrance to his progress, he lied about his age and made up a number of false identities so that he could manage several routes at once. The deal that he was able to make with the kid who maintained the local route, who was soon going off to college, helped in bringing him in $600 a week by the age of thirteen. His work ethic is legendary, often putting in late nights and twenty-hour days regularly. Most people who have accomplished his financial status would not be willing to commit to the level of work that he does. One of the best ways I have heard his work ethic described was from a person who was working for him as an intern who stated, "Diddy (Combs) works as if he don't have a dollar in his pocket."

Doing what others won't also works with implementing ideas others won't, which are against popular opinion. Sheldon Adelson is the founder of Comdex, the premier computer trade show in Las Vegas. When he built the Venetian Hotel casino in Las Vegas, he broke from the tradition of solely promoting guests to spend time in the casinos. Traditionally, casinos would keep guests on the casino floors to gamble by offering few amenities in the guest rooms, a strategy that most casinos have found success with to get them out of their rooms. Instead, each room in the Venetian is a suite and contains a minibar and fax machine, for guests to enjoy their time in their rooms not just when gambling. The hotel's business focus is geared equally toward conventions than centered specifically on the casino, and features the Sands Convention Center on the premises. Although critics were skeptical of his ideas, at a time, the Venetian was the Las Vegas Strip's second most profitable casino hotel. This is a new approach of profiting for a Las Vegas casino hotel, from an alternative source such as convention services instead of the traditional emphasis on solely casino profits.

Perhaps one of the best customer service stories that I have heard comes from the great service that Morton's Steakhouse was able to provide for an unexpecting customer. A person had been traveling by plane all day for business and was catching his last flight of the day back home to Newark, New Jersey. His flight was scheduled to take off at five PM and estimated that he would be at home at about nine PM, which would not allow him enough time to stop anywhere for dinner. He also did not want to grab fast food at either airport. So, before his flight took off back home he jokingly tweeted that he wanted Morton's to deliver a steak to the Newark Airport in a few hours when he landed. Keep in mind that the tweet was not an official order directed toward Morton's and there were no expectations for a response by the restaurant. It was simply a thought he was thinking which he decided to tweet, very much like many others do on a regular basis with comments like, "I wish it would stop raining," or "I hope that there is no traffic on the roads." Two hours later, they landed on time at their destination and he walked off the plane toward the parking area where his drivers usually waited. Then he heard his named called and much to his surprise there was a person in a tuxedo carrying a Morton's food bag. An employee of Morton's had actually delivered an order of a twenty-four-ounce Porterhouse steak, order of Colossal Shrimp, a side of potatoes, bread, napkins, and silverware. The person from Morton's actually took the initiative to take the order after seeing the tweet, had the cook make the food, drove over twenty miles to the airport, and found out all his flight information to meet him at the exact place he was going to land. Now that's service!

* * *

I was watching Netflix, and came across a show featuring Chef Gordon Ramsey called *Gordon's Great Escape*. I had recently discovered who Chef Ramsey was on *Hell's Kitchen*, a show featuring contestants competing for a chance to win a Head Chef position at a prominent restaurant and annual salary of $250,000. The contestants face various culinary challenges with eliminations at the end of each episode for those who do not perform to the Chef's exacting standards. The most appealing aspect of the show is Chef Ramsey himself, whose infamously short temper intensifies each situation, often screaming obscenities and throwing dishes to display his disappointment. It is quite hilarious to hear Chef Ramsey's insults, and you can't help but laugh at the misfortune of the contestants who must bear the verbal assault. As you watch the show you realize that there is actually a method to the Chef's madness, his sometimes brash and out of control behavior are really intended to fuel the preservation of his craft. It was truly his true passion for cuisine which moves him to act accordingly. He has a genuine desire to elevate the standards of the culinary arts, and if you examine the consistency of his body of work, all efforts which he engages in, proves this.

The Great Escape is a testament of these efforts, as he travels to destinations around the globe to experience first hand, the cooking of various regions in their most authentic form. The episode that I viewed featured Chef Ramsey traveling to New Delhi, to experience the true essence of his home place Britain's favorite genre of food, Indian Cuisine. The intentions of his travels, besides for the audiences viewing pleasures, are to learn the proper ways to cook authentic Indian cuisine to add to his own repertoire. His mission is to find out if Indian food created in the UK is comparable to that made in India. It is a personal voyage of discovery to find out how food back at home should be made.

He first visits a restaurant named Moti Mahal, which a food critic friend recommends, as the original birthplace of the popular dish, butter chicken. After tasting the dish first hand, his opinion of the dish is apparent by the next words from the Chef's mouth, "Bloody hell!" followed by, "Very flavorsome." He discovers that the food made in the UK is nothing close, and can hardly even be considered Indian food. The voyage is a success as he is now endowed with a whole new take on the making of Indian cuisine.

To understand my point in presenting this example, I first have to tell you that Chef Ramsey is a world-renowned chef who owns twenty-seven restaurants worldwide, is a bestselling author of a number of cookbooks, stars in a number of television shows, maintains the top position on the Forbes list of top earning chefs, and has been bestowed with the honor of a number of Michelin stars; the highest honor that is given to a Chef for his culinary abilities. In other words, he has little more to prove to anyone, let alone opting to travel to a third world destination positioning himself in an apprenticeship to learn more of his craft. Most other people in his position would be content with his myriad of accomplishments, leaving well enough alone. But that is exactly why he is so accomplished, and these efforts show his hunger to perfect his craft. He continuously pushes himself to learn new elements to become the best at what he does.

People who achieve great success do things that others won't do. They continue to work hard even after they find success, with the realization that there are always those out there who would be glad to take their place. They have a desire to keep improving their skill level so that they remain at the forefront of their profession. Business is a competitive entity and there are no assurances that a person will always remain in a prominent position. People like Chef Ramsey respect what it is they do and believe in contributing to their craft, not just benefiting from it. This is the sign of a person who loves what they do. It is no wonder why he has accomplished so many accolades in the culinary arts. No matter what trade you are involved in make sure that you are always aware of the new developments that occur so that you will evolve with the times. To perform at the highest levels of the Grind, you must always continue to progress and set new standards at what it is that you do, by taking measures others won't.

> *Today I will do what others won't, so*
> *tomorrow I can accomplish what others can't.*
>
> —Jerry Rice

The Grind

Some opportunities in life may not be glamorous and may even have a negative image in our society. They may test the limitations of your integrity. Pride prohibits the pursuit of these initiatives because most people naturally don't want to be looked down upon. By taking on these trivial challenges, you are exposing yourself to embarrassment. This is another case where you must be willing to do what others are not in order to reach success. From starting your employment in the mailroom as an intern to working as a personal assistant, some feel shame in taking on certain types of employment. However, sometimes these positions may lead to other opportunities that may be the deciding factor in finding success.

I had a friend that I often would see when I would visit the casinos on the Las Vegas Strip. He would position himself on the Strip and brought out an ice chest filled with water bottles for sale. The extreme heat of the Las Vegas desert makes water a necessity. He would catch pedestrians coming out of the casinos, and would sell them bottles of water and soft drinks. I remember a time when I had ran into him with a friend of mine who went to school with him. He was very condescending and commented that he felt sorry for him and that he didn't think that he would be reduced to selling water on the strip. Later, I saw my friend who sold water on the strip at the business license office and I asked him how he was doing. He told me he was doing very well and that he was able to pay his college tuition making several hundred dollars a day from selling water and drinks! It's funny how appearances make people think that a person cannot be successful because the type of work does not seem prestigious. There are plenty of ways to make money which are often neglected because they do not portray a flattering image. If you are only willing to do what other people do, you will be limited to what everyone else has. Being successful requires sacrifice and will sometimes involve putting your pride on the line. These small contributions may be the key to achievement. I always had a "whatever it takes" mentality when it came to any business venture. Sometimes it involves taking on even the most remedial requirements of your business. You may have to take on entry level responsibilities and involve yourself in an unflattering position of your business. When you are afraid to do something, analyze the situation and see what rewards may come as a result of taking this action.

I once worked as a bus boy at a restaurant and I experienced a situation where overlooking pride made the difference toward success. The owner would serve the customers himself, and would take the time to get to know them on a personal level. There were times when dishes could not be washed fast enough, and he wasn't afraid to go back to the sink and take on this responsibility. He also cooked when there was a shortage of chefs and was able to take on all positions of the business himself. He swept the floors and cleaned the restrooms to make sure everything was clean and presentable. There was nothing that he would not do for the business and ended up becoming very successful, later opening additional locations.

When visiting Thailand, I would often stay at my cousin's house. She told me a great story about her neighbor. This person experienced extreme poverty in his youth. He started recycling cans and bottles. There was no glory in this work but it was the opportunity that would change his life. He would jump in trashcans rummaging through trash to find any recyclables he could. He started hiring other people and bought a truck to carry more items. He pursued the success of the business diligently and was able to change his situation, eventually having enough money to buy the property next door to my cousin.

There are many examples of successful people who were able to put aside their pride and accomplish great success by simply doing what others would not. Unfortunately, I have also experienced people who could not get past the image of a certain field and ended up in bad financial resolve. I have seen so many situations where people were too embarrassed to do the very thing that may have made the difference between success and failure. Some even feel that it is beneath them and that they are overqualified to accommodate some duties. In these cases it is the people who are willing to do what others won't that will find success. I'm not saying you should ever settle for less than your potential especially when you can obtain more. The point is that you should not limit yourself because of pride, by not doing everything you can to accomplish your goals. Those who will do what others won't understand that a moment of vulnerability is worth the success that follows it. Nothing of any worth in life comes easy and without sacrifice. There is no less integrity in doing what you have to do to succeed. The only true embarrassment is failure.

* * *

In almost every success story you will find that the person took the initiative to do something others would not do. Taking risks is perhaps one of the most common ways of doing what others won't do. They take risks when others choose to play it safe or remain in a comfort zone. They take these risks knowing that there is a chance at failure. But with every risk, there is also a chance that you can find the success that you desire. The only way to proceed is initiate the process and give it your heart and soul. It is better that you try and fail, than to have the regrets of letting the opportunity pass you by without you even giving it a chance.

Vineyard Vines is a clothing and accessory brand started by brothers, Shep and Ian Murray in 1998. Miserable with the corporate jobs the two held at the time, the brothers decided to quit their jobs on the same day and begin the company. They took the risk of leaving their well paying jobs even though many said that they were crazy to do so and that it was a "dumb" idea. To finance the venture they took cash advances out of their credit cards, a big risk that eventually paid off. In one interview Ian even says that the two did not have any knowledge of fashion or the business when they started. In their early days, they started off by selling ties they made, one at a time out of their backpacks and from cars and boats. As stated on the company website, the brothers decided to start selling ties so they wouldn't have to wear them. Stocked with four different styles of ties, the duo were able to sell eight hundred ties within the first week. The brand later became an entire clothing line incorporating hats, shirts, shorts, and bags. Since the summer of 1998, the Vineyard Vines Company has increased their presence nationally with most locations on the East Coast. The brand also expanded further opening freestanding retail stores located nationwide, as well as being available in over five hundred stores around the country. An interesting story is mentioned on the website called "The Backgammon Story." Initially, stores outside of Martha's Vineyard were apprehensive on stocking the brand. In an attempt to get a store to stock his products, Shep challenged Zareh Thomajan, owner of Boston shop Zareh to a game of backgammon. The bet is that if Shep wins, Zareh will buy ties from Vineyard Vines. By a stroke of good fortune, Shep ends up winning the game and all the ties sell from the store. Between 2004 and 2007, the company's revenue tripled to thirty-seven million dollars, with projections of about one hundred million dollars in the upcoming years. In 2007, Vineyard Vines was placed on *Inc. Magazine*'s list of the five hundred fastest growing businesses in the United States.

Vineyard Vines would have never existed if the Murray brothers never took the risk of leaving their jobs that earned them a comfortable living. Shep was an advertising account executive and Ian worked at a public relations firm. They accrued a debt of forty thousand dollars on their credit cards to raise capital for the company and did not seek any funding from any venture capital firms. This was a move that could be viewed by many as foolish judgment, although it worked out perfectly for this situation. They took the initiative few are willing to do, selling their ties one at a time, hand to hand, out of their backpacks. By doing this they were able to move an impressive eight hundred ties in one week, enabling them to reorder more products and pay off debts. Shep and Ian may have not known about the fashion business, but their belief in themselves was enough to find success. "The Backgammon Story" is a great example of thinking of alternatives to solve problems which may be in the way of progress. Shep was able to use an unorthodox method to gain the attention of Zareh and get his products stocked in the store. Their story is filled with doing things that others wouldn't normally do. This can sometimes be a refreshing way of doing business that can gain interest from others opening up opportunities that conventional methods may not be able to do.

* * *

There is a saying which states that "if you are only willing to do what everyone else does, you're only going to have what everyone else has." How true is this? In the world we see that success is reserved for people who are willing to do what it takes to achieve it. Those who aspire for the best are willing to go above and beyond what everyone else will and they understand that these are the factors that separate them from the rest. Always look for opportunities to contribute more than other people in your profession are willing to. If other people are making the same efforts, then find ways to perform better than anyone else. Be the first to plan and act.

There is another great story circulated about Michael Ovitz. It involves a situation when he was trying to sign a couple writers to his agency. His partners in the firm were present also and they all pitched to gain interest from the pair. Nothing seemed to be working so one of them asked, "What do we have to do, tap dance for you?" Michael Ovitz then proceeded to get on the table and began to dance for them. The two clients, amused at the action, signed thereafter.

Others can sense when you possess a true commitment to your cause. When you do what others won't do, there is a perception that you will perform with equal intensity at all areas of your work. People gravitate toward this type of dedication and side with entities which will show them intensity. Acting in ways that are distinct definitely serves the purpose of being impressionable.

I conducted an interview with recording artist Mad Skills for my magazine many years ago and asked him about the events leading up to him receiving a record deal. He described the event where he met Q Tip, the person who would significantly help forward his career. Q Tip is a member of groundbreaking hip hop group A Tribe Called Quest. At a music convention, he encountered Q Tip who was surrounded by many other artists trying to be heard by the producer and artist. The artists were trying to take the opportunity to give him their projects and pitch the reasons why they should be granted a record deal. There was a crowd around him and Mad Skills was not able to get into a position where he could talk to him. He saw that there was a tree, so he climbed up and started reciting verses of his material. Not only did he stand out in the crowd with this act, but he was able to impress Q Tip with his lyrical skill. Q Tip asked him for his number and kept in touch with him, and this earned him a major breakthrough in his career. Mad Skills went on to be signed by a major record label and was able to secure production by Q-Tip on the album he eventually released, all results of the actions he took that day.

We come across so many people in life that most of the time we cannot even recall many of these encounters later. When you make a memorable first impression, this serves as a foundation to keep you distinguishable. When you are willing to do what others won't you put yourself in a unique position amongst a crowd of conformers. This does not mean that you have to be obnoxious or act carelessly to gain recognition but simply put forth your own individual characteristics into your efforts. Show people around you that you have the ingenuity and creativity to create your own options for progress. Let them know your individual importance and your abilities to think and act outside the box. Leadership is a position reserved for those who are entrusted by others to provide direction. When you do what others won't, you show that you are not merely a conformer but someone who has the instincts to lead by example. Your passion and dedication in exploring these outlets will highlight your efforts and will ultimately be noticed by others.

Grind Work Ethic

The dictionary is the only place that success comes before work. Hard work is the price we must pay for success. I think you can accomplish anything if you're willing to pay the price.

—Vince Lombardi

Opportunities are usually disguised as hard work, so most people don't recognize them.

—Ann Landers

Enjoy your sweat because hard work doesn't guarantee success, but without it you don't have a chance.

—Alex Rodriguez

I'm a greater believer in luck, and I find the harder I work the more I have of it.

—Thomas Jefferson

The Grind is very much a state of mind. Anyone who has ever tried to describe a distinct mind state understands the challenge of putting it into words. That is, to have the reader understand completely what it is that the writer is trying to capture through words written out on a page. The most difficult challenge for me when writing this book was to describe the full extent of the work ethic that is required to practice the Grind at its peak level.

I have best been able to express this intensity from the examples of successful people that I have included in this book who have used the characteristics of the Grind in pursuit of their goals. However, there is almost no way to fully detail and express the total extent of effort that was expended by these high achieving individuals during their accomplishments. That is to articulate their examples so that one would be able to read their stories and emulate or copy their efforts with the same intensity. One has to experience it first hand to fully comprehend. It is often a very personal experience and no one else could be present through the whole process to witness all that was required.

The best phrase that I have adopted to describe the effort needed to epitomize the performance of the Grind is "Whatever It Takes." This is the type of "fight" that is so compelling that it drives the individual to go to extremes such as staying up nights at a time to realize advancement in their pursuits, risking failure despite criticism from others, sacrificing years of their life to realize their dreams, or simply doing everything and anything in their abilities to achieve their desired goals. It is literally the willingness to go through the actual "blood, sweat and tears" that it sometimes takes to achieve success.

When practicing this extent of effort, you should feel like you are going through the "burn" stages that were described in the introduction of this book. If the degree of effort doesn't seem excessive, then most likely it is the level of performance that everyone else is performing at. However, I walk a fine line in this description as this can easily be misinterpreted to represent the very thing most people usually harm themselves with when practicing this subject.

I am not talking about the self-destructive misconception of working day in and day out to compensate for the failure that is present in another area of life. I am not describing the vicious work cycle that some people maintain because they are trying to prove something to someone else for some form of validation. For example, we see the example all the time of children growing up and working in a field that they despise just because they feel that this is what their parents expect of them. Or the other common situation of those who drag themselves through the rigors of work that harms their health because they feel that money will make them happy and fix all their problems. The truth is that there are many deep-rooted problems which cause some to inflict self abuse, for various invalid reasons, and hide behind the process of work to instill their blame. This is not the type of work ethic that I am describing.

I am talking about the type of work where the person rejoices everyday to wake up and go to work seven days a week because they feel they have found their calling in life. The type of work where the person loves what it is they do, and hours seem like minutes when they are participating in their profession. The type where an unquenchable need is present to see something you believe in, materialize into fruition, and the urge is so strong that there is no other recourse other than to proceed unyieldingly. The type of situation where the person would be doing the very same thing even if they were not getting paid. The life work that gives you true fulfillment and allows you to represent a cause you believe in. In these types of situations, this effort can hardly be described as work, and their work ethic is a direct result of their true desires.

> *There is no substitute for hard work.*
> —Thomas A. Edison

Former Disney executive and one of the founding partners of Dreamworks, Jeff Katzenberg exemplifies a prime example of a person who practices the work ethic of the

Grind. Katzenberg has earned the reputation of a man who would do absolutely anything to get a job done. Many in Hollywood will describe him as a workaholic, consistent with the 18-hour days he was often said to keep in the past during his days at Disney. He previously held the position of head of the studio at Disney and took on responsibilities such as reading scripts, engaging actors and actresses, deal making, talent solicitation and the numerous other duties it takes to run Disney Studios.

He would wake up at 4:30 in the morning and work out and exercise with his personal trainer. Then he would be in his office by 6:15, often holding down a seven-day work week, regularly even coming in on Sunday. He would then start on his routine of making his daily calls, staying consistent with returning his many phone calls within three hours every day. People have speculated that he maintains relationships with over a thousand people who he would keep contact with to keep the lines of opportunity open. He is said to have about five hundred phone numbers memorized in his head. Three assistants help him with his efforts, working in shifts from dawn until late at night. Katzenberg maintains a system of lining up in particular order on his desk, 3" x 5" note index cards which he makes notes on to reference the phone calls, projects, and plans which he had scheduled out throughout his work day. This process helps to keep his tasks organized and manageable. An agenda is planned out for all meetings that he attends. He was described as "tenacious" in keeping records and accounts to his projects. He was known to effectively strategize, read all scripts he considered personally, build lasting relationships with talent, pay great attention to the details of the accounting of projects, conduct extensive research, and many other exceptional actions which credited him as a major factor in the success of Disney during the reign of Michael Eisner as CEO.

Katzenberg maintained a fanatic, overwhelming energy and friend David Geffen once stated, "Compared to Jeffrey, everyone else in this town is on vacation." Other quotes describing his work ethic included, "The man is possessed," "The work ethic is off the chart completely. It is absolute and total fanaticism," "He has this compulsion to be on top of everything. A screenplay, a pitch, he wants it all, even if it's just to pass on it.," "Katzenberg doesn't let you go until you've said yes," "He gets things done immediately." One of his favorite famous quotes which give us an insight to his dedication for his work is the phrase, "If I don't see you here on Saturday, don't even bother coming in on Sunday."

* * *

More important than working long hours is working with focused intensity. It is of no benefit if your level of efforts does not yield equivalent results. In the Bible it says that you can judge a tree by its fruit, and the same can be said about the results that a person's efforts have produced. You can gauge the effectiveness of your work ethic by simply analyzing the results that you have had in your work history. Analyze whether or not your work habits are focused to the task at hand or tend to be generalized. In other words, are they being directed toward gaining results or do a lot of your efforts seem wasted? It doesn't mean that just because you are working harder than anyone else, you will be more successful than the rest. Focusing your efforts toward the right channels is a skill that needs to be developed. Periodically, assess what degree of return you are receiving for your efforts and this should give you an indication of the way that you should proceed.

Ryan Seacrest is definitely one of the hardest working people in Hollywood. He produces the results to justify his efforts. While most people are overwhelmed by a single duty, Seacrest continuously adds more duties to his workload. In addition to being the host of American Idol, he also can be heard on his nationally syndicated radio show *American Top 40* on KIIS-FM from five AM to ten AM, and seen as the anchor person of *E Daily News* seven days a week on the E! cable channel. As if taking on three jobs wasn't enough, he has also invested in eight restaurants, started a new clothing line, and is the new executive producer and host of the New Year's Eve show on ABC. He has also signed a three-year deal with E! worth $21 million for his company to produce original programming. Seacrest already maintains production credits for *Keeping Up with the Kardashians*, *Kourtney and Khloe Take Miami*, *Denise Richards: It's Complicated*, *Momma's Boys*, and other successful TV shows. He has earned two Emmy awards for yet more jobs he has held, as the host of the Walt Disney World Christmas Day Parade television special and producer for the *Jamie Oliver's Food Revolution*. He currently earns about $59 million annually. Seacrest is definitely a person who gets monumental results from the work that he expends. This is clearly shown from all the output that he is able to accomplish for his hard work.

In all of your efforts make sure that you are getting comparable results with the energy that you are burning. If you do not, then you are setting yourself up with the possibility of overextending yourself. This can result in burning yourself out or even loss of inspiration. You have to be honest with yourself. If you have been doing the same thing for years without any positive reinforcement or growth, then you might want to implement a new plan. You have to reevaluate your plan and explore the other options that you have available. Some things take a long time and I'm not saying you should change course every time you don't get immediate results but there should be some kind of indication that you are on course. Remember that hard work is of no relevance unless your work is directed toward the proper channels. Work harder but make sure that the results match your efforts.

> *No one ever drowned in sweat.*
> —US Marine Corps

It makes sense that most of the world's successful people, all possess a similar degree of work ethic. This serves as proof that work ethic is one of the most relevant contributing factors toward achieving a prominent position in their profession. The following individuals exhibit extraordinary work habits, accompanied by the practices which have made them successful. I would recommend that you research their stories further and identify the characteristics which have worked for them in their road to success. Acknowledge what it is that they practice, that others in their same profession are not willing to do, which you may be able to include in your own practice and situation.

Mark Cuban is a billionaire entrepreneur whose ventures include many diverse business genres, from entertainment to internet startups. He is most famously known as the owner of the Dallas Mavericks basketball team and his role as one of the investors on the panel of television show *Shark Tank*. When Cuban started his first company, he routinely stayed up until two in the morning reading and researching new software and technology. He also went seven years without taking a vacation. This work ethic was displayed early in his life, and by the age of twelve he was selling garbage bags door to door. Throughout high school he earned extra money as a coin and stamp salesman. He paid his college tuition by giving dance lessons for $25 an hour and starting a chain letter. When asked how to be successful as an entrepreneur he answered, "Busting your ass. It's not about money or connections, it's the willingness to outwork and outlearn everyone when it comes to your business. And if it fails, you learn from what happened and do a better job next time." After earning his degree, Cuban started a business selling local-area network and connectivity products, called Microsolutions. He funded the venture by convincing a customer to loan him $500 and by 1990 the business was grossing $30 million a year. Even though he did not know much about personal computers, he would spend his nights teaching himself about the business reading manuals and anything else he could get his hands on. He eventually sold Microsystems for about $6 million. He stayed true to his ways as a serial entrepreneur, and next started Audionet in 1995, a business streaming college games via the internet. Audionet became Broadcast.com and the company eventually went public. A year later Cuban and his partner Todd Wagner sold the company to Yahoo! for $5.6 billion, $1.3 billion of which was Cuban's share of the sale. To this day, Cuban is still investing in new business and most publicly offers investment funds to the contestants on *Shark Tank*.

Following in the footsteps of the most innovative leader of our time is difficult and Tim Cook has his work cut out for him as the successor to Steve Job's Apple. However, Cook definitely has the work ethic to fill those enormous shoes. He is a workaholic who gets up at 3:45 every morning. He starts his day with emails, then works out at the gym, then to Starbucks where he tends to more emails, then off to work. He has been known to hold Sunday night staff meeting on the phone in preparation for the coming weeks work schedule. Cook is usually the first one in the office and the last one to leave. His work at Apple has already proved effective, as he removed Apple from the manufacturing game, solidifying deals with contract manufacturers. This allowed Apple to reduce the length of time inventory stayed on its balance sheet from months to days and save costs by closing down manufacturing factories all over the world. He also switched Apple's line of computers over to Intel processors. He has had success shrewdly negotiating deals for components that has kept down costs and has increased the profit margin. Mark Briggs, Cook's boss when he previously worked at Intelligent Electronics, has said of him, "He just works all the time, that's his life."

Another great example of extraordinary work ethic, is Yahoo CEO Marissa Mayer. When she worked for Google she used to log in a staggering 130 hour work weeks, managing this intense schedule by sometimes taking naps under her desk! She has even been said to be strategic in taking showers for time management. She has stated during interviews that for the first five years at Google, she pulled an all-nighter every week. This insane work ethic did render its results and she has been credited with Google's functionality, look, and experience. The site's minimalist clean look with the single search bar in the center providing the site's simple functionality, accessing the complicated products Google provides; is said to be her contribution. Her tenure at Google has yielded products such as Google Maps, Google Earth, Google News, and GMail.

Tiger Woods is one of the most dominant figures to ever come along in the game of golf. In 1997 he won his first major title, the US Masters at Augusta, with a record breaking score of 270. He was able to accomplish this at the young age of twenty-one, and became the youngest man and first African American to earn the title. His career is full of record breaking statistics. Through the 2000s he maintained the number one ranked spot for a record of 264 weeks from August 1999 to September 2004, and 281 weeks from June 2005 to October 2010. Woods has been awarded the PGA Player of the Year for a record ten times. At this time, Woods has fourteen major titles and 77 PGA Tour wins. He has earned more money than any other golfer in history with his many wins and endorsement deals. Although there is no doubt that he possesses natural talent for the game of golf, it's his work ethic and determination that makes him great. Fellow PGA golfer and winner of the 2003 Masters, Mike Weir, said, "He's always working to get better, and I would love to have the strength of his mind and determination. I have it somewhat, I think, which is part of the reason I've been successful, but Tiger has taken it to a different level." It has been said that Tiger maintains the following work schedule while preparing for tournaments, "wakes up at six AM, takes a four-kilometer run followed by gym stretches, then half-an-hour for breakfast, two hours on the driving range, nine holes of golf, lunch, two more hours on the range, another nine holes, dinner and bed." Even when he is not preparing for competition he has been quoted as saying, "I decided a long time ago to treat golf as a sport and full-time profession. When I'm not playing in a tournament, I train from two to ten hours a day. I'm always trying to improve my conditioning so I can be a better golfer and athlete. Luckily, I like to work out, so training never feels like a chore." In fact, it was this work ethic that bought him back from the many adversities in his career including injuries, changing his golf swing three times and his much publicized break from golf after the infidelity accusations.

There is no doubt that these people are exceptional and it would be very hard to expect everyone to match their extreme work ethic. However, if you aspire to achieve similar results then you must ask yourself if you are putting forth the equivalent degree of effort. There is always room for improvement and analyze your situation to find any discrepancies in areas where you may be lacking. Great people do great things, and great results come from great effort. You definitely don't have to be famous to maintain these levels of work ethic and all these individuals started from modest beginnings before they achieved any success. Identify if there are any areas of your professional life, where you think you can be more productive. Analyze the work that you expend each day and acknowledge whether you can work even harder. Work ethic has to be improved gradually and you must condition yourself to do so. Take note of your current levels, and gradually add more to your workload in increments. Also, focus on your intensity and find ways for yourself to gain more results when you do so.

*Perseverance is the hard work you do after you get tired
of doing the hard work you already did.*
—Newt Gingrich

The most common mistake when considering working at these extreme levels is that you should do so no matter how detrimental it can be to your health. There is no doubt that it can breed great stress and lead to an unhealthy demise if you are not mindful of these issues. Of course, the intention to maintain an extreme work ethic is not to expose yourself to negative factors. All your efforts would therefore be in vein, and the hard work would be of no significance.

Most of the time, these negative occurrences happen because people are not doing it for the right reasons. They subject themselves to slavish labor because to them, they believe this will lead to a better financial future, and as a result, happiness. They do not have a true passion for what they choose to pursue and therefore begin to force themselves to act in ways they normally wouldn't. Therefore it is of utmost importance that you choose a profession that you truly love. It should mean more than a paycheck to you. It may be to further a cause that you believe in or be the change that you would like to see in the world. In most cases you should find something that you would do even if you were not getting paid for it. When you truly love something, the "work" that you expend toward your profession should actually seem minimal. This love will get you through the adversity that will surely arise in your pursuit for success.

"The thing about it is, when you love what you do, you don't really think of it as work. It's what you do. And that's the good fortune of where I find myself," is how Tim Cook described the feelings of his employment situation. Some of the following quotes have been made by Jeffrey Katzenberg to describe the love of his work and what he believes is required for success: "Because I have so loved what I do, for many, many years, I kind of do it morning, noon and night, 24/7.," "I genuinely loved my time at Disney, every day of it.," and "But, the truth is the only way you end up on the Fortune 10 Best List is if people genuinely are passionate and love their work and where they are working." You can see that both Cook's and Katzenberg's love for their profession is the motivating factor behind their work ethic. It is often the fuel that entrepreneurs use to keep them performing at an intense pace.

Make your profession a labor of love by taking the time to explore the many fields of employment that exist. Be thorough about considering a field of work you can fully commit to by conducting as much research as possible. You should never rush this process as this will be a life choice that can greatly dictate the outcome of your future. Better to take the time considering your choices during the initial stages, than pursuing a career that you will regret later and end up wasting more time changing course. Expose yourself to the choices available by asking many people what it is they do and what their work entails. Nowadays with the internet, research is unlimited and you have access to worldwide range of resources. It is solely up to you to dictate your future, so make every effort to find something that you can commit your life to that you truly love.

Of course, not everyone is fortunate enough to be able to choose what it is they want to do for a living. In these situations take employment that will enable you to acquire skills that you will later need for the profession you would ultimately love to do. For example, if you aspire to one day start a record label, you could take a job as an intern at a radio station, conduct street promotions for a record label, or work at a record retail shop. These may not be your ideal jobs but they will enable you to gain experience of one aspect of the music business you will eventually need to run a label. You can also gain insight to whether or not you would truly like to commit your life to this business before making any investments or further obligations. The experience will enable you to network with others who may already be involved in the business and you can start making connections that will help you in the future. In other words, try to secure employment which will educate you, not only pay you.

Also, if you are forced into a job that you may not enjoy, look for at least one of the aspects of the employment that you do favor. Identify the parts of the job that give you purpose and that keep you inspired. For example, a person may not like working as a bartender. They may hate to listen to the complaints and self pity stories that are told while the customer is on the "booze cruise." The late hours and the unwanted responsibility of tending to the demands of intoxicated customers may not be something that is tolerable. In short, the person may hate the job and would rather pursue a different field of employment. However, there is the option to find the parts of the job that can be enjoyable or provide some form of satisfaction or purpose. Maybe the person enjoys meeting people and this is definitely a place where you can practice your social skills. Bartenders can guide the conversations to topics of interest and that which can be a source of learning. For example, if someone is involved with a field that the bartender may be interested in, this can be a chance to learn first hand of the subject of interest. Flair bartending is the practice of bartenders who entertain guests and audiences of the bar by performing tricks involving bottles, cocktail shakers and other bar tools. This practice takes great skill and involves all kinds of tricks such as juggling, flipping bottles, manipulation of the bar tools and even magic tricks while serving drinks. These "flairtenders" are in demand by bar establishments as they provide performances to interest the attendance of customers. If the person likes to perform and gain the attention of others, he/she may take up this art form of flair bartending to bring new challenges to their job. This is a whole different approach to your employment and a great way to bring added excitement to the profession of bartending. The bartender can also make it a priority to network with the customers and even plan to open up a bar of their own in the future. There are many areas of the job that can be isolated and focused upon as a way to bring enjoyment or purpose to the employment. Whatever makes the job more bearable is an option. You may also find ways to combine activities you may enjoy into work that you may dread. For example, if you are an athlete and hate conditioning and working out, you can listen to music you enjoy while you train. If you are a student and hate studying, you can do so with a group of friends which may make the task easier. By being creative you can always find ways to make hard work seem more manageable or enjoyable. You must change your thought process if you are in a frame of mind where you hate your employment. Instead find the elements of your work that you do enjoy or provide fulfillment. It is very hard to continue in employment that you dread and most likely you will never exert your best efforts in this situation. You should be able to find the areas you do enjoy instead of grouping your job into one entire entity that you do not enjoy.

The other requirement of being able to maintain extreme work ethic is to maintain balance between work and life. You should be able to find an equivalent method to balance your life outside work and enjoy the fruits of your labor. Continuous work without an outlet for rest can slowly diminish the efficiency of your efforts, and soon you may be working just as much time with fewer results. If you do not already have these methods to unwind, identify ways that take your mind off your work and relax you. Whether it is fishing, meditating, sports, yoga, vacation, or any other outlet, you should identify the activities which bring balance to your life. These activities should help you to rejuvenate so you can continue to work at an intense pace. Everyone needs a break and in most cases these forms of rest helps provide the person more focus when they re-engage their profession. Maintaining a hard work ethic is not an easy prospect so give yourself as many advantages as possible.

We all have limitations. We cannot expect to perform at our greatest potential unless we provide ourselves all the requirements that both our minds and bodies need to function at their full capacity. The process of balancing our personal and professional lives involves giving ourselves an ample amount of rest in between the efforts that we conduct. We all need to rejuvenate after the extreme amounts of effort that are required of us during our professional aspirations. When you strive to exert high levels of effort and attempt to perform at the extreme levels required by the Grind, you must match the efforts with the equivalent amount of rewards.

Improving Your Professional Self

*When your life flashes before your eyes,
make sure you've got plenty to watch.*
—Author Unknown

Whether it is realized or not, I feel that everyone has some innate reason of why they were given this life. Without this purpose, there would be a void of meaning and worth in this lifetime. Some were meant for grand pursuits and others are grounded in simplicity, none of which are more relevant than the other. It is our own prerogative to take action and make our true, individual desires a reality. This is not always a simple assertion and some take a whole lifetime figuring out what it is they really want. You must be open to ideas, and exposing yourself to a variety of life situations provides you a better selection of options. Don't be so quick to take a stance and commit to a certain view until you have explored the options that exist. Take the time to really ground yourself in the cause which you choose to partake in. This involves taking into account the various perspectives that may be available. Be a sponge for knowledge and understanding and this will allow you to make experienced choices for all your endeavors.

Take the opportunities to travel or expose yourself to different cultures. People in all parts of the world have their own preferences and it is interesting to explore the reasoning. The discovery of various cultural values can lead to new viewpoints. Meet as many people as you can and take in different viewpoints. Always be quick to listen and learn, knowledge can be attained from the least likely of sources. Everyone has something to offer but it is up to the recipient to open up the channels to new sources of experience. Make sure to diversify the people that you congregate with, more exposure to a variety of people from different walks of life will yield additional channels of interest.

Read books and expose yourself to other subjects which you may possibly have an interest in. Biographies are a whole lifetime of experiences compiled into one source for your easy viewing. The internet makes the world more accessible and is a great tool for exposing ourselves to the varieties of life. The internet also opens the lines of communication to all parts of the world. It can provide an inexpensive means of communicating with associates and friends from all over the globe and expand your reach to different areas. Seek ways to pleasure your senses such as tasting different forms of food, viewing natural beauty, or listening for variations in music. This may give you insight to special interest you may maintain, or an ability you have not yet discovered in some form of arts, music, or lifestyle.

There is so much to experience and we have a lifetime to do so. All these are factors which may help you decide what it is that you really want out of life. Exhausting your options and getting a well rounded perspective of the world around you gives you more options to choose from. It helps eliminate the discovery of additional interests you may have pursued had you been exposed to these channels before making a decision. Be proactive in your determination of life pursuits, it is one of the most important choices you will have to make in life. There are so many who become depressed after finding that their pursuits have been misguided. They spend years of their lives pursuing something others want for them or what they feel was expected of them. They live their lives trying to make a reality of someone else's dreams or desires. Improve your professional self by gaining the experience it takes to make decisions which are right for yourself and help you live according to your own discretions. The more you know about yourself and your characteristics, the easier it will be to decide which options to pursue in your professional career. Knowing our true purpose strengthens our professional selves enabling us to live the life that we truly desire.

> *You can't build a reputation
> on what you are going to do.*
>
> —Henry Ford

In business we often live and die by our reputations. One of the most significant ways to improve your professional self is to make the effort to establish a reputation which is best conducive to succeeding in business. So much rests upon how we are defined through the actions that make up our reputations. It is the first thing people use as a reference as to what they can expect when they deal with us. It is the spoken resume that is shared between the colleagues in your profession about you. It is regarded as sound information due to the validations of others in your respective field. The merit of having a good business reputation opens up opportunities and may be a major factor in achieving great success.

In his book, *Pour Your Heart into It*, Starbucks chairman and CEO Howard Schultz describes a time when he was soliciting investment funds from investor Ron Margolis. Schultz needed capital to fund his new coffee-bar company, I1 Giornale. At the time Howard and Ron were complete strangers, making contact through the acquaintance of their wives. Armed with a business plan, financial projections, and prepared to answer any questions the prospective investor would inquire about, Howard went to the Margolis' home to present his proposal. Eager, Howard began informing Ron of the vision for the company growing more enthusiastic as he continued. Finally, Ron injected and asked how much he was looking for. Howard started to present his financial projections, but Ron waived them away and wrote him a check on the spot for One Hundred Thousand Dollars. Although, the book goes on to mention that Ron has made other investments based on the same instincts, I have no doubt that it was Howard Schultz's passion, knowledge, and past successes that propelled Ron to agree to the investment. Ron Margolis believed in Howard Schultz the person, not only the potential success of Starbucks.

A person's dedication and passion for their pursuits are often transparent. As in this case, it can get others behind your dreams to help in making them a reality. Evidence is stated in the book when Ron told Howard's wife Sheri, "If Howard ever starts a business, I'm sure he'll succeed, so I want to know about it.," even before Howard went to meet with Ron. The ability to Grind is greatly driven by our reputation. It can make all the difference in some situations. Our reputation can open up opportunities that are not available to every person. Always be mindful of the fact that it can take years to build but only one situation to destroy. Define yourself as someone worthy of professional respect and show it in all your actions.

* * *

Genghis Khan was the founder and emperor of the Mongol Empire who lived from 1162 to 1227. He, along with the Mongolian army, established the largest land empire in history. He united the nomadic tribes of the Mongolian plateau, and conquered large areas of central Asia and China. His children and descendents expanded the empire even further after his death advancing to areas such as Poland, Vietnam, Syria and Korea. During his lifetime, his armies conquered more land and killed and captured more people than did the armies of perhaps any other emperor in world history during their lifetimes. Many of the invasions of foreign land conducted by Genghis Khan resulted in large scale slaughter of local populations which gave him a fearsome reputation as a brutal pillager who showed no mercy to anyone in his path. According to some historians, they estimated that Genghis Khan's campaigns killed as many as forty million people. Genghis Kahn was known as a brilliant general and wartime strategist. One of his strategies included, allowing rumors of his atrocities to spread throughout the regions he was invading to encourage cooperation. He used his reputation to scare those who would otherwise resist his forces, into compliance and surrender. His reputation certainly preceded him and in 1215, just before Peking surrendered to the Mongol Army, sixty thousand girls from the town threw themselves from the walls to their own deaths rather than risking capture. The inhabitants of Peking were trapped inside the town walls, with the Mongol forces waiting outside, and there was a shortage of food. The fear was so great of the terrible retribution that was awaiting them that the terrified population resorted to cannibalism rather than surrendering to the Mongols!

Many Mongolians maintain that the historical records written by non-Mongolians against Genghis Khan are unfairly biased and that his butchery is exaggerated, while his positive contributions were underrated. Although, Mongols were often portrayed as bloodthirsty barbarians and not much else, Khan actually loved learning. He adopted the Uyghur script as the Mongol Empire's writing system and embraced learning about various forms of religions, enabling his subjects the freedom to do the same. During his time ruling the Mongol Empire he was responsible for creating a postal system, encouraging trade, abolishing torture, and advancing the rights of women in their society. He was one of the greatest generals who ever lived ruling a kingdom of nearly twelve million square miles. During his wartime conquests he was definitely violent, killing many and spreading terror amongst his enemies; but only for the purpose of expanding the Mongolian Empire and furthering their causes. Many present day Mongolians regard him as the founding father of Mongolia.

We can see by these facts that Genghis Khan was not only a great leader in times of war but also a great leader to his people. He used his wartime reputation as a tool to serve his purpose during his invasions of opposing areas. To his enemies, he was a bloodthirsty tyrant who had no concept of mercy. However, this was not the full extent of his character, and to his people he contributed much more than just war related progress. In business, your reputation can be used in the same way, manipulated to serve your best interest in whatever a situation requires. Many great business people have been known to maintain a completely different persona at their workplace as they do in their personal lives. It is your discretion as to what you will be known for according to the characteristics you show others when at work. Therefore, do as Genghis Khan has and use your reputation to serve your own purposes. Consider how you would like to be portrayed to your peers in your profession and what characteristics would help further your professional objectives. Be meticulous in establishing your reputation, as it is difficult to be undone once established. Read into the examples of any prominent business figures you can find, and examine how others interpretation of their reputations has served their purpose in finding success.

Reputation in business is one of the most effective forms of advertisement that you can have. One of the first things that people do when they want to find a doctor, lawyer, accountant etc. is to ask their family, friends, or associates for a recommendation of who they would suggest. These recommendations are priceless and are a direct result of how you have proved yourself in the past. Consistency is the key to establishing reputation and you must always be aware that every single action you perform may be used to assess your worth in business. Even one flaw in your efforts will damage how others view you. Negative factors will always be more focused on, than the positives. Remember the saying, "It takes a whole lifetime to build your reputation, but just one instance to destroy it." Always be mindful of your efforts when dealing with others. Even if a mistake is made, make sure that you make corrections and the other party walks away content. Remember, that a person who is not happy will go and tell many others. Preserve your reputation and acknowledge its importance by making the effort of doing your best work each and every time. In business, one of the most effective ways to improve your professional self is to build your reputation into the person you would like to be considered as.

* * *

Logically, most people will automatically assume that in order to better themselves, more focus should be placed in areas of weakness. Although I believe that you should not ignore the inadequacies of your professional makeup, there is a more balanced way to improve your overall business personality. When you focus on your strengths and abilities, there tends to be more success as a result of your actions. The opportunity to show your talents gives you an outlet for personal expression. The task at hand is more easily accomplished as it requires an area of your attention which you deem a strength from your past experiences. The higher rate of success of these actions leaves you feeling optimistic about additional tasks. Your strengths become greater and stand out more in a crowd of mediocrity. However, if you are focused predominantly in areas which require you to pull from the weaker points of your professional abilities, it becomes an arduous task destined for a higher rate of failure. The more of these conquests invade your workload the more you become complacent in efforts. Unproductivity becomes the result. These failures begin to take toll and buildup will pacify any chances for inspiration. Therefore, focus on your strengths and make them even better. Any person who is revered in any field is known as the best at what they do. The exception to the rule. A jack of many trades has the trophy of broad abilities but rarely does that constitute greatness in one particular field. As to not neglect your weaknesses, work on these areas in between tasks which require your strengths. This will balance your exposure to activities which require your strengths as well as those which may improve your weaknesses, and the potential to improve your overall traits are greater.

* * *

To increase your salary and further your position in your profession, you have to build your worth. Most of the times your potential to earn comes as a direct result of the abilities and benefits you can offer your employer or customers. With this in mind, seek to build your status at your workplace by focusing on improving your business potential. Acquire as much knowledge and skill as possible and you will be valued accordingly. The results of your work and the contributions you make to your profession will be used to gauge your worth and will ultimately dictate your employment reality. With all actions that you partake in, make sure they are done with the standard of excellence as this will be significant in building your reputation. Understand that each task is an opportunity to do so, and that you are always competing with others who are also making the efforts to build their worth. When you are a valued individual in your profession, you are regarded as someone whose skill is of importance and in high demand. Build and emphasize the parts of your business characteristics that are unique contributions that only you can provide.

One of the keys to Magic Johnson's success was his intuition to realize opportunity in areas not strongly targeted by others. He built his worth to other companies by being able to generate a customer base in urban markets, where others were seeking to expand. Magic was able to carve a niche as an entity who could successfully bridge the gap between well known brands and inner-city neighborhoods. Before him these companies were afraid of investing in these areas because they simply had no idea how to operate in them and felt they would lose money. He was able to close a deal with Sony, to open high-quality movie theatres, and soon bought other companies such as T.G.I. Friday's, 24 Hour Fitness, Starbucks, and others into the areas. Rather than having to travel outside their neighborhoods to the suburbs, urban residents could now stay local and enjoy a national chain which catered to their market. Many other companies followed suit, for example Best Buy sought out Johnson in 2008 for help on operating stores that appeal to the urban markets. Where others steered clear, Magic saw opportunity and was able to build his worth and professional value. When he first approached other executives, they would see him as a joke or simply a basketball player who had no knowledge on how to conduct business. Magic has since proven them wrong and now valued as a liaison to an expanding market. You can also do the same and become an asset to others who would like to utilize your services or talent. You should always be alert to ways that you can obtain an edge that no one else can offer.

The more individual and unique the contribution, the greater the value. When you focus on a particular area of expertise, you are able to target and emphasize assets others may not take the time to gain or have access to. This expertise may increase your worth as you are known for your skill in an area very few may provide. Seek to network with others who you have built a strong relationship with that can help further any cause. It should be understood that your involvement with any project, is an opportunity to gain from these relationships as well. You essentially establish a unified front, taking advantage of strength in numbers. Some business people cultivate a "team" under them. They may grow with, recruit, hire, train, mentor, and influence others in order to form a network of professionals who are cohesive in their intentions. Others who deal with these individuals understand that these people are associated and have each other's interests in mind. When they are fired, they may take others with them who hold key positions. When they are hired, it is understood that these relationships can add to available resources. Worth is increased due to this type of situation and must be acknowledged before others take action.

Another way to build your worth is to possess a well-rounded knowledge of your profession. The more working knowledge you have the more you will be considered an asset. Potential companies which you may like to work for will consider you for management and other prominent positions which require this well rounded knowledge. Current employers will want to keep you there, as they do not want your talents to be available to others who may become competition. Sometimes just stifling the options of competitors to gain from your abilities will be enough incentive to increase your employment security.

Ultimately, you must know what you are worth. This knowledge is significant as it provides certain guidelines as to how you should proceed in your profession. You must know what will be reasonable to ask for as compensation. Are you obtaining all the compensation you deserve and does your salary translate as your true value? You can use the measure of worth as an indication of what position you should be in and when to request promotions. Your worth can help aid you in negotiations and prevent you from being undercut. It is also an accolade that provides an indication of the progress that has been made in your career and how other entities value you. In your attempt to get to know yourself, carefully explore your business personality and consider the value that you provide to your profession. Update this information regularly and always be mindful and active in any ways that you may increase your professional worth.

* * *

One of the most important requirements of improving your professional self is to gain as much experience as you can in the business sector that you choose to involve yourself with. There are no shortcuts for acquiring experience and it is a necessity in securing your chances for success. Experience comes with time, although you can greatly maximize your potential by the intensity in which you dedicate yourself to your work. Just because you have spent years in your field does not mean that you have ample abilities, unless you have used the time efficiently and given your best efforts in acquiring the skill level that you need to excel. There is no substitute for time spent in the field, and every person must pay their dues. Besides acquiring the skills to become competent, there is an instinctual ability that can only be learned by putting in the time that is required. With time you develop a kind of "sense" that will help you in your profession. Too many people try to rush the process and make the mistake of prematurely involving themselves in something they are not ready for. For example, some may want to skip the steps that are necessary to start a business and will try to initiate the process before they are ready to. They may not have gained the proper funding, found the best location, gained enough operating knowledge, or other requirements that would place them in the best position to open a new business. This may greatly decrease the chances for success and put them in a bad position. Always be prepared to pay your dues and practice patience so that you can put yourself in the best position to succeed.

During my visit to Thailand, I went to the crocodile farm and zoo. They featured a show where a couple guys perform in a pit of crocodiles and conduct various feats like sticking their head and hands in the crocodile's mouth. They wrestle the crocodiles from the water and drag them up onto the main stage by the tail. It was very entertaining and amazing the comfort level the performers had in the presence of these deadly animals. There were about twenty crocodiles in the stage pit and they worked with as many as four at any given time. At the end of each stunt they performed, people threw money as tips into the pit. After the show, one of the entertainers was standing around talking to people and some people began to ask him a couple questions. They asked him if anyone had ever been hurt during any of the shows. He said that he had seen an instance when a coworker was not careful and lost his life after not being able to get his head out in time! He was also asked how he came to work in his current profession. He said he'd been doing this his entire life and being around these animals was second nature, and his actions had become instinctive. In essence, the knowledge he acquired over the years provided him a new sense on how crocodiles reacted in different situations. Time spent in the company of these animals provided a real life education and an opportunity to learn this unorthodox field of work. He familiarized himself with the many abilities needed to function in a profession where any mistakes could mean his life. There are no text books for this type of work and knowledge and experience must be acquired first hand.

Most of us don't have to operate in such extreme professions as wrestling crocodiles, but it is still important to acquire any knowledge that will help us maneuver in a business world that is filled with predators. It is the same in business and experience contributes to becoming qualified in the profession that we have chosen to pursue. You can study all the text books about a specific profession that you want, but this will never give you the same insight as gaining the experience first hand. There is no greater education than time spent on the job, and even if you have the knowledge about the subject, it is completely different when you have to actually experience these scenarios. There is a big difference between gaining knowledge and the actual application of the knowledge that you accumulate. With experience, the time dedicated shows that you have the ability to stick with the profession that you have committed to. You maintain grit to last and others know that it is a good investment to work with you because you will most likely be there tomorrow. You have also been through more situations related to your field and have the knowledge to accommodate change and adversity. You've had ample time to make connections, build relationships, and maintain a network at your disposal. With experience you have gained a reputation others may judge you by and gauge your skill level. Prepare yourself for the best possible outcome of your efforts, by taking the time to gain the experience necessary to perform at your best.

* * *

Distinguish yourself with memorable action, and empower yourself with unique characteristics. During my high school years, I worked as a waiter at a Thai restaurant. During this tenure, I came across many people and it took quite a long time to familiarize myself with the great number of customers. Many of them, I had become acquainted with because of the frequency of their visits. However, some of the customers were distinguishable to me by characteristics that made them stand out amongst the rest. Of course, it wasn't hard to remember the big tippers and I knew many of them by name. One of the customers, a professional cartoonist, would draw characters and various art work on the napkins. Another would always want his food a certain way and I specifically remembered how he favored spicy foods, pouring large amounts of chili sauce on his dishes. One loyal customer would actually order dishes be bought out to other customers because he wanted to have them taste the dishes at his own expense.

In life, you tend to remember people you meet who have unique characteristics and whose actions differentiate them from others. They are not hesitant to display the characteristics which make them different. These differences are not limited to action and can be displayed in the form of appearance, speech, habit, etc. In business, you may use these types of characteristics to separate yourself from the majority of peers in your profession. When you distinguish yourself you make it apparent that you are an individual whose abilities and characteristics are unique and should be valued. Others understand that they can only expect these benefits from you alone and cannot gain them from anyone else.

As much criticism as there has been of Simon Cowell, former judge of *American Idol*, the truth is that it is his reputation for being notoriously harsh that has made him a household name and has contributed to his extreme success. Cowell became widely recognized for his blunt criticism and insults of the contestants and their performances, as a judge on American Idol. He has been called "heartless," "thoughtless," and much, much worse, but even still, there are those who tune into the show just to hear his harsh wisecracks. He is known for his signature phrase, "I don't mean to be rude, but…," which he usually follows with a blunt opinion of the contestant's abilities, presentation, and even physical appearance. He doesn't hold anything back and is so harsh sometimes that he even elicits booing from the audiences and gets cut off by his fellow judges for being too mean. In 2003, Cowell was listed Number 33 on Channel 4's list of all time 100 Worst Britons. In 2006, he was voted the tenth most terrifying celebrity on television in a Radio Times poll consisting of 3,000 people. However, it is this same "tell-it-like-it-is" reputation that has contributed to the success of the Idol series around the world and provided promotions for his other shows and ventures, X Factor Franchise, Got Talent Franchise, American

Inventor, and Syco Records. This exploitation of his reputation, has earned him a staggering salary of up to $33 million a year on American Idol, $90 million annual salary in 2011, and a net worth of $550 million as of April 2012. He is a perfect example of an entrepreneur who has exploited his unique characteristics in his pursuit for success.

Bass Pro Shop is a company whose distinctive characteristics has attributed greatly to its success. Owner John L. Morris has successfully bought his consumers a retail experience rivaling the attractions of some of the most visited tourist destinations. In fact, the company's original Outdoor World location in Springfield has become the most popular tourist destination in the state of Missouri. Just to put the accomplishment of this feat into perspective, visitors to all Bass Pro Shops are expected to reach about one hundred million this year, which is about forty million more than the estimated number of visitors expected to visit Walt Disney World in Orlando this year! Bass Pro Shop's larger flagship stores, known as Outdoor World stores, are massive facilities up to three hundred thousand square feet in size offering fishing gear, hunting equipment, camping supplies, boats and golf and general sporting equipment. What makes them appealing however is the amusement features such as target ranges, fish aquariums, restaurants, and laser arcades. They are filled with free activities such as archery, rock climbing, fly fishing lessons, Dutch oven cooking, and wildlife exhibits. The decor of each store is themed to represent each location's geography. All stores have an indoor water showcases featuring game fish species that are indigenous to the store's area. Professional anglers and store staff hold demonstrations catching the fish and showing the use of artificial bait. The Springfield Outdoor World location boasts a four-story waterfall, a two-story cabin, hundred-yard indoor rifle range, twenty-five-yard range for handguns and archery, book and gift store, a wildlife art gallery, a taxidermy shop, a large selection of stuffed animal and mounted fish displays, a stream stocked with trout, barber shop, and a 250-seat auditorium! Bass Pro Shops are ranked in the top 200 on Forbes list of the 441 largest private companies. They currently bring in an estimated annual revenue of over $2.5 billion.

Some of the people considered icons in our society such as movie stars, singers, and other people of high recognition have their own signature characteristics. Actors coin phrases that we repeat over and over and can immediately identify if inquired about. Donald Trump firing the contestants on his show *The Apprentice*, Simon and his insults on *American Idol*, Marilyn Monroe's birthmark, Michael Jordan's competitive nature, and Martin Luther King's passion heard in his speech, are just a few examples.

The same can be said about any circumstance where a person displays a distinguishable trait in the work they engage in. This can be done to your advantage to separate you from the many people that others may come across in their professional lives. These unique actions do not have to be completely original but may be actions which are not regularly exercised by other peers in the workplace and that make you stand out in some way. One example may be sending handwritten letters to customers thanking them for their continued support. Even something so simple as this gives you a personal touch that people remember.

Assess your professional characteristics and bring to the forefront, traits which you feel will improve and differentiate yourself from others. Highlight the genuine qualities that only you possess and examine how these may help you in your professional life. Such actions and characteristics must be genuine and uncalculated as others may sense insincerity or view you as manipulative. Factors such as communicative style, or even wardrobe will better solidify your presence in another person's mind.

There are a number of ways that you can also make your presence felt. If you present yourself differently than others when meeting a person, the likeliness of that person remembering you is greatly increased. Set meetings in memorable places so the person will remember you every time they come across the place. Try to memorize stories for situations which may come up in your profession. Memorize some jokes related to your field which will be remembered and told again. Read news columns and periodicals which may be used as a conversation topic. Watch sports or TV shows that can help you make a connection. Use certain words that will make you stand out that only maybe you would use. You should practice developing your charm and wit and take note of these types of characteristics that you appreciate in others.

So few people take the time to develop their true selves as most are busy trying to conform to others and fit into a crowd. It is very appealing to meet people who bring a new approach to life and who possess a distinctive personality. All of us have our own characteristics that we often hide which we need to unlock and learn to display to others.

* * *

You can greatly improve your professional self by being a person who takes the advice of others. Sometimes pride may prohibit us from doing so, but if it is advice that can help out our cause, then we should take the advice into consideration. Being a person who is accessible and welcomes ideas from others helps open up the lines of communication for improvement at your workplace. No matter what level of employment you are involved with, there are great benefits to keeping your ears open for new ideas and better methods of getting things done. Sometimes these ideas, which may come from inside or outside the company, may give the company the improvement that is needed to grow. We are sometimes limited in our own perspectives and it can be helpful to obtain other points of views.

Meg Whitman, former CEO of eBay, can attribute part of her success to taking in the viewpoints of others. She was always open to listen to advice and suggestions on how things could better suit the buyers and sellers of the eBay marketplace. One suggestion from both customers and staff led to the purchase of PayPal, which provided its customers with a highly effective online portal for banking and payment processing. PayPal works seamlessly with eBay and provides great ease of sending and receiving payments for items bought and sold on the site. In the company's San Jose headquarters, Whitman even set up an office in cubicle space amongst all other coworkers to be readily available and in close contact with her employees. Being amongst her employees on the work floor, she was able to gain insight to how the company would best improve its functionality. This was in direct contradiction to the practice of most executives who alienate themselves in their offices, never being exposed to the day to day experiences of coworkers. She would personally screen emails and phone calls to obtain valuable insight from eBay's customers. She not only listened but also implemented the ideas at every stage. She balanced the scales of making eBay appealing to larger companies while keeping the loyal base of small buyers and sellers which the company had started with. Whitman is also a customer of eBay herself, and employees are encouraged to shop and sell on the website to gain the customer's perspective on its usage. By remaining accessible and welcoming ideas to make the company better, Whitman was able to provide eBay's customers the direction they requested. She promoted a work environment of sharing ideas within her company and as a result has gained the benefits of sound input from the people who best know the business. Plenty of competition has tried to establish themselves and provide the same outlet as eBay, but the attention she paid to her customer's requests was a great advantage in making it the industry leader. She has successfully put herself in the position to gain insight and knowledge of a pioneering new business which set the trend for its genre.

It is of utmost importance to be open to the advice of others. Everyone views various situations from their own unique viewpoints and it can be a great asset to gain another perspective. Always stay accessible in your professional career so that you can obtain the benefits of others' good ideas and solutions to problems we may not be able to think of ourselves. Improve your professional self by giving yourself a more well rounded perspective from the input of others and the helpful advice they may be able to impart on us.

* * *

Another beneficial way to improve your professional self is to welcome the resources of people who you are currently working with. These people may include lawyers, accountants, managers, or others who you may already be working with. Be receptive to the flow of information from all business relationships and ask a lot of questions. For example, an attorney can provide limitless information on the field that you are pursuing. Instead of just seeking their traditional services, you may also benefit in such ways as gaining new contacts and references to individuals you should familiarize yourself with. They are great sources for information and other resources as they deal with a varied client list that you may seek exposure to. They may represent others who can help you with your career, and have strong relationships with people you may not otherwise have access to.

Others such as bank tellers are a great resource for information. I regularly ask them which businesses they have seen that are successful, any current news and trends they come across, the numbers of businesses in the field in question or the level of competition that might exist, and a myriad of other questions that may benefit me in future goals. The merchant tellers are exposed to customers who operate or own a variety of different businesses and are in touch with these individuals on a daily basis. You essentially have the access to individuals who are a gateway to other professionals who conduct business in your particular demographics and possess up to date information in the ever changing world of business. Bank tellers witness the birth of new companies and the demise of many others and may have talked to certain professionals who maintain information from real world experience that can better the chances for success.

Your accountant most likely has extensive knowledge on the finances of different fields of business as they also represent a number of clients in a variety of different professions. They can give you a broad overview of businesses you may have in question and the profits or financial burdens that may be unique to certain others. They may be able to tell you from their experiences, which businesses have been most consistent or have a high percentage of success. As they may deal with many different entities in the same particular field, they have the advantage of acquiring information from a number of different perspectives and viewpoints which gives them a better understanding of all aspects of the particular business. An accountant would have the knowledge of the profitable areas of their clients' businesses and can tell you where others have faulted in expending of capital and other resources. They may also inform you which businesses are volatile in nature and which may be risky endeavors.

Do not neglect the resources that may be available to you from others you may work with. One person may be an outlet to a number of others and you may exploit this situation to gain additional knowledge or business relationships. When inquiring about information, do so in a respectful manner which does not cause them to divulge the personal information of their clients. They must always maintain the integrity of their relationships with their clients and can not provide specifics which may compromise any situation. Simply ask questions specific to your interest in a way that does not directly violate any professional standards. For example, if you are interested in finding out how coin laundry businesses have faired in your area, you may question a bank teller without specifics such as naming a particular business or identifying exact figures from a third party model. Seek to find and work with entities who can provide not only traditional services, but may also offer information and other benefits. Those that are prominent in their field have most likely gathered a great deal of resources throughout the years, and have much more to offer than just the services that they advertise.

Habits

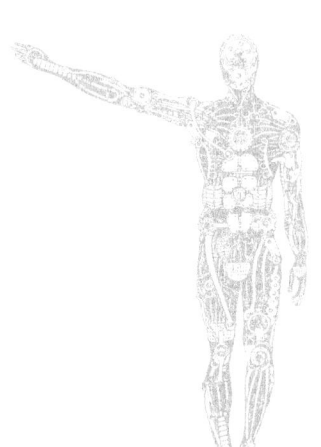

Motivation gets you going and habit gets you there.
—Zig Ziglar

Motivation is what gets you started.
Habit is what keeps you going.
—Jim Ryun

Another significant way to better position yourself to perform at your highest potential is to establish and practice efficient habits. Habits can be defined as behaviors that are implemented in such repetition that they become automatic action. In light of all the information gathered throughout the years from research of the subject of habits, it has been found that we can manipulate them to improve work performance and benefit our lives as a whole.

Remember that the Grind involves any way in which to bring about your peak level of performance. Once a habit is established, it then becomes subconscious in nature and requires hardly any thought process to conduct the action. You may utilize habits to get things done with automatic reaction which will lighten your workload and enable you to concentrate on other areas that may require your attention. As a result, the brain does not have to work as hard to accomplish tasks. It frees up mental resources which you could devote to something else and enables you to accommodate an increased workload. That is why you can take on other tasks while performing actions which you have already established as habit. For example, you can carry on a conversation while driving a car or watch TV while brushing your teeth. These actions have already become automatic behavior and you do not have to expend much focus in performing them, so conducting other actions at the same time are easily done.

Without the benefit of habits, our brains would be overwhelmed from all the focus we would have to exert for every single action. A Duke University study in 2006 found that more than forty percent of peoples' actions performed each day came as a result of habit instead of actual decision. Therefore, we must acknowledge that many of the current actions that we exercise come as a result of how we have established our habits in the past. With so much of daily action being governed by routine and automatic behavior, it is important that time is taken to form good habits and modify bad habits so that they are consistent with how you would like to establish your business performance.

* * *

Habits consist of a psychological pattern called the habit loop. In his book *The Power of Habit: Why We Do What We Do in Life and Business*, author Charles Duhigg details how the habit loop has been used to transform people's lives. Success in multiple areas of life has been achieved through altering people's habits by focusing on this three-stage process.

The first is the "cue," which is the trigger to initiate an automatic behavior or the habit. Researchers have discovered that most cues fall into four general categories: a location or time of day, a certain series of actions, particular moods, or the company of specific people. Second is the "routine," which is the behavior itself. Last is the "reward," which is the conclusion which tells our brains whether or not we should use this habit in the future or not. It is an outcome that your brain strives for by conducting the habit.

The main way that a habit is established is through repetition of the behavior. It has been said, arguably, that a habit takes about two weeks of repetition to establish. Others have concluded that there is no definitive time frame to do so. Things that we really enjoy are quickly established into habit, whereas tasks which we find difficult, may take longer. Factors such as the level of difficulty to carry out the habit may also be significant. Remember that the main objective to establishing the habit is to conduct it in such repetition that it becomes automatic. This is the time when we do not have to expend any effort to perform the habit.

* * *

There are many techniques that help in successfully establishing habits. Trial and error can be used to see which of the following may be effective for your own situation. Remember that the main objective is to make the behavior automatic and you will know that you are successful when the particular action no longer requires much effort to perform the task.

As repetition is the main way to establish a habit, you should commit to a few weeks of repeating the same behavior. The initial phase is usually difficult but should get easier as time passes by. Keep in mind that there has been no proven time frame that has been established to create a habit. You will know that it has become habit simply when the action is performed subconsciously. Missing a day will not ruin your efforts but you should make every effort toward making the habit stick on a daily basis. Try to make things as simple as possible and try not to make major changes too suddenly. For example, if you would like to commit to a two hour workout daily, start off with a half an hour and condition yourself to take on more gradually. Exercise maintaining the habit consistently. Try to perform the habit at the same time or place, as keeping the circumstances consistent makes it easier to establish.

Adding a trigger can help you in your efforts and you can do so by keeping a ritual or routine before executing your habit. Let's say you are trying to get to work at a certain time each day, you may want to set an alarm to remind you to do so. The sound of the alarm is a trigger and every time it sounds it tells you to wake up and get ready for work.

Accountability is also very effective and telling others of your goals makes you more likely to follow through on your efforts. You can let your friends know of your intentions as you are likely not to want to look bad in front of them by giving up.

If by attempting to establish a habit, you will have to remove behaviors from your usual routine, try to replace them with another instead of just removing them altogether. It has been found that it is much easier to alleviate behaviors you are trying to remove from your routine by finding replacements to fill the void. It will also be easier to establish a habit by removing any temptations that may be in the way. For example, if you are trying to establish the habit of eating healthier, you could remove any junk foods from you living space that would make it difficult to follow through on your intentions.

Just like with anything else, it can be much easier to accomplish a task by recruiting the help of others. Habits are no different, and you can enlist the help of others who will keep you on course. Create simple plans that you may follow with ease.

Don't overlook the effectiveness of writing things down. This provides you a reminder and keeps your intentions clear. Write down an action plan that you can follow and keep a checklist so you can see your progress.

Always keep in mind that there will be failures along the way and that it may take a few attempts until you find success. Do not judge yourself too harshly and do not give up when things do not go your way.

* * *

Just as important as creating good habits is the process of changing bad habits into good ones. Neurological studies have discovered that once a habit has been established, it becomes encoded in the brain structures and can never really be completely eradicated. Behavior is represented in our brains by a neural pathway that becomes thicker as the behavior becomes more automatic. If you stop a behavior the pathway doesn't go away, it becomes dormant. When you wish to replace a bad habit, the best thing to do is not just stop that behavior altogether. Instead of saying "I am going to stop doing X," you should say that "I am going to do Y instead of X." By doing this you are acknowledging that it may not be realistic to erase the habit from your mind, but that you may instead overwrite the habit and change the behavior for the better.

This can be done by focusing on the habit loop described above. The cue and the reward would stay the same and a new routine would be established which would replace the undesired old one. First, identify the cue triggering the routine, which can include a mood, time of day, location, person you are with, etc. Next, identify the reward that the habit produces or the desired outcome of the action. Once the cue and reward are realized, you will then come up with a new routine to replace your current one. This technique has actually been used to successfully treat such conditions as procrastination, depression, alcoholism, smoking, gambling addiction, anxiety, and other behavioral problems.

A good example of the use of this technique is one that has been used by AA to treat drinking problems. The cue may be that a person may feel depressed or stressed out and decides to go to a bar to drink. The reward may be that you will have an outlet to forget about your troubles and also find the company of friends and others to help comfort you. As mentioned above, you can use the technique of keeping your cue and reward but changing the routine. In this case, instead of going to get a drink at the bar, you may want to go to a support meeting, finding an activity that keeps you busy and that can involve many of your friends (i.e., set up a bowling game, meet with your friends for a card game, etc.) or other activities which would provide the company and comfort of others. This way you are still able to obtain emotional support without the negative behavior of drinking and relapsing. You are able to attain the same rewards that you would which would be to gain comfort to all the things that you are depressed about while keeping you involved with an activity that takes you away from thinking about your troubles.

You can also implement this technique to change any bad habits that hinder your business performance and make you fall short of working at your best. You can take the same steps of identifying the cue and the reward and replacing the routine to produce the desired results.

* * *

In *The Power of Habit*, Duhigg gives us a great example of how implementing habits has been used to benefit a real life situation. Tony Dungy was head coach of the Tampa Bay Buccaneers from 1996 to 2001, and head coach of the Indianapolis Colts from 2002 to 2008. Dungy's coaching strategy involved transforming his players' decisions on the field into habit, making their reactions automatic instead of responsive. Instead of the players' having to make immediate and instinctive decisions for each situation that was encountered; they would be trained to react out of habit that was established during practice, and later during competition. The focus was not on sophisticated offensive and defensive playing schemes but rather to respond immediately and instinctively to various situations encountered while competing. There was no need for a thick playbook but instead focus on where the opponents lined up and moved on the field. They practiced responding to behavior patterns until their performance became precise reacting to everything habitually. He was able to get his players to react automatically to opponents' visual cues, eliminating the need for decision making and momentary hesitations. This coaching technique made them perform faster and with less error than their challengers. Results were proven when the Bucs moved on to become division champs and a decade later, Super Bowl champs. The Colts also went on to win the Super Bowl in 2007. This was all a direct result of training his players to use habits in their performance.

* * *

There are many ways that you can implement habits to improve your business performance. For example, let's say that you are having problems with procrastination and would like to create and modify current habits to make it easier to change the bad habit of procrastination. One of the reasons why we procrastinate is because we often have other matters we must deal with before we even initiate the thing we intend to accomplish. For example, let's say that you are trying to eat healthier and therefore decide to prepare to cook a meal instead of going to get fast food. Maybe you do not have the pots and pans already cleaned. Maybe it is other factors, like having to wait until the food is marinated, having to go to the store to get the ingredients, or other obstacle. Some of these things will attribute to not wanting to cook and procrastinating until another time. Even washing the dishes which have been sitting for a week can be a deterrent to start to cook and follow through with our intentions to eat healthy. Therefore, the key to not procrastinating in this situation is to set the habit of preparing for the task beforehand to make it as easy to accomplish. In this case you may want to set the habit of always washing the dishes right after every meal, shopping for ingredients in advance on another day, or preparing your food beforehand.

At the work environment this may include keeping your desk clean and organized, getting to sleep at a good hour as to be fully refreshed, or planning and preparing before we even start the action. Always set up the things you will need in advance so you will make your activities as easy as possible. This will take away or hinder your tendency to procrastinate.

In 2008, psychologist Shane Owens and his colleagues at Hofstra University found that procrastinators who formed "implementation intentions" were about eight times more likely to follow through on a commitment than those who did not. Implementation intentions are established to specify when and where you will perform specific behaviors you set out to accomplish. Instead of saying, "I am going to be more productive," you would set up an implementation intention including the specific timing and location. You may say, "I will be going to work earlier at six AM and have the project finished in two weeks." This will make you much more likely to follow through on your intentions and inhibit the tendency to procrastinate.

Procrastination may hinge on your unwillingness to go through frustration at the current time or your reluctance to add difficulty to your schedule. Perhaps it may be disorganization. Whatever the reasons may be, you can establish habits that make the likelihood for success greater. The more habits you discover and establish that will help your situation, the less effort you will need to expend. Things will become more automatic and the tendency to procrastinate and other bad habits will be easier to remedy.

* * *

The fact that almost half of our actions performed each day are attributed to habits, shows us the necessity of focusing on this subject for the betterment of our professional careers. It is vital that we discover all benefits that can be derived from the habits that we establish. Just being aware of these advantages can contribute greatly to our chances for success in business and our professional lives.

The formation and modification of habits takes practice and the more that you do so, the better you will become at this process. The advantages of the use of habits are many and you will discover more applications as you experiment with what behaviors work best for you. You can use them to practice automatic reaction to decrease errors from the decision making process or utilize them to change bad habits to ones which will help you perform.

Take the time to take inventory of your current habits and the effects that they have on the outcome of your work. Make note of all bad habits that may be hindering your performance and implement action plans on how to modify them to your advantage. The ideal situation would be to establish habits that would allow you to exert extreme effort as a normal occurrence. This would involve being able to create and make routine all behaviors that could contribute to working at your best. In other words, make high achievement so common during your performance that it becomes the standard of your output.

So, consider the formation of habits as necessary resources in the goal attainment process. Elimination of bad habits and the replacement with efficient habits can greatly contribute to the requirements of success. These habits can be maintained to strengthen your business personality, a trait which is ultimately essential for the theory of the Grind.

Matters of the Mind

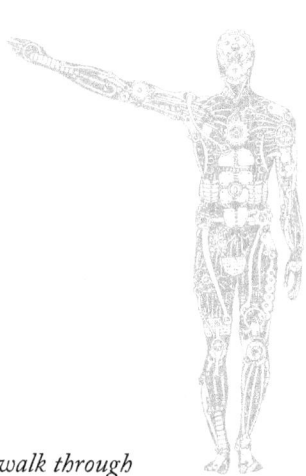

*I will not let anyone walk through
my mind with their dirty feet.*

—Mahatma Gandhi

Since everything we do is a product of our mind and our thinking, it is vital that we take the steps to maintain our brain for healthy cognitive functioning. The practice of the Grind requires that your mind is working in optimum condition, so you should take any measures that will help it perform at peak levels. Just like a computer or a car, our brain functioning is dependent on how we take care of it and our maintenance of its needs. It also begins to deteriorate with misuse and neglect, and has its own requirements to operate at a maximum level. The following are a number of ways that we can enhance the well being of our minds to optimize our thinking and generate its peak performance.

First, we must feed our brain and make sure that we provide the proper nutrients for a healthy diet. Different foods benefit our brains in different ways. Our brain draws its energy from glucose and foods rich with carbohydrates, such as fruit, whole-wheat bread, brown rice, oatmeal, high-fiber cereal, lentils, and whole beans. The best time to fuel your mind with these types of food is four hours before you will be working, as this is approximately how long it takes for your body to make use of complex sugars. Omega-3 fatty acids help form its cell structure and help strengthen the synapses in our brain related to memory, which you can obtain in foods such as wild salmon, tuna, halibut, spinach, broccoli, soybeans and flaxseed oil. Antioxidants that you can find in tea, fruit or vegetables help regulate the oxidative stress that destroys the brain cells. Amino acids help connect the neurotransmitters which are essential for keeping your brain sharp and can be found in foods like fish, meat, eggs, cheese, yogurt, and other protein rich foods.

Make sure that you get lots of sleep, about seven to eight hours per night, and rest so your brain can cement neural connections. A good night's sleep is said to trigger changes in the brain and can boost your memory levels. Daytime rest is also critical to fueling the brain and helps to prime it for critical tasks of thinking and problem solving, so take naps when you have the chance.

Give your brain a break by not always trying to remember what to do, but by writing things down which you have to do. This way you can conserve the mind's energy to draw upon functions that are creative and productive. When you overcrowd your brain with memory, your thinking slows down, so set up another type of method to organize and prioritize your "to do" list. This can include a list made daily on paper or a schedule you can make on your computer that you can use instead of your mind, in order to give it a break. When you allow your mind to wander, it begins to scan the environment for subjects that peak its interest and focus becomes scattered. Try directing your brain to focus on the subjects that you choose. By doing this you help your brain focus on one thing at a time instead of attempting to multitask your efforts.

Just as it is for your whole body, exercise is also good for your brain and has been shown to improve short term memory and other functions. Studies have revealed that 30 minutes of walking daily can improve blood flow to the brain, boosting neural growth and brain connectivity. Running will increase the levels of oxygen in your brain and body and release endorphins which make you feel energized. Engage in other activities such as golf which stimulates use of decision making to plan stroke strategies and control of repetitive movements which instills mind body discipline, or yoga which forces you to focus on controlling your muscles and breathing to give you a rest from stress. Try to establish a workout schedule, maybe in the morning before work, where you can go to a gym and get some exercise.

You can also further exercise the brain itself, with activities that challenge the brain like playing Sudoku or crossword puzzles. These have been shown to improve our intelligence and also help prevent Alzheimer's disease or dementia. The more that you challenge your brain, the more new nerve pathways you can form. You can give your brain a workout even by using everyday tasks like brushing your teeth or washing the dishes, but instead using the opposite hand that you usually use. This helps strengthen the pathways in the opposite side of your brain. You should also try to use more of your senses in these familiar tasks such as opening the lock on your door or combing your hair with your eyes closed to stimulate your other senses. When you learn new things, it promotes the growth of new brain cells and the connections between them. Try learning new languages or activities like cooking to keep your brain challenged.

Meditation is now considered a useful tool for business success. More and more corporate executives and companies have been using meditation techniques as a powerful tool for increasing mental clarity and performance. Companies such as Google, Target, and General Mills have embraced the practice of meditation, providing courses and opportunities for employees to learn more about the subject. Business schools are also increasingly teaching mindfulness, a Buddhist form of meditation which increases awareness of oneself and one's surroundings. Meditation includes practices such as quieting the mind, mentally focusing your attention on your breathing and away from everyday thoughts and worries, and being fully and attentively present in the moment using the breath as an object of awareness. It has been shown to be effective in improving focus and memory, lowering stress levels, and even preventing mental illnesses. There are a number of books and references that can give you ideas on different techniques and practices of meditation, so research what will work for you.

People are social beings and maintaining healthy relationships stimulate our brains. Interacting with others may just be the best kind of brain exercise. A recent study from the Harvard School of Public Health found that people who have the most active social lives experienced the slowest rate of memory decline.

Remember that our minds are our most important tool that we have available for our use in the Grind. We must make sure that we take all measures to ensure that our brains are functioning at its optimum level. Anything that can contribute to helping your mind function better and reduce stress levels can be a useful ally in leading a more successful professional life. It is only logical that we emphasize the maintenance of the instrument that we use the most in everyday business functioning, and give the brain the attention it truly deserves.

* * *

Multitasking may be a feature that computers are endowed with but for the human mind trying to do the same, it is just not practical. The term multitasking is the act of performing two or more tasks simultaneously. It can also involve going back and forth between various tasks, doing several different things at once. In the past, it was considered a good way to be more productive and take on a greater workload throughout the day. The logic was that if you were able to work on several different things at once, you would be able to get more things done. The fact is that it actually costs us more time than it saves, as well as diminishes the quality of the work that we are able to output. When we switch between tasks, our minds must readjust to cope with the new information. When we begin to add more tasks, we can't devote our full concentration and focus with every switch, so the quality of our work suffers. This is even worse when the task is more complex or technical. Another negative to multitasking is that doing so often increases our stress levels, making us overwhelmed.

In a recent study published in the August 24 edition of *Proceedings of the National Academy of Sciences*," Stanford researchers Clifford Naas, Eyal Ophir, and Anthony Wagner tested a group of one hundred college students with a series of three experiments that consisted of organizing things in their working memory, switching among tasks from doing one thing to another, and filtering through relevant and irrelevant information. The students were separated into groups of "high multitaskers," who were those who regularly used four or more forms of media (texting, chatting or texting on phone, reading emails, watching TV, etc.) at one time, or "low multitaskers" who used no more than an average of two types of media at one time. The goal was to determine what elements of multitasking the high multitasker group performed better at in comparison with the low multitasker group. Surprisingly in every test, students who spent the least amount of time multitasking performed the best, or better than those who did so frequently. People who are regularly multitasking several types of electronic media do not pay attention, control their memory, or switch from one task to another as well as those who attend to and complete one task at a time. Multitasking is not efficient and does not get more work done faster. Instead, one task interferes with another, so everything actually takes the brain longer to function. Nass concluded, "Multitasking is a problem, and people should not be deluded into thinking that it works. It hurts productivity, and it may be hurting your thinking process." Social scientists have long assumed that it's impossible to process more than one string of information at a time, and another report from the Institute of Psychiatry at the University of London found that when people constantly juggle emails, text messages and phone calls, their IQ actually falls ten points.

Our fast-paced world of business makes it very hard to refrain from trying to take on a number of responsibilities at once. It is almost forced on you in some instances, and becomes an automatic occurrence with all the distractions and added interference that comes a person's way each day. There are a few strategies that you can implement to stop yourself from multitasking. First, you can set aside specific time periods for your tasks. Assign a part of the day for each responsibility such as checking emails, returning calls, conduct research, etc., so that you eliminate the time you will spend going back and forth between them. When you are working on one task, turn off or eliminate any distractions that can take you away from your current task. If your computer may signal you of new emails, or phone notifies you of a text or message, or someone can walk in your office because your door is open; do what is necessary to eliminate the distraction. Have a system in place that you can conveniently file away new "to-do" items, so that you have easy access to them at a later time. This way you don't feel pressed to take care of the issue immediately for fear of forgetting about it and you can organize them according to their urgency. If you find your mind wandering or starting to multitask, practice refocusing your attention back to the matter at hand. Do not allow yourself to multitask at any time. You may need to take a quick break, so implement a system that works for you which will enable you to take a breather as well as bring your mind back. Even short breaks can refocus your mind, lower your stress levels, and improve your concentration. Learn to concentrate on one thing at a time, and practice finishing one task before starting on another. It may take time to break any habits that you may have already established, but practicing concentrating on one thing at a time will improve your focus. There is a lot of research available on these subjects and you should take the time to further read up on any issues that you are having problems with.

* * *

We have to take the responsibility of controlling what we intake into our minds as these things can sometimes negatively affect our thinking. Studies have shown that the more a person is subjected to negative issues the more likely the person is to demonstrate negative behavior. That is the reason practices like visualization can work for us, but can also work against us when exposed to negativity. As research has determined, our minds cannot distinguish between real and imagined practice. Try to shield yourself from external influences that do not have a vested interest in your well-being. Distance yourself from negative news and conversation, as the effect on our brains is the same as if we have lived through these events ourselves.

Research revealed that exposure to thirty minutes or more of negativity, including bad news on TV, complaining, or gossip, compromises the effectiveness of the neurons in the brain's hippocampus area. This is the area of your brain that aids in problem solving, reasoning and memory, so all these will be diminished by exposure to these factors. In studies, exposure to complaining and negative people caused the same emotional reactions that are experienced when going through stressful situations. Keep in mind that the longer you endure these negative states or the longer the duration of exposure to these elements, the worse it is for your brain. Always make the effort to avoid people, environments, and other sources that are negative. Anger and resentment are said to be the most contagious of the emotions, and exposure to people feeling this way often causes you to become quickly angered or resentful. Try to use self assuring positive language that will promote encouragement and good mood.

When you use self-defeating language, you promote a negative outcome. Have you ever heard someone tell you, "You look tired," and automatically felt like your energy had diminished and you actually started feeling like you were tired? These suggestive words actually have an effect on your emotions so always be mindful of your exposure to them. Also, try to begin and end all your communications with positive words, as these also have an effect on the thoughts of yourself and others around you.

Like the concept of advertisement, the more you hear a message, the more you are likely to believe it. By repeating positive affirmations to yourself repeatedly you will eventually start to internalize them. Just like a song that you don't like the first few times you hear on the radio, but then start liking it as you begin to hear it often; the messages you repeat to yourself often may also have the same effect.

* * *

The expectations of both yourself and others, has significant effects on business performance and motivation. A person's opinion and self expectation of themselves and their abilities, dictates their performance. This is called the Galatea effect. In other words, if you believe that you can succeed, then you most likely will. The more you believe in yourself and the higher your self esteem, the better your performance.

A study by Robert Rosenthal and Lenore Jacobson was conducted as an experiment to support the hypothesis that reality can be influenced by the expectations of others. The Pygmalion effect states that people perform in ways consistent with how others expect them to perform. This study was conducted at an elementary school where teachers administered to each of the students a Test of General Ability (TOGA) which measures a student's IQ. After the test, some students were chosen at random and labeled as "academic bloomers" and their names were given to their teachers. Keep in mind that these students were not actually "bloomers" but were chosen at random. At the end of the year, the students were tested again and those who were labeled "academic bloomers" received a significant increase in TOGA scores, more so than those who were not. The test concluded that the teacher's expectations of the students can influence the student's abilities to perform according to what was expected. This in part may result because teachers may subconsciously behave in ways that facilitate and encourage the students' success because of what they were told. In any case the expectation was an effective factor in influencing the "bloomer" students to perform in the way to make what the teacher expected, a reality.

In 1968, a teacher named Jane Elliott divided a group of third graders into groups based on eye color. One group was told they were superior and the others were told they were failures. Elliott then gave spelling tests to both groups on each day of the experiment. The next day Elliott switched the groups and told the groups they were the opposite of what they were told previously, either superior or failures. The results indicated that the students scored very low when they were told they were failures, and very high on the days they were told they were superior. This illustrates another example of the power of expectation and it's influences on reality.

It is believed that once an expectation is established, a person tends to act in ways that are consistent with making what is expected, a reality. He/she will then turn the expectation into a reality as a result. Just like the example of a bad day. The person becomes so adamant that nothing can go right with their day that they end up subconsciously acting in ways that will bring about negative results to match those bad expectations. Even the smallest inkling of negativity will show through body language, speech, demeanor, etc. and ultimately effect the situation in some way.

Nothing goes right in the day because the person does not expect it to.

Surround yourself with people who believe in you and expect the best for you. This will help your performance. Also remember that it isn't only what others expect of you that determines results, but also the expectations you have for yourself. What you expect from yourself is equally as significant and you must take the time to organize your thoughts to bring about the most beneficial expectation of yourself. Make it an effort to expect only the best results from yourself and your efforts. Your expectations will make you consciously or subconsciously work to make your perception a reality. Build up your confidence and define who you are through your actions and continued accomplishment.

A person who practices positive expectancy is more likely to maintain successful habits such as finding solutions to problems, embracing responsibility as a means to finding opportunity, and welcoming adversity as a way to progress. If you want to live with positive expectancy, you must vividly imagine great accomplishments. Always be mindful that your expectations contribute to your future, so it is vital that you take the time to consider the exact expectations you currently maintain about yourself. Ask yourself questions which will help you establish your expectations as well as understand where they currently stand. Analyze what you expect from yourself and why. What expectations do the people you work with have of you? What do you expect from others that you work with? Where do you expect to be in the next few years? How have your expectations been established? Do you feel what you currently expect of yourself is accurate and justified?

If you only expect the worse then you are setting yourself up for failure or loss. You must find any way to increase your self-esteem and confidence. See yourself the way that you want to be in the future. The depth of your success greatly depends upon your commitment to your positive expectations, so make sure your beliefs are grounded in achieving success.

* * *

Self-efficacy is a term that can be defined as our faith in our own abilities to accomplish a specific goal. It is the trust we have in our own competency to achieve success at a particular task. Those who have high self-efficacy are those who are more willing to take greater risk in the attempts of achieving challenging goals.

A research study conducted by J. Robert Baum, from the University of Maryland, is a good example of the significance of self-efficacy. The goal of the study was to measure the level of significance of the factors that contributed to new business success. Baum examined 442 newly established architectural woodwork firms over the span of six years. He questioned the CEOs and their employees as a way to measure the motivational factors which led the CEO to start the new business. For the next six years, he kept record of the growth of the firm. In conclusion of the study, he compared the CEO's motivational factors to the growth of the firms. Of all the motivational factors that were examined, the most significant with relation to long term success was the CEO's self-efficacy. This study showed that self-efficacy was the strongest, determining factor leading to the long term growth of the firms.

Self-efficacy is the faith you hold about what you are capable of, or not capable of making happen in your life. It does not refer to the actual abilities that you have, but instead what you believe you can accomplish with those skills. It influences the choices that people make and the course of action they will pursue. Most people tend to gravitate toward tasks they are confident they can accomplish and avoid those which they feel they can not. Self-efficacy also determines how much effort a person will exhibit toward a goal and their level of persistence. The greater the level of self-efficacy, the greater the effort, perseverance, and determination exerted.

Those who are confident anticipate success. They are more likely to engage in difficult challenges which yield greater rewards. They maintain a greater interest in the tasks they pursue. Those with high self-efficacy recover quicker from failures and setbacks. The confidence helps them approach difficult tasks calmly as opposed to those who will not maintain this composure and feel things are more difficult than they really are.

It is important to increase your level of self-efficacy which can be done in a number of ways. First, welcome the emotional support of family, friends, partners, peers, etc, which will gain encouragement to improve your performance. Be aware of those who criticize or undermine you and try to stay clear of these people. Try to maintain a positive productive mood, and try to steer away from bad moods which may bring negative results. Seek the examples of others who are prominent in your field and who can aspire you especially in tough times. Don't be too wrapped up in the advice of others or become dependent on requiring their advice. This dilutes the significance of your own opinions and insight and lowers your confidence levels.

Keep in mind that studies have shown that a person's belief in their own ability to cope is a stronger predictor of success than possessing the knowledge and abilities necessary to get the task done. In other words, believing in yourself and your abilities is one of the greatest contributors toward finding success at a particular goal. Part of changing your ways of thinking for the better include building up your self-efficacy and believing that you are capable of whatever you aspire for.

*   *   *

Creative Visualization is a practice that uses the resources of the mind to make positive change in a person's reality by first engaging the subject in their mind. It is a practice maintained by high achieving individuals that can help achieve success and accomplish goals by mentally visualizing a scenario and the outcome in advance. The mind thinks in pictures, and your thoughts are actually pictures appearing on the screen of your mind. The act of visualizing is simply the process of playing images through your mind. The mind does not know the difference between something vividly imagined or something that really occurred. In other words, visualizing an action has the same effect on the brain as doing it or going through the experience. This is why visualization works as this activity is recognized by the brain in the same way as something that had taken place. The brain doesn't know the difference between visualization and the real thing, so we can use this to our own advantage. While visualizing, the brain sends neural signals in the same patterns to the muscles, thus training them for the particular activity.

Athletes have been using the practice of visualization as a way to improve performance for a long time. A study was conducted by Dr. Blaslotto at the University of Chicago in which three test groups practiced shooting free throws. One group physically practiced shooting free throws for an hour a day, the other group only visualized themselves shooting and making the free throws but did not physically participate, and the last group did nothing. After thirty days, all three groups were tested again. The first group who practiced the free throws physically improved by 24 percent. What was surprising was that the group who visualized themselves shooting free throws but did not physically practice actually improved by 23 percent! This example clearly proves the effectiveness of visualization.

In another study conducted by the Harvard Medical School, a group of adult volunteers were split into three groups and put in a room with a piano. None of the participants could previously play the piano. One group was provided intense piano lessons over five days. The second group was in the room with the piano but did not practice playing. The last group was told to imagine that they were practicing playing the piano and used creative visualization to do so. In conclusion, all three groups were tested. The second group's brain activity did not change as nothing was done. The first group who had taken lessons revealed structural changes in the area of the brain related to the finger movement of playing the piano. The third group, who used visualization, was discovered to have changes in the structure of the brain that were similar to those who actually played the piano. Again, this study showed that creative visualization had a real and physical effect inside the human brain.

What you can think of or imagine can be made a reality through the method of creative visualization. Therefore, you can adopt the practice of visualizing your actions before physically initiating any activity, to improve performance. It is essentially the process of seeing success before it takes place. When you visualize, the key to success is to envision as much detail as possible. Try to involve details of all the senses including touch, smell, taste, hearing, and vision. Also to be effective you must visualize everything in first person, from your own eyes and not as in third person like you would do if it were a movie. Let's say you are visualizing shooting free throws, you would look at the situation through your own eyes and notice where you are positioned on the court, feel the ball in your fingers, aim at a certain point of the basket, feel the release of your shot, see it going toward the basket, picture the net, and hear the swish noise that comes when you make a shot. Remember, the more detailed the better.

Every time you use the method of creative visualization and picture the same scenario over and over again, it's just like you already experienced this scenario a number of times. It is a mental rehearsal of the event. If you can imagine something in your head, you can make it a reality. Let's say you would like to use this method for a presentation you are giving to gain an account. Visualize all the details surrounding the event such as where you are, the people that are in the room, the time, what you are wearing, the visuals that you are using, how everything looks in the room from the desk to the walls, any noises that you may hear, how the paper copies in your hand feel, and every other detail that you can possibly imagine. Picture yourself giving the whole presentation, every word that you say, and how you say it, the reactions of the people you are presenting to, the usage of charts and diagrams, your movements; in short every little detail from the beginning of the presentation to the end of it. Picture the use of all your senses, including how you felt whether confident or nervous, the sound of every person's voice, the decor of the office, the taste of the mint that's in your mouth, and even the smell of the newly vacuumed carpet. It is imperative that you add as much detail to your visualization as possible. For better results, continue to repeat this scenario in your mind a number of times, over and over again. Do this until you know that you feel completely comfortable and well versed at giving the presentation, until your actions become automatic. To utilize visualization properly, you must believe that you can actually have whatever you are picturing. This comes from having total faith in yourself and your abilities. Try using this method in any task that you may have coming up and take note of your results. Visualization requires lots of practice to be effective but once you do, this process can benefit you in many ways. Give it some time and you will see the difference that it can make.

Performance

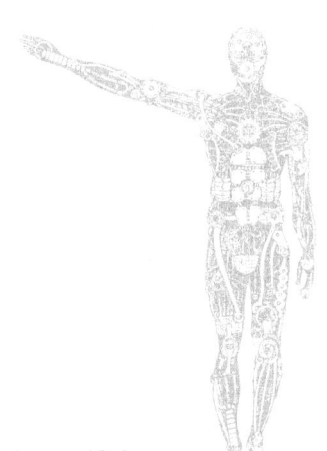

*Some people dream of great accomplishments,
while others stay awake and do them.*
—Author Unknown

When I was a child I enjoyed watching magicians perform magic tricks. On one occasion, I had the opportunity to travel to Las Vegas to attend one of the shows. I remember sitting around afterward and trying to come up with theories on how I thought they created the illusions. Then one day I saw a TV show which displayed magic tricks followed by a detailed explanation of the methods used for the illusions. I later went to a magic store and saw items and books for sale that I was able to learn from. After getting a "look behind the curtain," many of the tricks were no longer a mystery and I could sometimes even tell how some magicians performed tricks while watching their performances. However, I realized that as many people were exposed to these secrets, there were always many more who would still be enchanted by these illusions. Knowledge is not the only criteria required to perform these illusions. Although I may have acquired some of the techniques that may enable me to conduct a few of the tricks, I am far from a magician. Being able to display the skills from this knowledge is what is relevant.

In business, it is the same process, and even with the know-how to become a success, you must be able to translate this knowledge into action. Many magicians use the same techniques as their counterparts to create their illusions. The difference is the way each magician conducted their own distinct performance. The way that each one of them incorporated their own methods in their performance is what distinguished them from one another. Theatrics, flair, skill, timing, attention to detail, and other contributions from each performer enhanced the illusions, and those who became prominent gave that extra effort that made them unique.

The business world and the journey toward prominence in any field require the same type of translation of knowledge into action. The knowledge is much more common than the practice. Instead of slight of hand, business professionals must develop techniques of usage from the information that is acquired. The use of the methods in practice is what will determine the quality of your performance and what ultimately gives you a competitive edge. It is always easier being the spectator than the performer, the person gathering the information rather than the practitioner.

Performance is the stage of the Grind that places emphasis on the action part of the process. There are no magical set of rules in which you can pattern yourself for success. The key lies in how you will process and utilize the information that you acquire. The following paragraphs focus on suggestions which may help you in your working performance.

> *I have not failed. I've just found 10,000 ways that won't work.*
> —Thomas A. Edison

One of the best ways to proceed when facing adversity while performing your duties is the practice of exploring alternatives for a solution. A roadblock in progress does not necessarily have to result in the abandonment of an effort. Sometimes it requires intense contemplation and the use of your creativity to come up with the best possible solution for these types of situations. You should always focus on the possibilities that may exist and your ability to come up with alternatives may be the deciding factor of what makes you more successful than others.

Elvis Presley was known as a poor money manager and when he died in 1977, his estate of $4.9 million was quickly depleting. It was estimated that within several years all of the money would be gone. With the pressure of paying bills that were accumulating, the Elvis financial legacy seemed to be coming to a demise and the option of selling off assets and the estate seemed like the only option. Instead of succumbing to a negative outcome, Priscilla Presley, Elvis's widow, considered the alternatives which could be exercised and decided to push toward turning the company around. She took matters into her own hands, taking control of his finances and forming a company called Elvis Presley Enterprises, Inc. Over the next few years, she focused on developing the Elvis Presley brand, building up the worth of his estate. Priscilla chose to open up Graceland, Elvis's home, to the public and charge admission. She expanded the merchandising potential of the company and went after merchandisers who were using his likeness without paying the estate. She further recouped unpaid royalties from Presley's music catalog. As a result of her exploration of the alternatives of the situation instead of giving up to financial pressure, she was able to turn the Elvis legacy into a completely new business. About eleven years after the death of Elvis, Elvis Presley Enterprises was taking in $35 million in a year, making more than her husband did when he was alive!

Sometimes you simply have to try out a number of alternatives and options and hope something works out for the best. Especially if you hit a roadblock and cannot immediately come up with an option to remedy the situation. At the age of twenty-nine William Wrigley Jr. moved from Philadelphia to Chicago to start a business. He began to sell soap for a living, giving his customers a complimentary can of baking powder with each purchase. The baking powder ended up being a better sales item than the soap, so he eventually ended up switching up his business product. Just as he did before, he gave away two packs of chewing gum as an incentive to customers who bought the baking powder. Once again, the incentive product became more popular than the baking powder, so Wrigley ended up switching up the business product once again. This made way for the early couple types of chewing gum that he produced, which was Juicy Fruit and Wrigley's Spearmint. This time the product stuck but it was difficult to get a foothold on the chewing gum business with competition from several other companies. Several times his new company was on the verge of going under, but he continued to work hard selling the product personally in the early years of the company's existence. Wrigley was said to have a gift of seeing things from his customer's points of view and inspiring the enthusiasm of those who worked for him. He was also credited as one of the pioneers in the use of advertising branded merchandise through newspaper, magazine, outdoor poster, and others. Today Wrigley's is a household name synonymous with gum, with sales of over five billion dollars worldwide in 2008. Wrigley became the biggest gum manufacturer in the world by trying out new product alternatives until something eventually worked for him. His perseverance through the early days delivered him out of several possibilities of bankruptcy. Instead of giving up, he continued to switch up the products he was selling until he found success in the chewing gum industry.

You should never quit any pursuit, unless you first contemplate any alternatives that may exist to remedy the situation. Be comprehensive and think outside the box. Research and study other people's problem solving methods and solicit the advice of others who may have gone through the same experience. The only way to get the best results in any situation is to explore the possibilities that may exist. Contemplate whether the results that you have come up with can be improved upon. Part of the process of the Grind is not to only continue what your doing in the same ways, but finding new and better ways of obtaining successful results. In order to achieve higher standards, you must increase your skill in seeking out options.

Offering options and alternatives to those you are dealing with can also contribute toward progress. People naturally do not like to feel like they are getting boxed in or forced to make a decision based on limited options presented by the opposite party. Limitation leads to feelings of contempt and may cause resistance in entering into any transaction. Good business entails giving people options and enabling them to gain what they want out of any business transaction. It has been said that good business exists when both parties walk away happy and satisfied at the end of the day. With this occurrence there is a greater likelihood of additional future dealings amongst these parties. I have noticed that sometimes an opportunity for a deal or work related progress can be stifled because one member does not have clarity of the choices they have available. Looking through their eyes and having empathy for what the other person wants can be the missing link for progression. Sometimes as the negotiator you may get better results if you help others with the direction they may exercise. Conceiving new and alternate ideas for the opposite party may end up helping to finalize the deal. You must understand that the other party may not realize what your perspective of the particular situation may be and may not be considering possibilities which will help both parties. Establishing alternatives for both your own and others' situations may be the key to success. Make sure you are at all times considering the options that place you and your peers in the best possible position for advancement.

It takes the same energy to think small as it does to think big. So dream big and think bigger.
—Author Unknown

In your performance, make sure that you maintain high standards of output. There is so much competition in business these days and it takes more effort than ever to distinguish yourself from others. Focus on quality control in all of your efforts, and take the additional steps that are necessary to provide the very best, each and every time. There is no more room for mediocrity in today's business climate, and the current volatile economic state ensures that success is limited to those who raise the bar.

Krispy Kreme Donuts is a company that maintains some of the highest food standards in the food business. They are definitely proud of this and the company's retail outlets proudly display their donuts being made, out in the open where the customer can watch the process through a window. They are so obsessed with the consistency and quality of the product that each batch of wheat flour is sampled and tested in a lab first. When the trucks pull up to the loading dock, an employee climbs up and takes a four-foot-long core sample of each and every delivery. They test for moisture content, protein, and ash with an infrared tester. Furthermore, all of the raw ingredients such as shortening, flour and sugar are tested even before the batch is made. If the flour is not exact according to their standards, they send back the twenty-five-ton shipment. This happens with a frequency of twice a month. The donuts are made from 2,500-pound batches of mix and each is tested to make sure they are blended correctly. These batches are also rejected at the frequency of about one per month, despite the costs. They have found that the mix does not taste its best if used immediately, so they make sure that each is seasoned in its sack for about a week to exacting standards. This type of attention to quality has spread the popularity of their donuts all over the world. They test and sample the ingredients and batches frequently to ensure consistency and quality, in efforts to produce the best donuts possible each and every time. Today, Krispy Kreme has grown from a one-person donut making operation to the opening of over seven hundred retail locations globally with sales of just under $1 billion dollars in 2012.

Over the years, luxury retailer Nordstrom's has established a reputation as a company that maintains exceptionally high standards in customer service who will go through great lengths to please its customers. They are said to maintain a "no questions asked" return policy, which allows customers to return items without receipts, sometimes even years after they have been purchased. Nordstrom employees have been known for pushing the boundaries for better customer service, and there have been numerous instances and examples of these efforts over the years. One story that has become legend in Nordstrom's customer service history is the one about a man who had bought tires from an auto shop that occupied the same space prior to Nordstrom's moving in. It is said that the man came into a Nordstrom's in Alaska trying to return the set of tires even though the store doesn't even sell tires! To everyone's surprise, consistent with the company policy, the salesperson accepted them and the customer received a full refund. The validity of this story has come into question, but there have been many employees as well as a company spokesperson who have said that the incident actually happened. Whether or not true, this type of story is one that accurately illustrates the company's devotion to their customer's needs. Another famous story which was definitely factual was about one of the employees who had noticed a woman was on her hands and knees searching for something. When he was told that she was looking for a diamond ring that she had lost while trying on some clothes, he recruited several other employees to help her look as well as getting down on the floor to help search for it himself. They eventually found the diamond, going as far as searching through the dirt and debris inside one of the store's vacuum cleaners. Another story that I read was a story about another Nordstrom's staff member who had discovered a customer's shopping bag in the parking lot, along with a receipt and flight itinerary showing the customer was due for a flight later that day. The employee looked up her phone number on the ticket and tried to call but because there was no answer, he drove to the airport with the bags. He then had the airport page her to let her know where he was in the airport to pick up her items. There are countless other stories that reaffirm Nordstrom's unyielding commitment to serve their customer's needs. Employees also conduct simple tasks like sending thank you letters and calling their customers when sought after items arrive in the stores. The store provides pen and paper at all of their registers, so that customers can share more stories of their exceptional experiences while shopping. Every morning before each store opens, Nordstrom employees are gathered in the main lobby for the store manager to share some of the best stories and provide rewards to those who have made the efforts. Although they face competition from many other luxury fashion retailers, research have shown that Nordstrom's has realized stronger sales per square foot than their competitors as well as receiving the most word of mouth promotions as a retailer and is considered the "best in its class."

Businesses that maintain high standards gain an advantage over their rivals. As competition builds in various fields of business, standards are raised and there is a certain level of quality that customers soon become accustomed to expect. Make sure that whatever business sector you are involved with, you have a good understanding of what your customers expect from you. Provide the standards that exceed the expectations of your customers, and you will be in a good operating position. Initiate some form of quality control system in place, which maintains the quality of your work or product. Just as in the examples of Nordstrom's and Krispy Kreme, notice the extra efforts they are willing to take to ensure high standards in quality and service. By implementing measures that may seem excessive that none of your competitors are willing to practice, your customers will appreciate your efforts as attempts to provide them with the very best. By doing this you will establish a reputation as a professional who can be trusted to perform good work and one who values the standards that you provide your customers and employers.

> *In the end, you're measured not by how much you undertake but by what you finally accomplish.*
> —Donald Trump

In your performance, try not only to work harder, but also try to work smarter. Working smarter can intensify the results of your hard work. It is very important to always be alert to new ideas and opportunities to do so. Forced and misdirected efforts do nothing but diminish efficiency and waste needed energy. What good is working hard if no results come from these misdirected efforts? What good is a circumstance where the amount of work does not translate into comparable results? Working hard without working smart is similar to the example of machine gun fire as opposed to the single shot from a sniper's rifle. With the machine gun, many rounds are fired to better the chances that at least one bullet will meet its target. A sniper's shot is conducted with meticulous aim and focus to waste no other resources to hit its target. Similarly, strive to work with a purpose aimed at directly accomplishing your goals with no wasted energy. To do so involves thorough consideration of the alternatives to best accomplish you goal. You must have a broad view of your goal and locate the most effective method in which to proceed. Your action plan should narrow down all alternatives and conclude the most efficient course of action. Careful planning will eliminate overextending your efforts.

One great example of working smarter is a trend being practiced by many A-list movie actors. They have figured out how to increase their earnings exerting the same amount of effort as before, by negotiating better terms. Jack Nicholson touched on an ingenious new revenue stream when he accepted the role of the Joker in the movie *Batman*. He accepted a salary of $6 million instead of his then-average quote of $10 million, and in return negotiated earnings of a percentage of the film's total earnings. By doing this he would sacrifice $4 million he would normally make in advance, but instead this entitled him to the back-end profits, which could earn him an amount which was much greater than any amount he could earn from his quote. He was also able to strike another major negotiation point which was to secure a percentage of the film merchandise sales also. The movie became a major success and the movie ended up grossing $411 million worldwide, and Nicholson ended up earning more than $50 million for the role. This increased his average-earning per film by $40 million! Tom Hanks also capitalized on this trend and agreed to star in *Forrest Gump* for a portion of the box office earnings. The movie ended up earning $680 million worldwide, earning Hanks over $60 million dollars for his work on the film. Taking it one step further, some actors have also signed on to movies as both an actor and producer, opening up their salary to further income. Tom Cruise signed on to *Mission: Impossible 2* as the star and producer, negotiating a salary that included 30 percent of the film's gross earnings. Cruise walked away with a staggering $75 million for his role as actor and producer.

David Gold of the 99 Cent Store, was able to come up with a smart promotional ploy which didn't require him to put forth much effort, and also encouraged others to do the promotional work for him. During the stores early days, he would go out and buy about thirteen black and white TVs for $150 a piece and offer them at 99 cents in the store on a first come, first served basis. He would then flood neighborhoods with flyers mentioning that his 99 Cent Store was offering televisions for only 99 cents! This created a gathering of crowds lined up around the block of the store. Then, Gold and his family would take turns calling local television stations asking what the frenzy was about. This scheme attracted film crews from various local stations which would run the story on the evening news. The TV coverage further led to newspapers covering the event the next day. As a result, Gold was able to have his customers, TV stations, and newspapers conduct the promotional duties on his behalf and at no expense of his own! This was definitely a smart way to get the most results he could with a small amount of his own efforts.

The Mongols were able to gain the upper hand against their enemies by using cunning tactics to outsmart their enemies in war. They would use a number of strategies to make the sizes of their armies seem greater than they really were. In the daytime, they would make life-sized puppets they would position on their reserve horses, appearing as if they had additional warriors with them. When seen from a distance these looked realistic and the enemy could not distinguish them from the real soldiers. They would also make the prisoners they had captured march in battle order to make them seem like they were part of their army. When it was dark they would have each soldier light three or more torches, at some distance from the other, so it appeared as if each of them was holding their own torch. In the darkness this made it appear as if each torch represented one warrior, also making their numbers seem greater. They would spread rumors, by sending spies traveling separately from them to say that they were twice as numerous as they really were before advancing on the cities they were about to invade. This strategy enabled them to outsmart their enemies by intimidating them into surrendering without even taking additional action. Their reputation preceded them and struck fear into the areas they were going to pillage. They used their reputation as bloodthirsty pillagers who spared no one to pacify their enemies and induce easy defeat.

Always consider ways to work smarter, instead of expending any unnecessary energy that can be saved for other required tasks. Any ways to save your resources should be considered, so that we do not overextend ourselves with unnecessary work. Working smarter should translate to working less with greater results. Some feel that just because they are exerting immense amounts of efforts toward their goals, they will eventually realize success from their work. They feel that this is always a way to get better results. The truth is if not directed toward the right areas, the work may be done in vein. There is the possibility that you may even end up with the same results as someone who put forth half the effort you did. In your performance, identify what it is you want accomplished followed by the smartest way it will take to meet this challenge. When you approach any task, do so by looking for ways to work smarter for better results and not necessarily always harder.

* * *

You can greatly improve your business performance by taking every opportunity to cater to the needs of your customers or the people that you are conducting business with. Doing so will strengthen professional relationships and can open up a number of additional opportunities. People tend to conduct repeat business with those they are comfortable doing business with. Certain practices that can be improved upon such as showing up on time, being easily reached or easy to communicate with, quick to act on your responsibilities, sympathetic to their specific needs, or any other way of making yourself easier to deal with; should be focused upon. Simply listening to their needs can make such a difference in the progress of any situation. Take the time to understand who you are doing business with. Do your research of their business history for points which may be relevant in your dealings with them. Remember, that the people that you deal with on a daily basis are the same ones who will be responsible for establishing your business reputation, as well as referring you to others.

In the music business, superstar recording artists will usually gravitate toward the most prominent record companies who have maintained a proven track record for success. When John Lennon of the Beatles came back from retirement after a five-year hiatus, he decided to sign with David Geffen's Geffen Records to release the project. Many major record labels jumped at the chance to include this project on their roster's, but Lennon decided to give Geffen the chance because he was the only one with enough confidence in him to agree to a deal without first hearing the album. Another contributing factor was that Geffen was the only label head who would pay attention to the views of Lennon's wife and partner, Yoko Ono. The album, *Double Fantasy*, ended up selling triple platinum and won a Grammy Award for the album of the year. A short time after, Lennon was fatally shot and as it usually is when an artist dies, the project became a massive seller. This was one of Geffen's greatest attributes as a label head, as he was able to maintain great relationships with the talent, and would strive to understand the creative side of the business, and not just the business itself. When you keep the needs of your customers or people you are dealing with in mind, they will help you to succeed. This form of synergy helps bring out the best results for both parties involved.

Too many people neglect the process of taking the steps to make it easier for the customer to conduct business with them. Customers are more likely to do business with those who are going to make the transaction as convenient as possible for them. They want to be in a situation that caters to their needs whether this involves finances, convenience, comfort, speed, support, etc. In the above example, Geffen was able to add Lennon to his roster because he took the time to find out what factors were important to Lennon, which other companies were not in tune to. He was able to provide a business transaction that truly catered to Lennon's needs, which considered his wife's input and showed him the trust of agreeing to the album without first hearing it. Nowadays, it seems to have been forgotten that "the customer is always right," and that catering to them is a key aspect of business. Make sure you take the time to keep current with technology and all other new practices in your field that add convenience to your business transactions. It is also vital that you show your customer and employer the respect of taking the time to cater to them by finding out what they want out of each situation. Improve your performance by always keeping the needs of the people you are working with and for in mind and strive to be an entity that is easy to work with.

> *A person who never made a mistake
> never tried anything new.*
> —Albert Einstein

While performing your duties, look for ways that you can be innovative by implementing new creative ideas in your pursuit for success. Doing so, separates you from your competitors, and makes your efforts stand out amongst the crowd of conformers. While others in their same field are trying to compete in the same ways, innovators look for alternatives to find success in an entirely new approach. Over time, many fields have become stagnant in the way that their business is conducted which becomes uniform or done with a "cookie cutter" approach. Therefore, there are no new developments or breakthroughs that are made and all parties begin to follow the same formula for success. People who seek to perform at a higher level, bring a different approach to the way they do business and pioneer new ways in which business is conducted. This not only rejuvenates this particular field of business but creates a new experience for the customers to enjoy.

People often forget the "professional" in professional sports, and just like any other company, a professional sports teams may also benefit from an owner with the business savvy to make them a success. The Los Angeles Lakers had this with owner Jerry Buss, who turned the franchise into one of the most exciting teams in basketball history. He was an innovator who combined show business dazzle with basketball magic enlisting the talent of players like Magic Johnson, Kareem Abdul-Jabbar, Kobe Bryant, Shaquille O'Neal and Dwight Howard. Celebrities showed up for games encouraged by his "Showtime" management style including Hollywood regulars Denzel Washington, Dyan Cannon, Leonardo DiCaprio, Penny Marshall, and Jack Nicholson. Before Buss, most people weren't that excited to go to the games and would just watch them at home, but he changed the format to include entertainment all the way through the game. He was the first to innovate the ideas of adding cheerleaders (the world-famous Laker Girls), added attractions and fanfare during the breaks of the game, and a band to play live music. He transformed the Forum, where the Lakers played, into the place to be seen which attracted the Hollywood celebrity crowd. More fans began to come out with the added attraction of seeing their favorite stars as well as their favorite team play. Before Buss, courtside seats were reserved for the press and media, but thanks to his innovations, they became a high ticket valuable attraction and a profit generator for the team. He also created the Forum Club, a VIP attraction for celebrities and LA's elite to engage socially and have drinks before the games. In all, he was able to turn the Lakers into a true Los Angeles home team which fit perfectly into the Hollywood identity lifestyle.

* * *

When you perform your duties, stay alert for ways that you can cut costs and conserve your resources. One of the ways to increase your earnings is to not only earn more, but to proceed by spending less. There may be situations that may arise when you must compromise due to lack of some form of resources. In these cases the option is to be creative and generate ideas which will gain effective results while not depleting too much of your resources. Many times for a new startup, the problem that is often encountered is a lack of capital. Again, you must consider the alternatives that are available and determine what options you have to proceed.

During the early days of building FUBU into a success, the company would use creative low cost options for promotions. One of these ideas was because the company could not yet afford billboards, so they would pay retail stores in key promotional areas to spray paint "FUBU" on the roll-down security doors. In many ways this may have been more effective than a traditional billboard as it stood out amongst the clutter of the other advertisements. What a great economic alternative to expand the presence of the company while not expending a lot of financial resources! The Magic Convention is an apparel convention held in Las Vegas twice a year. This is where all members of the apparel business including retail, wholesale, sourcing, marketing, publicity, etc. attend to do business. A booth at the event comes with a pretty high price tag, and as FUBU was not yet in the financial position to afford this, they instead rented a hotel room as their showroom. Founder, Daymond John, and his team bought back buyers to their room to show them their clothing line, and were able to come home with $300,000 worth of orders. Not long afterward, they acquired a contract with department store chain Macy's, and a distribution deal with Samsung which allowed their clothing line to be manufactured and delivered on a massive scale. FUBU has gone on to achieve much success, selling over $6 billion dollars in products worldwide.

There are so many ways to save money if you just take the time to be creative and think of ideas to make the same impact by spending less money. You can gain ideas by following the examples of company's and entrepreneurs who have used money saving strategies to better their situation in the past, like the example detailed above. Remember that every dollar saved can be a resource to potentially help open up further opportunities. Strategies such as buying in bulk instead of increments, obtaining purchase orders before manufacturing, involving yourself in cooperatives for advertising and promotions to share costs with others, drop shipping instead of stocking merchandise, and many other's should be explored as options. If you're in a situation where you are an employee and do not take responsibility for the finances, you still have to remember that your choices will show how you can handle a promotion or a position where you may have to maintain this responsibility. Also, if you aspire to one day own your own business, you can observe strategies which are being used in your current situation by those who are responsible for the finances. Remember every dollar counts! Always stay alert for ways to save resources, cut costs, and spend less; and keep in mind that this process of conserving is extremely vital in determining the outcome for success in all areas of your profession.

> *We have two ears and one mouth so that we can listen twice as much as we speak.*
>
> —Epictetus

The Grind

In your performance, be receptive to the helpful advice that others may give to you that will improve your situation. There is significance in the input others give us that we cannot always provide ourselves. Constructive criticism and opinions give us insight from a different perspective, a view that we may never discover on our own accord. Our views often become pigeon holed as they are often confined to only our own experiences in life, and the knowledge that we have accumulated in our years. As a result, our work often comes from one perspective, and therefore doesn't have the potential to represent a diverse perspective.

Stephen King is one of the most famous and accomplished horror and suspense authors of our time. A number of his books have been adapted to become successful movies, including *It*, *Needful Things*, *Cujo*, *Misery*, and others. King has published over fifty-five books which have sold more than 350 million copies. His first published novel was *Carrie*, about a shy high school girl who uses her newly discovered telekinetic powers to seek revenge on those who have teased her. The main character was influenced by a couple girls King went to school with and based the story on the reversal of the Cinderella fairy tale. This was actually the fourth novel King had written but none had been published at the time. At the time of writing this book, he was still using his wife's portable typewriter. He began writing this short story which was originally intended to be featured in a magazine, but didn't like how it was shaping up and ended up tossing the pages he wrote in the garbage. The two were living in a trailer at the time, and his wife saw the work and retrieved the pages out of the garbage. She encouraged him to finish the story, so he continued and expanded it into a novel. He persisted and finished even though he didn't like the book at the time. Carrie went on to become a major achievement for Stephen King. His paperback rights alone earned him $400,000 at a later date. The book was adapted into a feature film, a Broadway musical, feature film sequel, a television movie, and a new theatrical adaptation of the book is said to be in the works. Imagine if his wife had left it in the trash!

Every 99 Cent Store location opens their stores fifteen minutes before operating hours and keep their doors open an additional fifteen minutes after they close. They never want to lose out on sales because a customer may show up a few minutes late or earlier, which happens regularly. Founder David Gold does not allow any signs to be put up which may have a negative connotation, such as "No shoes, No service," which will turn away any potential customer. They are always mindful of consumer wishes such as placement of stores in middle-class neighborhoods, in contrast to their competitors who will place stores in lower pay grade areas. They do this with the understanding that lower income customers will travel to nicer areas, whereas middle class or affluent customers won't generally travel to neighborhoods they consider poor areas. Another interesting story is that Gold has been known to give out vouchers for one free item at his 99 Cent Store when leaving a tip for waiters and busboys after dining out instead of the traditional currency. He has figured that when they use the coupon, they will most likely end up spending additional money picking up other items since they have already made the trip to the store. What a great way to turn the tables from a situation of spending money, into a potential situation to earn.

While you are performing your every day duties, try to welcome any ideas to improve your business practices. It's often the small things that make the biggest differences in success. Ideas can come from a number of sources such as coworkers, customers, or any other source that will help you improve your business practices. These ideas can include any strategies, no matter how small; which may bring in even the slightest additional profit, make the customer experience more pleasant, improve a service or product, differentiate your business from others, give you a competitive edge, or any other improvement that can be realized. Ideas for improvement usually present themselves while you are working, as their need becomes evident. Always stay alert for these potential improvements, and embrace them to add to your business practices.

> *A professional is one who does his best
> work when he feels the least like working.*
> —Frank Lloyd Wright

To compete in today's business world, you have to proceed with constant progression. Your performance should always include measures that will keep you ahead of your competition. If you stand idle, the world will pass you by and today's successes will quickly be tomorrow's forgotten past. Remaining active includes seemingly passive actions such as planning and research, which do not seem like they involve any momentum. Staying active includes practicing restraint and preparation, not just actions toward growth measures. Considering our options is vital. You have to constantly keep current with the trends and practices of the day and make sure that your decision making is not outdated. Efforts must be taken to stay one step ahead in your respective profession.

Home Shopping Network was the first TV channel devoted to solely presenting merchandise to television viewers for purchase. Joseph Segel noticed the potential of TV shopping after watching HSN and felt he could outdo them by adding a few improvements they were lacking. He started by thoroughly describing each product in great detail when being presented, instead of HSN's quicker "order now" style. He gained credibility by making deals with established businesses such as Sears to offer their products. All items prominently displayed shipping costs which was not always the case with HSN's products. QVC also delivers each order in about four days as opposed to a few weeks. They concentrated on customer satisfaction, making all efforts to make sales a satisfactory experience. These factors were enough to place QVC ahead of the Home Shopping Network as a viable alternative choice for consumers. QVC now generates nearly $9 billion in annual revenues and is available in 300 million homes worldwide.

On my trip to Thailand, I was often burdened with the presence of mosquitoes. There are so many rivers, lakes, and basins which act as the perfect breeding ground for these pests. They constantly make their way into your room at night and will keep you up all night biting and pestering you. One of the things I noticed is that when they bite you and have their fill, they begin to fly slower and often take what seemed to be long breaks sitting on a wall or the floor. They will let their other counterparts take over as they seem to be content. When they achieve their desired outcome, this is when they are most vulnerable for people who would like to swat them and act on their demise.

This happens all the time in business to companies and individuals who have achieved some form of success. Sometimes we justify these accomplishments in our mind as a substitute for the completion of the ultimate goal. This takes away our drive and intensity we had for our overall goals and slows us down. It can also be a reason for missed opportunity. The rewards make us comfortable and usually more complacent. Instead of encouragement to continue in the right direction, these rewards can act to pacify us. When we experience growth, more action should be taken to prepare for the additional responsibility we may not have expected. Usually the bigger you are the slower that you will move. Companies and Individuals that last in business realize that there are always the emergence of competitors and new challenges in business. With growth comes more ground to cover, and there is a greater need for attention to detail. In the Bible it says that, "What more a person is given, more is expected." Even if you enjoy a comfortable position, just realize there may be many others out there who desire to be where you currently are. Staying active helps ensure that you are one step ahead of any would be competitors. Always seek to do what your competitors do better than they can. Success in one instance is not a reason to decrease your intensity. If anything further success may just be that more difficult to obtain the next time around.

* * *

When at work, attend to all the tasks you despise the most first. All the duties you define as your weaknesses or the ones which you dread to address. Get these out of the way first, before you attend to your other responsibilities. The tasks which you enjoy doing or find easy to accomplish should be scheduled for the later parts of the day. In the beginning of the workday is when you have the most energy and retain the most focus. A whole day of effort has not yet worn you down or taken away from your full potential. You are in a better position to tend to difficult situations and the help you may need from others is still a fresh prospect in the earlier parts of their day. Everyone winds down at the end of the day but you will most likely still maintain the ability to tackle the easier parts of your workload then. These don't require your full potential and by following this schedule you will be more efficient in dealing with a broader range of tasks.

If you have a great number of various responsibilities in a day, I recommend the following strategy. Separate your tasks into three main categories of difficultness. You will have a "difficult or things you hate to do" category, a middle level or moderate category, and a category for ones in which you find easy or enjoyable. Start with the middle category first. The moderate level of ease will enable you to start off with a greater chance at success and build momentum in preparing for the difficult tasks. This way you are less likely to hit road blocks at the beginning of your day from the difficult or hated tasks. You will not be discouraged and unmotivated to accommodate other challenges in your day.

For those days where there are only arduous tasks planned for the entire duration of the workday, utilize your breaks or lunches in the latter parts of the day. These will provide a retreat and chance to refresh yourself to continue to deal with these tasks. It would be the ideal situation to split your breaks into many smaller ones if you have the liberty to do so, as this will give you more opportunities to rejuvenate.

* * *

Enforce measures in your performance to make the execution of your work easier. In other words help make it easier for yourself to work harder, by making all employment conditions ideal for productivity. In this book I mention a strategy to help encourage the involvement of another person or party you would like to work with. You may accomplish this by making their involvement as easy as possible. In some cases performing some of their duties for them to promote the initiation of their contributions.

The same can be considered for yourself, and you can encourage yourself to work hard by making your responsibilities more ideal for productivity. You should make a list of these possibilities. For me, as a writer, I never know when I will get some inspiration or an idea. Some of my best ideas come to me, not at a time I have dedicated to work, but instead when I least expect. I even come up with ideas when I'm in the shower. One idea or phrase can be a potential strongpoint in the book which can make all the difference. Every word counts and ideas can really come at any part of the day or night. Sometimes, even the inconvenience of finding a pen or trying to remember everything can make you lose an idea. Therefore, I carry a small notebook and pen with me everywhere that I go. This promotes me to be as productive as possible. I am always ready and in a position to contribute to my craft. Some of my friends in the music business carry a mobile recording studio with them when they are on tour. This way they can work on new material for their next album while touring and promoting their current release. The feedback from the fans they are performing for every night can be great motivation, and this can be captured by recording at their convenience in the mobile studio. It would be very difficult to book studio time and record while they are on the road, and this can cause them to lose material that they may have been inspired to create at the current time.

If you feel yourself becoming fatigued earlier in the workday, you can explore options such as implementing a workout schedule, buying healthier foods, sleeping more hours, taking vitamins and supplements, or any other way that may give yourself more energy to keep you at your full potential. If you are a business owner, executive, or any professional with numerous responsibilities, you can make the investment of hiring a personal assistant to help you with time consuming duties. This gives you more time to dedicate to work and allows you to work on responsibilities which require more of your personal involvement.

Any idea which will enable you to better perform your duties should be adopted. You can use these methods of making it easier to work harder, in any field you are involved with. Whatever it is that can inspire you, motivate, or make it more convenient to attend to your duties, should be practiced. It is surprising how even small conditions can affect our work, and we have to be aware of all the factors which have the potential to improve our performance when we are tending to our workload. It doesn't matter what the idea is as long as it enables you to work harder without any negative effects. You can get as creative as you would like and remember that there are endless possibilities.

If you're interested in balancing work and pleasure, stop trying to balance them. Instead make your work more pleasurable.

—Donald Trump

Try to bring out the fun and enjoyment in your work day. If you choose a career which you have a passion for, it should not be difficult to find the lighter sides of your work. Take your work serious but don't take yourself too seriously. Being in a good mood can limit your stress levels and lift the spirits of the people who work around you. Life is just too short to not enjoy the activities of everyday life. It makes you more approachable. Those around you will contribute ideas more liberally if they feel they are not under intense scrutiny. It also allows them to be themselves and confident to bring about ideas they may otherwise be apprehensive to show to others. There is a time for everything and you should always accommodate every situation with the requirements needed for that particular instance. Actively search out for ways to make your work more enjoyable. If you are in the position, you can set up activities at work that may help the performance in the office. You can organize contests with prizes for those who perform the best. You can dedicate some time, during breaks or lunchtime, to get to know your coworkers and enjoy the company of those you work with. Many companies set up corporate functions such as dinners and retreats to bring the workforce together.

Another area that you can make more enjoyable may be the environment and surroundings that you choose to function in. Sometimes the way that an office is set up can make a difference. If you spend countless hours in an environment, you might as well make it as pleasant and accommodating as possible. Whether it is a fish tank, office furniture, pictures, decor, or view that will enhance your workspace; maintain your work environment to your own standards if you have that liberty. Whatever factors may bring enjoyment into your work should be addressed and explored.

The Nike World Campus in Beaverton, Oregon, keeps consistent with the company's involvement in the fitness and sports world. The buildings in the company's headquarters are named after sports legends like Michael Jordan, Dan Fouts, Bo Jackson, and John McEnroe. Included on the property is a fitness center where the employees can work out. There is the presence of sporting images displayed throughout the location. The company endorses and hosts bike races and sporting events, and the families of the employees can partake in some of the many activities. The company even pays its employees to ride a bike or in line skate to work to promote fitness. There is no smoking on the grounds as can be expected as it is an opposition to the maintenance of healthy living. You can witness pregame shoot-arounds by professional teams and famous athletes can be found on the grounds on a regular basis. Employees have been known to remain at work until late hours such as eight PM and they have the outlets to get haircuts, messages, fitness evaluations, shopping, and restaurants. The company realizes the importance of making their environment one that is enjoyable to their employees. They feature outlets which promote fun, but also keep in line with the company's philosophies. The environment enhances the performance of the employees and promotes a culture of fitness.

Zappos is a company known for the value that it places on maintaining its corporate culture of a fun and enjoyable work environment. The company's leader and CEO, Tony Hsieh, makes it a company mission to provide an enjoyable work environment for his employees. His aim is evident as he has stated, "There are companies that focus on work-life separation or work-life balance and at Zappos we really focus on work-life integration and at the end of the day it's just life…and especially if you spend so much time at work you better enjoy the time that you're spending there and people that you're with."

The company's headquarters strives to promote friendliness amongst their employees and everyone is required to wear his or her nametags. The building actually has multiple doors where employees may exit but they have been intentionally locked so that everyone has to go through the front entrance reception area which has become a central hub for everyone to pass through with the intention to build community and culture. They also have their names hanging above their desks, in hopes that knowing everyone's name makes the place more sociable. Each of the company's departments has its own decor ranging from a log cabin themed decor to a rainforest themed decor, and even CEO Hsieh's desk is in the middle of a cluster of cubicles and features jungle vines and inflatable monkeys. Employees enjoy amenities such as free lunches and no-charge vending machines to get employees together to interact with each other and socialize.

Pretty much anything that any employee has a passion for is highly encouraged so that the passion is shared with other employees. They encourage a lot of interaction outside of the office, having employees organize golf tournaments, hiking trips or happy hours, and it is even a company requirement for managers to spend 10 to 20 percent of their working hours "goofing off" with employees outside of the office. Employees can be seen holding an office parade or doing the "wave" like crowds do at sports games. The company even provides a nap room for those who need to energize.

To maintain the hiring of only like-minded employees to uphold the culture, Hsieh says that no matter how talented an applicant is, if they don't fit the culture, then they won't hire them. They must fit into the company values and be talented; otherwise, they won't get a job at Zappos. In short, it is serious business for Zappos to provide a fun working environment for their employees, and this has also been a major factor contributing to the success of this company.

There are always areas in your profession which you can exploit which bring out the fun and synergy in what you do. Always intently seek for these areas so that you can bring added enjoyment to your profession. Doing so will bring more fun to your job as well as make the efforts of hard work during your performance more manageable.

* * *

Sometimes it can be a great benefit to challenge yourself by putting yourself in positions which will force you to perform. Some people actually work better under pressure. When you place yourself into a situation where you will be affected personally by the outcome, you are forced to do your best work. This is so because you personally have something to lose if you do not perform well.

When actor Shia LaBeouf was preparing for his role in the sequel to the classic movie *Wall Street*, he chose to put himself in a position to quickly learn the subject by investing twenty thousand dollars of his own money. By going through the actual process of investment, he was able to gain insight into his role from the position of a real investor. With help from finance royalty such as Donald Trump, Jim Chanos, and George Soros, he surrounded himself with those who possessed the knowledge to contribute to his upcoming role. What was interesting was that LaBeouf was eventually able to turn this initial investment amount of fifteen thousand dollars into about three hundred thousand dollars in two and a half months. Twenty thousand dollars is not an amount that would break an actor of his earning potential, but the gain he was able to realize was enough to acknowledge this investment as significant. His direct involvement and potential for loss forced LaBeouf to learn quickly and educate himself of the subject first hand.

Most of the time, the lack of accountability has it's negative affects on performance. For example, some managers never gain insight to what their staff may have to go through when dealing with customers. It can be a situation on the phone when the employee must deal with the customer directly and bear the burden of hearing complaints or other dissatisfaction. Because the manager does not have to deal with the consequences directly, he/she never gets the full perspective of the situation and the priority to correct mistakes can be distorted. Sometimes, in business, we sometimes get so far removed that we never fully realize what we stand to lose when we fail at even the slightest task. Putting yourself in the position to deal with the consequences or losses may raise your awareness and increase your levels of performance as you now have something to lose. When you "put your money where your mouth is," you are really putting yourself in the position of necessity to perform.

* * *

When you are in a situation where you are attempting to find success in a field of business that is highly saturated and has many competitors, look for ways you can differentiate yourself. This involves notifying and making your customers aware about the current differences that are present between your business and your competitors. Highlight these variations and determine whether you can make use of these to add to your appeal and make you stand out amongst your competitors. If there are no significant differences, then you should take the steps to add some new features such as improving quality, changing price points, or differentiating your business in some way to establish a new marketing position. Look for any ways that you can modify your products, services, goods, etc. or add features that can give you a competitive edge and make you stand out.

In the middle eighties, the denim market was regarded as "casual" wear, worn by the working class usually on the weekends. When Renzo Rosso attempted to break his brand Diesel into the US market, he set out to reinvent the market, transforming jeans into a luxury item that could be worn during any occasion, even formal events. He was the first to introduce the premium denim concept, offering a product with special washes and vintage treatments, manufactured wear and tear, and high quality fabrics, at a higher price point. Diesel didn't just set out to sell a new product, they chose to sell a whole new lifestyle, "for successful living," as Rosso would say. Rosso felt that there was a style conscious, consumer base of the Wall Street boom era that would pay a premium for jeans that were brand new but looked vintage, manufactured with wear and tear. This was during 1986, when the most expensive pair of jeans in the US was made by Ralph Lauren for $52. Diesel's cheapest pair of jeans was being offered at $100, first sold in the LA boutique Fred Segal. The price point was justified by the quality of Rosso's fabrics, which was attributed to the location of Diesel's factory. The factory was located near rivers that contained water ideal for denim production, since textiles absorb conditions from the ground like food. Soon, stores in Boston, Seattle, and New York were stocking the brand, partly attributed to the guarantee that Russo made, he'd buy them back or pay for the retail square footage wasted if the clothes didn't sell. Diesel did sell, with sales of $2.8 million in 1985, $10.8 million in 1986, and $25.2 million in 1987.

Renzo Rosso's first business venture began when he was given a rabbit by a schoolmate. He realized the rabbit was pregnant and as a result he began a breeding business for some extra pocket money. At age fifteen, he used his mother's sewing machine to make his first pair of jeans. He found that he could make a couple dollars sewing jeans for his friends, and this was the inception of his career in the fashion industry. At twenty-three, he cofounded Diesel with his mentor, Adriano Goldschmied, and later bought the company outright in 1985 becoming the company's sole owner.

Recently, Rosso has been conducting business through a holding company called Only the Brave or OTB. He has been spending the last decade buying up majority stakes in small prestigious fashion companies across Europe such as Martin Margiela, Viktor & Rolf, Marni and DSquared2. He also bought out high end manufacturer, Staff International, which has allowed the company in house design, production and distribution as well as manufacturing and distribution for a list of companies such as Marc Jacobs Men, Just Cavalli, and DSquared2. In 2012 OTB reported revenues of $2 billion. Diesel, of which Rosso owns 100 percent of, is worth over $3 billion. The brand maintains presence in over eighty countries, employs about 1,300 people, and maintains about 10,000 points of sale, about fifty which are company owned.

The clothing business is a field of business that maintains a great deal of competition. Diesel's success can be directly attributed to their ability to reinvent the denim market. They were successful at transforming the image of denim from "casual" wear, into a luxury item that can be worn during any occasion. In your performance, when attempting to reinvent your own business, use the same strategies that have worked for Diesel and other companies who have been successful at differentiating themselves from their competitors. Implement any features or modifications that can make you stand out and give you a competitive edge.

* * *

The reasons for success can be derived from all types of contributing factors. In some cases, a cause is attached to the business, helping to contribute to its success.

Consumers support these businesses because they believe in the cause that the company stands for. They feel that by supporting these businesses they are somehow attaching themselves to the cause, becoming proponents of the effort. This is a great way to add more fulfillment to the work that you do, while also helping your business in a positive way. This situation also allows you to be working for two goals simultaneously making success that much more gratifying, which can only make you want to work harder. In your performance, determine whether you can further a cause you believe in while you are pursuing your professional aspirations. By doing so, you are also welcoming the support of others who believe in the same causes while increasing the success of your business.

When you think of the traditional business for a cause, the Body Shop is as good an example as any. Anita Roddick decided to open the Body Shop, to support her two daughters while her husband was away fulfilling a long-standing personal goal she was in full support of; to ride a horse from Buenos Aires, Argentina, to New York. The small shop provided cosmetics made from natural ingredients she picked up on her visitation to the areas she calls "the hippie trail" which was her travels through Europe, the South Pacific and Africa. During her journeys she learned the rituals and customs of many Third World cultures, including their forms of health and body care which she brought to her shops. The first shop opened in Brighton and carried just fifteen products in refillable containers which were packaged in five sizes to make it look like the store had a lot more selection of products to choose from.

Besides the great success that The Body Shop went on to become, Roddick's true achievements came by way of her social activism and creating a cosmetics company retailing products that shaped ethical consumerism. Since products were sourced from ancient hill tribes and third world cultures that had used all natural ingredients on their skin for centuries, they were able to become one of the first to prohibit testing on animals. They offered only biodegradable products and provided refillable containers, not only for concerns of waste but to keep costs low. The company fought for environmental protection such as saving the rainforest, corporate responsibility, community activism, and fair trade with third world countries. They supported causes such as Greenpeace and Amnesty International, which set the company apart from its competitors and generated a loyal customer base. Consumers believed in the company's positive action and felt good about supporting and buying Body Shop products, as they felt that they were also contributing to the causes by doing so.

Roddick added her own creative efforts to stimulate business like leaving a trail of her strawberry essence fragrance on the street in hopes of luring customers with the smell. She used her natural talent to garner free publicity for the store. Next door to her shop, there were morticians who ran a funeral parlor who were complaining that her store's name was hurting their business. So she leaked a story to the press saying the morticians were picking on a woman shopkeeper who was just trying to get by. This publicity stunt worked as people who read the article began to visit the store to see what the commotion was about. The combination of well defined values and unique products generated a buzz and within a year, Roddick was able to open a second location. When her husband returned home, The Body Shop had become so popular that they began selling franchises. By the fall of 1982, there were Body Shop stores opening at the rate of two per month. The Body Shop went on to expand to more than two thousand stores worldwide, and was bought by competitor L'Oreal for $1.5 billion. Next time you doubt the change one company can make, just repeat one of Roddick's favorite quotes: "If you think you're too small to have an impact, try going to bed with a mosquito."

To this day, The Body Shop Ltd. franchisees must agree to support some local community or environmental project to be a part of the organization. The company also encourages each store's employees to become involved, on company time, with at least one volunteer community project.

It is no doubt that one of the key ingredients to Roddick's and the Body Shop's success was due to their social activism and support for various causes. People often want to be a part of positive action and in the Body Shop's case, their concern for the causes they support translated into sales and success for the company. Furthering your own causes with your profession may be a great practice and may also contribute to your success, so look for any opportunities to do so in your performance.

* * *

Make every effort not to limit the degree of your success by alienating any groups of potential customers. Try to increase your opportunities by welcoming as diverse a customer base as possible. If possible, maintain elements in your business that are in demand and needed by a wide variety of people. Of course, there are times when certain businesses are targeted for a specific customer base, and may be specialized in nature. Sometimes products and services are targeted to specific groups, sexes, races, etc. However, if this is not one of those situations, diversity will help in attracting as many customers as possible. Increasing selection of products and services may also help in broadening the appeal to others and makes them accessible for all instead of just a select few. During the performance of your duties, take the extra step of auditing your current business characteristics and determine whether any of your practices may deter any groups of potential customers. Eliminate any factors that may be limiting your potential and always strive to think of other ways to appeal to more customers.

MAC is an acronym for Makeup Art Cosmetics Inc., one of the most successful cosmetics companies in the business. The company was founded by Frank Toskan and Frank Angelo with the mission to create make-up which would hold up under the most grueling of conditions, even the rigorous wear of photo shoots. Before he partnered with Angelo, Toskan would spend hours experimenting with formulas at his kitchen table using his high school chemistry book for reference. He enlisted the help of chemist brother in law, Victor Casale, to help him with blending new colors and working on a tiny range of lipsticks, eye pencils, bases and powders. Angelo was a veteran entrepreneur who was the owner of a successful chain of beauty and hairdressing salons in Toronto. When Angelo was only seven, he showed early entrepreneurial instincts starting a business showing movies to neighborhood children. The two Franks formally established the business in 1984, originally created for professional makeup artists and distributed among friends in the high fashion industry. It was eventually launched to the general public after gaining a great deal of popularity when word got out of their color range selection, dense pigments, and non oily finish in the foundations. The synergy of the two Frank's, combining Toskan's ideas and Angelo's business acumen, led to enough demand of the product to open the first MAC store in New York's Greenwich Village in 1991. In addition to the MAC stores, the company signed distribution deals making their products available in several department stores in the US and Canada, including Nordstrom's and Macy's, and later on to outlets all over the world.

MAC can attribute a large part of their success to their ability to appeal to a diverse consumer base. With the usual representation of beauty consisting of an image of a skinny, white, teen, blonde model, a large part of potential consumers has always been neglected and alienated in the fashion and beauty industries. MAC broke through these stereotypes and stayed consistent with their motto of catering to "all sexes, all races, all ages." Their commitment to this motto was apparent when they made Rupaul, a 6'7" drag queen, their first spokesperson. Their enormous range of colors includes more than 160 shades of lipsticks in seven different finishes, 150 eye shadows, and 60 blushes and always growing. Their product contains something for everyone. By expanding their product's spectrum of skin shades, they became hugely popular with customers with darker skin. Known to maintain a cult following in the cosmetics industry, MAC quickly established a large following of very diverse consumers who were previously unsatisfied with the limited selection of products available from other companies. MAC continuously stays active in increasing their product lines, and every season they launch additional cosmetic palettes that are current with trends and seasonal color. The brand's appeal to the masses was furthered when it began to spread to the celebrity scene endorsed and worn by the likes of Pamela Anderson, Boy George, Lady Gaga, Fergie, Victoria Beckham, and many others. MAC has even been mentioned in pop songs such as "Unpretty" by TLC. During the opening of their first store in New York's Greenwich Village in 1991, women stood in line for hours for their lip pencils. Growth was very rapid, and they had such a great demand for the product, they were not able to respond quickly enough. Products which were being sold in North America, were being taken and sold in other countries, particularly in Asia, sold on the black market for three times the original price. They began to feel the weight of the challenges of expanding globally, as well as the demand to open other retail stores. This became a large distraction from product development and marketing and soon their infrastructure began to suffer.

This led way to the two Franks selling the company in 1994 to Estee Lauder who bought a 51 percent stake in the company for $38 million. This was an ideal merger, which gave MAC the ability to concentrate on building the brand and image, while Estee Lauder managed the business responsibilities and expanded the company. They initially kept the arrangement a secret as to not take away from the street credibility that the brand had built throughout the years. Then tragedy struck in 1997, Angelo died of complications during a surgery. By then MAC was making $250 million annually. Without his partner, Toskan no longer wanted to continue the business and sold the rest of the company to Estee Lauder for an estimated $60 million in 1998.

The key to the success of MAC was in great part due to its ability to appeal to a wide range of consumers. They never alienated any groups and continued to expand the line to appeal to a wider customer base. When possible, make certain while operating your business not to alienate any potential customers or cut off any opportunities. Find ways to gain additional customers by making a conscious effort to add any elements to your business that may increase your appeal, without compromising the original direction of your business. For example, the casinos in Las Vegas target adult visitors who are legally allowed to gamble and enjoy the attractions that the area offers. Of course, this is their primary business and dedicating all their available space to gambling and the attractions that draw patrons to gamble, is in their best interest as all these features add to their ability to profit. However, casinos such as Circus Circus have taken a different approach and added additional ways to attract clientele such as appealing to tourist's children and those taking family vacations. They have chosen to add carnival games, circus stunts, video games, rides and many other attractions that appeal to children. This gives children something to do while their parents gamble and participate in adult activities that they are not legally allowed to be a part of. In similar ways, find ways to add elements to your business that may contribute to increasing its appeal and expanding your customer base.

* * *

In your performance, make sure that you plan for the future and anticipate any upcoming trends that may affect your business. The prominent position you may enjoy today, can quickly be upstaged by another company you may not currently feel is a threat. You never know the progress others in your field may be achieving, so it is imperative that you always remain current and welcome any changes and developments. All necessary measures should be implemented today, in preparation for tomorrow to keep you competitive and ahead of the curve in your particular field.

One of the cautionary tales of a company that stayed idle instead of keeping up with the requirements of success is Blockbuster. In 1997 Reed Hastings founded Netflix, after he became disgruntled paying high late fees when returning a video he had rented from Blockbuster. Netflix is a subscriber based provider of on demand movie and television selections via internet streaming media, and DVD by mail offering hundreds of thousands of titles. In their early days, Blockbuster didn't take Netflix seriously and didn't feel that they would be any competition for the media giant. Barry McCarthy former CFO of Netflix recalled in an interview that he, Reed Hastings, and Marc Randolph (Netflix Co-founder) met with Blockbuster CEO John Antioco in 2000 in Dallas, Texas. Reed proposed that they ran Blockbuster's brand online, and that Blockbuster would run their brand in the stores. He recalls that Blockbuster's response was that "they just about laughed us out of their office." In fact, in 2000, Blockbuster turned down several opportunities to purchase Netflix for a mere $50 million. This was pocket change for Blockbuster, a company that had held a $5 billion IPO the previous year. Instead, the company inked a twenty-year deal to deliver on-demand movies with Enron Broadband Services, a subsidiary of energy trading giant Enron. Just a year later, Enron files for bankruptcy during the infamous accounting scandal. Not until 2004, six years after the inception of Netflix did Blockbuster feel they had to establish an online DVD rental by mail service. By then, not only did Netflix already begin turning a profit, but a company called Redbox soon launched DVD rental kiosks. By the time Blockbuster began taking serious measures to compete, the new upstarts were already establishing themselves. Even as late as 2008, Blockbuster was still not taking Netflix as a serious threat as CEO Jim Keyes says in an interview, "I've been frankly confused by this fascination that everybody has with Netflix…Netflix doesn't really have or do anything that we can't or don't already do ourselves." It is no surprise that in 2010, drowned in revenue losses of $1.1 billion, Blockbuster was delisted from the New York Stock Exchange and filed bankruptcy.

This example is proof that no matter how much success has been gained or how large an entity a company has become, there is still a need to plan for the future and take measures to remain competitive. If you expect to sustain your success, you have to always embrace change and think ahead to the future. It's usually a fact that the bigger you are, the slower you become. The slower you become the more you are a target for others to try to overtake your success and outdo your efforts. Remember that business is a perpetually ongoing effort and your responsibilities rest in always staying ahead of the competition so that you do not one day find yourself obsolete. Don't just plan for success but think to the future and put measures in place to keep this prosperity going.

Excellence

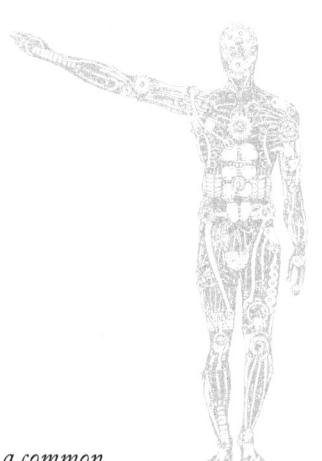

*Excellence is to do a common
thing in an uncommon way.*
—Booker T. Washington

*The quality of a person's life is in direct proportion
to their commitment to excellence, regardless of their
chosen field of endeavor.*
—Vince Lombardi

Those who practice the Grind seek no standard less than that of excellence. There is no other standard that is considered acceptable to those who strive to achieve greatness in their profession. Excellence yields one of the great rewards of hard work, the respect from your peers and those around you. This establishes your reputation as a person who may be counted on to produce quality results. Accompanying this reputation comes benefits such as promotions, higher wages, increased demand, and the many other rewards this status has to offer.

People who seek this standard understand that no effort should be considered finalized until the results are perfect. Excellence requires you to focus intently on each and every aspect of your efforts, and no area can be neglected. The steps of following up and continuously rechecking your work should be incorporated into all tasks and considered mandatory for any process.

Donald Trump, along with his many accolades, is considered a real estate developer whose projects are regarded with standards of excellence. Since his earlier conquests like Swifton Village, a 1,200-unit apartment development in Cincinnati, he has used exceptional building materials to develop his properties. He turned the property from a rundown condition to a fully occupied residence which helped beautify the neighborhood. It is no surprise that years later, the reputation surrounding the Trump level of excellence helped make The Trump International Hotel & Tower Waikiki Beach Walk the fastest selling single development. In one day, all 464 of the development's residences sold, bringing in over seven hundred million dollars. Keeping consistent with the other past Trump offerings, the development featured the very best in design, amenities, services, materials and accommodations.

The Grind

Marilyn Monroe was much more than a pretty face, she was a person who constantly pushed for excellence. In preparation for her career she dedicated hours in front of the mirror practicing her body language and facial expressions. She continuously looked for the perfect image that her audience appreciated her for. She took her trade seriously enough that she was known to wash her face up to fifteen times a day to avoid sweat and spots. When she wasn't wearing any make-up, she would apply olive oil to her face to provide a protecting agent. Ever aware of her image and in efforts to maintain her legacy, she asked her personal makeup artist, Allan Snyder, to make sure that he did her makeup when she died. Excellence involves the process of paying close attention to details and putting forth effort others do not do.

Learn to be very meticulous and calculated when you work. Excellence is not an easy prospect, so approach it with the same intensity as if you only had one attempt at a particular effort. Once you have established excellence as your only acceptable standard, your mind can be habitually conditioned to pursue nothing less. Once an individual discovers the rewards that this standard brings, no other results are desired.

One person's definition of excellence may vary from another. This definition is usually determined by what that particular individual was exposed to or what has been revealed to the person through experience. You really have to be cautious of what examples you choose to associate with your definition of excellence. Consider a sufficient number of results from a wide variety of examples so that you will have a thorough determination of what the standard of excellence consist of. Take the time needed for you to thoroughly comprehend what the term excellence means and identify all its requirements that exist in your particular profession.

* * *

Zappos is a great example of a company who strives to practice excellence in their corporate functions, especially customer service. Their customer service can arguably be considered the best in the business and they are also known for their work culture which has received inclusion on the Fortune's list of "The Best Companies to Work For." Although they are in the internet retail shoe business, the company's CEO, Tony Hsieh, promotes the company to perform as if the Zappos is actually a customer service business that sells shoes. In fact, some of the stories of their outstanding customer service have become legend.

In December 2012, a customer service rep dedicated a record ten hours and twenty-nine minutes to a call helping out a customer! On one occasion a woman called Zappos to return a pair of shoes her husband had bought after he died in a car accident. The next day she was sent flowers. Hsieh once called the Zappos hotline anonymously to win a bet that the employee would locate the nearest late-night pizza delivery places if he asked. Two minutes later the call center employee actually came back with a list of the five closest late night pizza restaurants. If a customer calls for a product and Zappos does not have the item in stock, they recommend a competitor who has it despite the chances of losing the sale. The website indicates that delivery will take between two to five business days, but it is not uncommon for customers to receive free overnight shipping for no reason, at no expense.

These standards of excellence were appreciated by customers and they began spreading these stories by word of mouth, which has contributed to the success of the company. In fact, 75 percent of Zappos orders consist of repeat business due to this extraordinary customer service. Zappos has taken most of the money they would have spent on advertising and marketing, and instead invested in the customer service and experience, letting the customers do the promotion through their word of mouth. Zappos employees are encouraged to go above and beyond traditional customer service which has been the norm at most other companies. They empower their customer service reps to decide what's best for the customers instead of having specific policies for each case.

Zappos has also maintained the reputation of being one of the best places to work. Every employee goes through a four week training process. They learn the company strategy and culture, as well as the emphasis on the customer service philosophy. They spend two weeks in the call center. One interesting company fact is that at some point during the training, they are routinely offered $4,000 to simply quit and walk away from the company! The company does this to weed out people who are only there for a paycheck, and they believe this process makes the employees become much more passionate and engaged because this proves that it's a place they really want to be and contribute to.

During the interview process, they are not only interviewed for traditional characteristics such as skills, experience, competency, etc; but also if they would be someone that Hsieh would like to know personally and would fit into the culture. If they are hired, they enjoy many perks that you would not find at other companies. Employees enjoy free food and items from the vending machines, free health care, and have access to a company library and even a nap room! They are encouraged to decorate their work spaces in fun ways to create an enjoyable atmosphere.

Managers are even required to spend 10 to 20 percent of their hours on the clock "goofing off" with employees outside the office.

This type of corporate atmosphere worked perfectly for the company, and Zappos has grown to become the largest online shoe store, with sales reaching $1 billion annually. In 2009, they were acquired by Amazon.com, a deal worth about $1.2 billion.

> *Excellence is the gradual result of always striving to do better.*
>
> —Pat Riley

One of the key requirements in the process to achieve excellence is to always follow up on your efforts and make sure you conduct quality control each and every time. Following up your efforts involves revisiting your work to make corrections, additions, modifications, or whatever else it would take to get flawless results. This stage is so vital, as it is your last chance to make sure that all the work that you have already contributed to the effort will not be a waste. Letting one mistake pass you by can contaminate your whole effort. It is similar to pouring clean filtered water into a dirty cup.

There are a couple questions that you may ask yourself in these follow up stages that can be asked in any case, no matter the field. Do you have any examples that you can compare your work to which was deemed a product of excellence? This example should be applicable toward your field and a similar, if not exact same task. Is there any other area that can be improved in the effort and can you do any better? Simply put, if there is anything that can be improved then it is not yet perfect! Would someone who is considered prominent in your profession, be content with this outcome? If you are not truly happy or content with your effort then chances are that others won't be either.

Fred Trump, the father of famed billionaire real estate developer Donald Trump, set high standards for his family's professional direction. Even after he had achieved success and acquired great wealth, he would continue his practice of spending hours of every day on the work site, consult with architects and contractors on a regular basis, kept accessible with a phone nearby at all times so he could be reached, and continuously followed up on details of his business over and over with frequent repetition. He was said to often have more knowledge of his projects than the people that he hired to do the job for him. Trump once told a reporter, "You have to follow up and follow up and follow up and follow up." This is a great example of the level of effort required to achieve excellence. Notice in this example, even in this position of prominence, Trump is still willing to do the things that others in his position were no longer willing to do. He made himself accessible to his employees and peers enabling them the outlet to express their thoughts and provide contributions which may help maintain this standard of excellence. He spent hours at his work site so he could confirm that all employees were producing quality work. There is no doubt that Trump acknowledges the importance of following up efforts as he is clearly quoted stressing its value in his own situation. He continuously contributed his own abilities toward excellence as he often had more knowledge about the work than most of the people he hired to do the job.

Excellence requires the commitment of as many efforts that are needed to achieve its standards. The way that we fall short of its requirements is when we settle for mediocrity and are no longer willing to follow our work up. In all your tasks, allocate more time than you would normally dedicate to rechecking your work. Each revision is an opportunity to find a better way to do something. Do not be lazy, but always take any chance to go over your work and analyze how you can get even better results with each follow up.

Next to excellence is the appreciation of it.
—William Makepeace Thackeray

I enjoy the pastime of smoking cigars and collecting them as a hobby. Over the years, I have sampled many different brands originating from all over the world. I am far from an expert but have acquired a decent understanding of my preferences. When I first started smoking cigars, I really could not distinguish the unique characteristics that each type possessed. They pretty much all seemed the same. With trial and error and communication with other cigar enthusiasts, my knowledge of the subject grew. It took me some time to gain a pallet and acquire the ability to identify the qualities that I enjoy. With additional experience, I eventually made a breakthrough.

The term *breakthrough*, as described in this book, is when you actually realize the criteria that would be required to reach a standard of excellence in a particular field. In other words, a breakthrough is the point in the process that is reached when an individual has gained enough experience and knowledge of a subject to be able to relate to other experienced members of that field. At this point you retain a level of knowledge when you can give accurate opinions, be able to educate others on the basics, and feel like a part of the culture, pastime, or profession. With more discoveries of characteristics, both good and bad, I was able to understand what the cigar experts determined as quality. My standards were increased and I began to truly appreciate the qualities that came with a good cigar. I even got to a point where I would only smoke certain brands and types as my taste had become more distinguished.

Each respective field of employment requires that you learn its unique requirements in order to understand what superior results consist of. Only with this knowledge can you understand what direction to strive for in order to become successful. Therefore, the more time that you spend getting familiar with a trade, the better the chances you will understand what is considered quality. The only way to gain an understanding of any subject is to actually experience it. You can read countless books about the subject but you'll never get a true sense of what the true life experience is really like. No matter what field you choose to pursue, directly expose yourself to it and take the time to gain the experiences it takes to make a breakthrough. The breakthrough is made in the previous cigar example, when after some time I was able to get past the novice position and discovered what cigar enthusiasts regard as quality or excellence. This is why it is significant not to quit early, but to always take the time necessary to discover the alternatives which may help you make a breakthrough.

There is no excellency without difficulty.

—Ovid

Gordon Ramsey can arguably very well be considered the world's most famous chef, starring on several popular TV shows including *Kitchen Nightmares*, *Hotel Hell*, and

Master Chef. He has authored a number of bestselling cookbooks and maintains a restaurant empire including over twenty-seven establishments worldwide. At age thirty-one, Ramsay founded his namesake restaurant, Restaurant Gordon Ramsay, which boasts the most prestigious accolade in the culinary world, three Michelin Star Awards.

Hell's Kitchen, another one of the reality cooking shows he stars in, trains contestants to become America's next culinary star in a high pressure competition setting. It features the foul-mouthed Chef Ramsey hurling insults at the contestants struggling to win his approval and challenges that he presents them in each episode. Starting with about sixteen to eighteen contestants competing, the numbers dwindle as they are subjected to elimination rounds for those who poorly perform. The winner of the show is rewarded with the position of head chef in one of his, or his choice of restaurant establishments with a salary of $250,000 per year. The contestant chef's are thrown in the hot seat, at times having to cook for a restaurant full of customers, learning the skills to do so as they compete. The widely popular show has now run over ten seasons and has greatly increased the spotlight on the culinary arts.

To justify his sometimes shrewd actions and his aggressive style on the show, Chef Ramsay states, "I've always extracted the best out of individuals because I push them to the absolute max. That's how you get perfection." If you have seen the show, you know exactly the extent of intensity that is exercised on the show and in the kitchen. Chef Ramsay pushes for perfectionism and wields numerous insults with his infamously short temper to get nothing short of those results. In the competition he sends the chefs running, scrambling as they must prepare their dishes under time restraint all the while paying attention to each minute detail. They are chastised with every mistake showered with insults such as, "It looks like dehydrated camel turd," "You got a pallet like a cow's back side, that's disgusting," "Finally your head is coming out of your ass, now sit down," "It looks like some bear sh——t in the woods…I can't believe I'm eating this," "It feels like I'm eating donkey d——ck," "How long have you been cooking? What a waste of ten years," "I think you're a plank…plank means an idiot so be a good plank and get back in line," "You fat bastard, is your brains in your f——g ass?"

He does not allow anything out of the kitchen that does not meet his exact high standards and the customers often must wait for hours to be served. There are no heat lamps and all dishes are made to order. Only the best ingredients are included in his dishes and are never frozen or compromised in any way. In fact, if one of the dishes in the order has to be recooked, the entire table's dishes have to be redone. Visually, the plating must look like a work of art and everything from the aroma, taste, temperature and any other detail are intensely scrutinized before service.

The pursuit of excellence strived for on this show is very much the standard aimed for when practicing the Grind. However, in business you do not always have the advantage of someone scrutinizing your faults and pushing you to perform at your best. It is almost solely an individual effort and you must at all times remain resilient in your efforts, especially if you own your own business and have no one to answer to. You will not win any contests with each challenge but there is just as many stakes involved. In life and business, you will instead strive for prizes such as promotions, financial superiority, professional control, and the many other perks that a person works for. You may not face elimination, but there is no doubt that the casualties of not exceeding in business are far worse. When I watch the show, I am reminded of it's similarities to the world of business which can get equally or more chaotic. When practicing the Grind we must proceed with the same intensity in order to obtain the standards of excellence.

* * *

I have a friend who works in the film industry and is currently producing for various networks. One day I went to the movies with him and discovered that his perspective is different from most people who view a film. Perspective can be defined as the way that you view a certain situation. It is the way that an individual perceives anything, according to their past exposure to the subject. Perspective is gained from the person's educational experience of the subject and what was learned in traditional education outlets and during time on the job. After we watched the movie, I asked him what his opinion of the film was. In his critique of the film I could tell that he pays attention to specific details such as lighting, angles, costumes, plot, setting, acting, dialogue and other intricacies that the average viewer does not. The average will view a film and follow the storyline or seek only the entertainment factor. People involved with this field such as producers, directors, or actors more times will tend to focus on the specifics which go into the production of the film. This is so because their perspective of their profession is more experienced than others. They have a deeper understanding of the field as they are directly involved. Their perspective contains greater insight and is more detailed.

From this example, you can see why a detailed perspective is significant when you are aspiring for excellence. What you are able to perceive as the conditions which contribute to excellence, are ultimately what you will strive for. These are the steps you will include in your action plan. Without being aware of these requirements, they are neglected from your actions, inevitably falling short of excellence. This is so because your perspective would not be experienced enough to identify the conditions of excellence. As previously mentioned, this is when you have not yet made a breakthrough.

Contemplate what your current perspective of your profession is. Do you know enough about your profession that you know what is required for excellence in that particular field? Is your perception of excellence similar to those who are prominent in your field? Without this knowledge you can never establish superior standards in your profession. I was watching a documentary of Mike Tyson and in one of the scenes he was talking about how he would regularly study other fighters and review past fights. He would watch footage of old bouts and would study the greats in order to add to his existing talents. By viewing other great fighters, Tyson was able to gain an accurate perspective of what actions made them great. As a boxer who is considered one of the greatest of all times, you can see that he was able to use this research to benefit his own career.

You too must do your homework to determine what it exactly takes to achieve the standard of excellence. Exposure to qualities of excellence, and identifying its practitioners is not a difficult prospect. Those who have become prominent in their fields are usually considered with great respect from peers. They are the same individuals who have pioneered new developments in their profession. They are the same individuals who are featured in books and interviews when the subject is mentioned. Others associate their name and likeness with their specific profession, and they are considered for their contributions to their work. Their reputation is associated with excellence.

Try to identify many examples of those in your field who are keeping up with these standards. One person's definition of excellence can sometimes be different from another person's. It is all just determined by what you were exposed to. Your exposure to the characteristics will be determined by who you are observing. This is why careful consideration must be taken to ensure that you are choosing examples which are relevant. To be able to achieve success, you must establish a perspective which will help you define the qualities of excellence for your field of work. You will then use this perspective as your guide to establish your goals.

> *We are what we repeatedly do. Excellence,*
> *then, is not an act, but a habit.*
>
> —Aristotle

To this day, founder Jim Koch is still committed to the standards of excellence that has made his Sam Adams beer a success. He still tastes a sample from each and every batch of his Boston Lager to ensure flavor and quality. He also constantly tests for consistency between breweries located in different cities and visits retail sites to check the date stamps on the beer they stock to ensure quality. Koch personally travels to England and Germany each year to hand pick the hops that will go into the ingredients to make a dozen different varieties of his Sam Adams beers. On an average day, Koch will be at his Jamaica Plain brewery at 4:30AM in the morning and regularly won't leave until eleven PM in the evening. From the products to the people, he makes sure that the quality is up to the standards of when he first started the company. He still meets with every employee that works for the company. He does what few founders of their company will do, and continues to be involved in the company's day to day operations ensuring that Sam Adams will continue to have success for many more years to come. His on going efforts has kept his Boston Beer Co., the largest US owned brewery, producing about two million barrels of Samuel Adams brew each year. His beer has won more awards in international beer tasting competitions in the last twenty years than any other brewery in the world, including the "Best Beer in America" at the Great American Beer Festival.

Excellence is a standard that must be continuously maintained, and it takes ongoing attention to details to keep up this level of quality. It is very easy to allow the standards of your work to decline, as there are so many distractions in the business atmosphere. You have to take the time to implement quality control even at times of prosperity, and realize that your continued success and reputation depends on it. It is the time when we achieve initial success when we tend to decrease our intensity, but in actuality this is the time when we need to be even more focused on our level of quality. These are the times when we enjoy the most customers and patronage, and we want to make sure that each and every person receives our best.

You will come to find that as you practice maintaining standards of excellence, other levels of quality will no longer be good enough. It truly becomes habitual to practice perfection and you will find that when others appreciate this standard of output, your reputation will reflect this level of effort. The praise and being known for quality work is a new form of reward, and provides satisfaction that will give your work more purpose. Soon you will find that you almost get a sense of guilt when you are not giving every effort your best. Other rewards also accompany high levels of achievement such as increased pay, worth, promotions, opportunity, and others. So start today in giving every effort your best. Make sure you understand what the standard of excellence requires in your particular field of work, so that you are able to achieve these standards each and every time.

Criticism

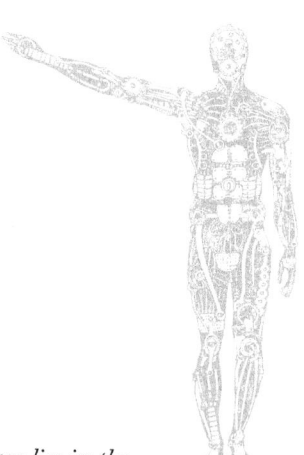

The strength of criticism lies in the weakness of the thing criticized.
—Henry Wadsworth Longfellow

Few people have the wisdom to prefer the criticism that would do them good, to the praise that deceives them.
—Francois De La Rouchefoucauld

In some cases, criticism and other's opinions can be the great destroyers of dreams. Criticism about our work, characteristics, thoughts, etc. can lead to low self esteem and reluctance to act in realizing our future goals. Who knows what the world would be today if some of the great dreamers and innovators of our time took heed to the opinions of others and never graced the world with their ideas. What if Thomas Edison would of listened to his teachers when they told him that he was "too stupid to learn anything."

What would the world be like without his groundbreaking inventions such as the light bulb, recorded music and electrical power? What if Oprah Winfrey had listened when she was told that she was "unfit for TV" early in her career? Would she still of became one of the most successful and iconic women in the world, bringing the world shows like the Oprah Winfrey Show which became the highest rated program of its kind? What if comedic great Jerry Seinfeld quit comedy when he froze and was booed off the stage the first time he performed? He may have never became one of the highest paid comedians with his show, *Seinfeld*, or became twelfth out of one hundred greatest comedians of all time ranked by Comedy Central. It was a good thing he went back on stage the next night, completed his performance and gained the laughter and applause we are used to seeing after his performances. Think of how many times in your life that you or someone you knew was talked out of initiating action due to someone else's doubt of your potential. Imagine what kind of different reality you may be living in had you or others you knew followed their dreams or bought some of these neglected ideas to fruition. Never let your potential be stifled by the unwarranted negative criticism from another person. Most of the time, criticism and other's negative opinions are spoken out of jealousy. Most people don't want to see other people find success as they may feel inferior while they remain in the same stages of procrastination. They would rather keep you at their level so they don't have a negative self image of themselves. It is always easier to criticize someone else than to put forth the work to satisfy the requirements of your own success.

> *The trouble with most of us is that we would rather be ruined by praise than saved by criticism.*
> —Norman Vincent Peale

On the contrary, criticism can also be the positive factor which causes us to reflect on the standards that we uphold. It can be done constructively, a viewpoint from others who give us their input as to how we can improve on our shortcomings. We can use this input to better our performance and gain the perspective from the viewpoints that we may not see when limited to only our one set of eyes. Two views will often provide a more complete perspective of any situation. Don't be too proud to limit yourself by not accepting the views others are willing to give you that may benefit your situation. Many times we are only willing to listen to praise, as we don't want to acknowledge anything that can hurt our pride or ego. The problem with this is that people are more prone to giving us positive feedback, even if untrue, as they do not want us to feel bad or make us view them in a negative light. Of course you have to examine the motivation behind the criticism and determine whether they are given to you with good intentions or out of jealousy or some other form of negativity. Next time you are offered criticism, determine whether it deserves any merit or should be discarded as a negative attempt to hurt your situation. If the criticism can benefit you in any way, then consider how you can use it to improve your efforts.

* * *

In some instances, you must be willing to go against the grain and implement your own ideas, even if others do not agree. This takes confidence in yourself and the vision to see the potential that others may not see for the future. It is a vital skill that requires trusting in your own instincts and ability. The only person who truly and completely understands a vision is the person who came up with the idea. Therefore, it sometimes requires the person's personal touch and input to make sure that their vision is carried out accurately. You should always be willing to inject your opinions and ideas when you feel that the situation requires your contributions. It may be imperative to the process in order to achieve success. Your input should be well thought out and planned. If you decide to go against any traditional reasoning, make sure it is substantiated by you exhausting all other options to see if this is in fact the best way to proceed. Your actions should be driven by the need to see things carried out in the best way and not just motivated by pride or ego to prove a point against any criticism.

Many of the decisions Isadore Sharp, founder of the Four Seasons hotel chain, made during his career went against the grain of what others thought was conventional wisdom. He trusted his own instincts despite the criticism of others and believed in the vision that he had for his company. He had no experience in the hotel industry and it took him five years of knocking on doors to secure financing to open his first hotel. After convincing subcontractors and vendors to extend credit, he collected enough funding to start construction of his first venture. From the beginning of the company's existence, the decision to place the location of his first hotel in a seedier area of Toronto, bought opposition from the opinions of others. Many thought no one would stay in rooms in these parts of the city. Instead, the fact that it was located close to a major hockey stadium and growing television station added publicity at no cost. The location wasn't far from the more prominent areas of the city. Also, the land was cheap, making the investment less of a risk. Sharp's intuition proved to be correct and the first Four Seasons location quickly became a success leading to the expansion of the company with additional locations. During the economic downturns of the company's history, Sharp refused to cut rates or luxury amenities, which others felt would lead to professional suicide for the company.

However, it was his maintenance of the values and worth of the company that kept its reputation sound and got them through the recession. As a result, they were able to charge a premium because their customers acknowledged that they offered a fair value for the price, with amenities and services that few others could rival. Many critics felt that he gave front line workers and employees too much authority. In reality, this is what led to the reason the company has become a success, the superior customer service. Sharp treated all employees with equal respect no matter their position on the employment hierarchy. It was the trust in these team members that resulted in the elite customer service standards the Four Seasons is known for, allowing team members the freedom to implement their own ideas. Treating their employees with respect kept consistent with the Golden Rule of the company, and the employees in turn treated the customers with the same respect and superior service. It is no wonder why the Four Seasons is repeatedly recognized in Fortune's "Top 100 Companies to Work For." Many managers and hotel industry people thought he was spending too much on amenities and felt that most customers wouldn't even know the difference. However, the amenities and services that he pioneered providing guests early in the company's history, such as complimentary bathrobes, shampoo, quality towels, shoe shines, minibars, gyms, nonsmoking rooms, twenty-four-hour room service, etc., has now commonly become accepted as the norm in the hotel industry of today.

Although many of the ideas that Sharp implemented were initially against the opinions of what others thought was best, the company ultimately flourished due to his input. It was Sharp's attention to detail and innovations, that established the Four Seasons as one of the most prominent luxury hotel chains known for their exceptional five star service. The company's hotels have received a number of Five Diamond awards from the AAA, Travel & Leisure, and the Zagat Survey. Four Seasons also maintains one of the best ratios of room occupancy to room rate in the industry. Many of the ideas that Sharp pioneered has become the industry standard and eventually copied by most of those in the hotel industry. Sometimes what's best for any endeavor includes ideas that are nontraditional or nonconforming and it takes a leader willing to go against the grain to find success. Make sure that you are always willing to do what is necessary to find success, even if you have to take such actions and go against the views and criticism of others.

Keep away from people who belittle your ambitions. Small people always do that, but the really great make you feel that you, too, can become great.

—Mark Twain

People gain inspiration from many sources. Sometimes it is the encouragement from friends or family. Sometimes it's an idea that comes to mind that stands out. Maybe it is inspiration from the progress that's been made in your workload. However, there are also times when inspiration comes from a painful incident, compelling the person to take action to overcome the circumstances. A person may be belittled or criticized for their ideas or actions and may react in a number of ways as a result. They can either listen to the criticism, and possibly become negatively affected or use it to drive them to want to do better. The criticism may be used as motivation to give them the drive to do better and to prove the other person wrong. In the case of Debbi Fields, she took what was negative criticism as fuel to prove that she had the ability to become a success despite others' opinions.

One night Debbi Fields and her husband went to dinner at one of her husband's client's homes. At the time, she had not started her company yet but was instead taking on the responsibilities of a housewife. The man asked her what she did, to which she answered, "Oh, I'm just trying to get orientated." The man then stood up, pulled out a dictionary from the shelf, and put it in her lap telling her, "The word is oriented. If you can't speak the English language, you shouldn't speak at all." She described her reaction to the event and her thoughts as, "Incredibly embarrassed, sitting there in his library with tears streaming down my cheeks, I realized I wanted to be somebody. I could hear my father's voice telling me that wealth was doing what you loved, and what I loved was cookies." That night she decided she was going to set out to be somebody and start her business, Mrs. Fields Cookies. From the start her ambitions were met with discouragement from everyone from her family and friends, to her husband. They felt she had no business starting her own company. She had no formal education, no experience, no significant product, and no money. She had married her husband, Randy Fields, a Stanford graduate, when she was nineteen years old, and for the first year played the role of the dutiful housewife. As a kid she loved making cookies and when she obtained her first job at age thirteen, she even used her first paycheck to buy ingredients including vanilla, butter, and chocolate chips for baking her cookies. It was no surprise that she decided to enter the cookie business years later when deciding what business she wanted to start. So at the age of twenty, Fields ignored the criticism and armed with her business proposal for her new cookie business, began to solicit banks for a loan. She eventually secured a loan at 21 percent and in 1977 opened the doors to her first store in Palo Alto, California, under the name Mrs. Fields Chocolate Chippery. The morning of the first day, her husband made her a bet that she couldn't make $50 in sales. She took the bet but halfway through the day there were no customers and no sales were made. So she took the initiative to walk up and down the street, handing out samples of the product, and by the end of the day ended up selling $75 worth. As a result, providing free samples to potential customers remains a cornerstone tradition they still practice at their shops to this very day. A couple years later, she realized enough success to open a second store at the Pier 39 shopping area in San Francisco. The store was so successful that the long customer lines caused problems for nearby businesses. From then on the race to open more outlets began. Fields went from baking and managing her first small shop in Palo Alto to franchising more than nine hundred stores worldwide. In 1993, realizing her dream of growing her company into a worldwide entity worth $450 million, she sold her interests in Mrs. Fields Cookies to private investors to turn her attention to motherhood.

The best outcome when faced with criticism is to use it as encouragement to promote yourself to do better. Unfortunately, many end up taking heed to the criticism and allow it to affect them negatively. By succumbing to other's negative comments without evaluation, we are giving up on our initiatives and accepting failure. You should listen to the criticism to determine whether it contains any advice that you can use to improve the outcome of your task. Determine whether the intent of the criticism is made as "constructive criticism," which may contain advice that may be utilized for better results. Alternatively, determine whether it is just criticism that is meant to undermine you and not help in any way. In this case, try to use it in the same way as in the example of Debbie Fields, who used it in a positive way to motivate herself to follow her dreams in the cookie business. Either way, make sure that you use the words of others to your advantage instead of only negative criticism of the things that you are doing wrong.

* * *

There have been situations where people have been successful in both furthering their professional goals as well as a cause that they believe in. The cause may have even been incorporated into the corporate culture or mission statement of the company that they have been involved with. Companies such as The Body Shop strive for success while also promoting social activism for causes such as rainforest preservation, corporate responsibility, fair trade, and others. In doing so, they sometimes face criticism and opposition from other parties who do not necessarily agree with their views. Opposing groups may even take action to stifle the prosperity of the business in order to cripple the causes that are related to them. Religion has often been a subject of great debate which has caused much fighting amongst various groups throughout history. In the following example, religious beliefs have become a major issue for Hobby Lobby and opting to maintain their beliefs can greatly risk their future professional prosperity. However, sometimes you must maintain your integrity, continue to fight for a cause that you believe in, and continue to strive for success, even despite the opposition of others.

David, Green founder and CEO of Hobby Lobby, is living proof that you can find success while still maintaining your core values and beliefs. Hobby Lobby is a retail chain company with more than five hundred stores in forty-one states which carries products such as a vast selection of well-priced arts and crafts supplies, home accessories, and holiday decorations. While most succumb to the demands of their work and live according to what is dictated by their profession, Green has found success basing his business practices on biblical principles and the way he has chosen to live his life following God. He has shown us that you can use your work as a tool to benefit and enhance your life and promote the change that you wish to instill in the world, without going against the things that you believe in. He stands by the principles of his beliefs even in cases where it takes away from his bottom line profits, most notably by giving his employees more time to spend with their families by closing at the early hour of eight PM nightly and on Sundays. By closing on one of the busiest days of the week, he sacrifices an estimated $100 million in sales annually, which shows where his priorities really lie. He also believes in the biblical principles of sharing your blessings by paying his full time employees almost four dollars above the Federal minimum wage, something he isn't obligated to do. Hobby Lobby Stores Inc. is self insured and provides full health coverage to over 13,000 of its employees, and also runs a clinic that provides free health care to its insured employees and reduced cost health services to others. It has been speculated that Green gives over $300 million a year to his religious causes and has personally been responsible for putting Bibles in over 400,000 homes in China. He has truly been blessed by his actions and has turned a business he founded in a garage in 1972 on a loan of $600 into a company with sales of over $2.2 billion a year. It is clear by these examples that Green is more concerned about the way he looks in the eyes of God rather than his standing in the business world. His business practices are firmly rooted in his deeply held Christian values, and remain unwavering even in the midst of a situation that could potentially close the doors of the retail giant in the future. The health insurance that Hobby Lobby offers pays for a limited form of birth control, but does not include "morning after" pills which are considered against the teachings of the Evangelical Christian faith that Green has built his business based on, since the drug may induce abortions. However, this is against the new Federal employer group health insurance coverage mandates issued by the Department of Health and Human Services, which state that all insured must be offered birth control, including "morning after" contraceptive treatments. As a result, the Green's filed suit claiming that the mandates violated their First Amendment rights that would force them to engage in practices that were contrary to their religious beliefs. The courts ruled against them, saying that the Hobby Lobby Stores Inc. did not meet the definition of a "religious group." If they do not comply, the company faces fines of $100 per day for each insured employee which equates to a total of approximately $1.3 million per day. But Green who has always maintained the operation of his business in compliance with his biblical principles, announced through his attorney a statement saying that they had no intention of complying with the HHS mandate which takes effect on January 1, 2013, and that he would vow to pay the fine until his lawsuit is finally settled.

David Green's action is one of true commitment and at the time of writing this book, there has been no final resolve to the outcome of these matters. Green has always been consistent in operating in compliance with biblical beliefs, and any changes put him at the risk of changing the very practices that have always bought the company success since its beginning. It is not always a simple prospect to remain steadfast in your beliefs and doing so may sometimes risk your chances for continued success. It is your choice as to what extent you will stand your ground, but you must always acknowledge that in some cases criticism will be followed by action as in the case of Hobby Lobby. Make sure that you anticipate any possible repercussions that may occur and that you are always ready for these types of situations that may arise in opposition of your beliefs.

There is only one way to avoid criticism: do nothing, say nothing, and be nothing.

—Aristotle

There will always be people around you such as friends, colleagues, and family which will be apprehensive in supporting you in taking a risk. Because they don't want to see you fail, and often because of their own apprehension to take risks in their own lives, they may advise against you taking any chances no matter what the situation. To be successful in life you have to be the type of person who has faith in yourself and your abilities, and one who does not need the validation of others to take action. You will also encounter those who do not have your best interest in mind, and would like to see you fail. In the following examples, it took the courage and foresight of an individual to look past the criticism and doubt of others to continue with their aspirations. No matter how unlikely success may appear, they must have seen potential that others could not realize. We have to take into account their examples and apply this to our own situation when relevant. Analyze these examples and determine how we can use some of the actions they took, in our own situation. Sometimes only the person with the idea or vision is able to articulate the outcome in their mind. When this is the case in your own situation, proceed with confidence and put all your effort into making your aspirations a reality. You may be the only one who can make the success a possibility, so take the initiative to do so.

When the owners of Red Bull Energy Drinks hired a market research firm to gauge how the public would receive their product before its release, the response was that Red Bull would fail! Other research concluded that people didn't like the taste, logo, or the brand name. In fact, critics feel that the success of Red Bull defies odds because it simply doesn't taste very good, with descriptions like "cough medicine in a can" or "another flavored sugar water." Dietrich Mateschitz, the man behind Red Bull's meteoric rise, didn't care about the criticism and believed in the products efficiency, and its ability to improve endurance, concentration, speed, and other benefits. Mateschitz traveled to Thailand in 1982 and was introduced to an uncarbonated "tonic" called Krating Daeng, which piqued his interest after he tried it and it immediately cured his jetlag. Not long afterward, he set up some meetings that led to him meeting and cofounding the company with partner Chaleo Yoovidhya. The two decided they would introduce the drink to the rest of the world after carbonating it and repackaging it. Red Bull has achieved massive success, currently selling over four billion cans per year, with more than a billion in the US market alone. Sales are in excess of $5.1 billion. This was the beginning of the energy drink revolution and their belief of the product has made both partners very rich. Mateschitz is now the richest person in Austria, and Yoovidhya is the second-richest person in Thailand.

What's worse than criticism from people who know nothing about the profession you are trying to pursue, is criticism from those who have extensive experience in your prospective field. Under these circumstances, it may be harder to maintain your confidence. However, it must be acknowledged that each situation is different and your situation may just be the case that defies the odds. Jim Koch, founder of Sam Adams Boston Lager, decided to join a business that five generations of his family had done before him. His father, who had been driven out of the business by major beer corporations like Anheuser-Busch, thought it was a bad career move. In fact, Koch said when he told his father he was going to start a brewery, his reaction was, "Jim, you've done a lot of stupid things in your life, but this is just about the stupidest thing you have ever done." In his father's experiences breweries were destined to go out of business, bankrupted by the big companies. However, Jim believed in himself and his beer and decided to leave his current job as a consultant where he was earning a good living. He took $100,000 of his savings, secured a second mortgage, and raised additional funds from friends and family to start the venture. Jim began brewing his old family beer recipe in his kitchen and began packing samples in a suitcase. He couldn't get any of the distributors in Boston to deliver the beer so he rented a truck and went from bar to bar, getting people to taste his Samuel Adams Boston Lager. Today, his Boston Beer Co. is the largest US-owned brewery producing more than 2.5 million barrels of Samuel Adams brew each year, representing about 1 percent of the US beer market. The company has generated revenues of $629 million and a profit of $60 million in 2012. Even to this day, Jim Koch still tastes every batch of Sam Adams beer and meets every one of his employees personally. It is no wonder that Samuel Adams has won more awards in international beer-tasting competitions in the last twenty years than any other brewery in the world.

In order to achieve any success in this world you must be immune to criticism and the doubt that it may cause. Risk taking is a very important aspect of the Grind and to do so you must not be affected by the misinterpretation of others and their opinions on how you should proceed in your professional life. You must always maintain a great deal of confidence backed up by reasoning of why you should maintain this belief in yourself. Your confidence should be substantiated by factors such as knowledge about your pursuits, the skill level that you have acquired, past success and accomplishment, etc. Remember, you are the only one who knows what you are truly capable of. So, if you believe that taking the risk is the best way to proceed, then do so with full confidence in yourself. Follow the examples of Dietrich Mateschitz and Jim Koch mentioned above, and take the action necessary to make your dream a reality.

A successful man is one who can lay a firm foundation with the bricks others have thrown at him.
—David Brinkley

You will always have to endure criticism and opposition from others in your quest for success. It is just a part of the process. Make sure you filter through the criticism and determine whether it may actually be useful "constructive criticism" or just an attempt to bring you down. Sometimes, what you feel is criticism is actually, sound advice that you should listen to and use to better your objectives. You should never let your pride get in the way of listening to the truth, or neglect any opportunities to gain the views of others that will benefit you. In other cases, criticism and others' opinions are just meant to promote doubt and negativity. The world would probably have become much more of a creative or dynamic place to live had it not been the input of these naysayers. However, the people who succeed are those who will throw caution into the wind, ignore the criticism of others, and proceed with an aspiration that they feel can bring change to the world. Even the wildest of ideas deserve some merit. To be an entrepreneur you must believe in yourself and your abilities.

Although you should always take heed to the advice of others, you should never neglect belief in yourself and your abilities. You must consider the motives of those who are giving you their advice and determine whether it is provided for your best interest or not. The method that I have implemented to consider the use or nonuse of another person's advice is to consider the consistency of their actions over time. Have they been supportive of your profession or showed consistent opposition? How well do you know the person giving you the advice? Does the person stand to have anything to gain or lose by giving you this advice? How have they treated others who they have a professional relationship with, and in these relationships has there been any reasoning as to take or not take their advice? These and other questions will give you a better indication of their motives. Make sure that the criticism that you consider is from reliable sources, people who are competent in the subject that they are giving their opinions of. It is also a good idea to take criticism from a number of different people to get a variety of perspectives. If you have carefully considered your decision as to whether or not to trust the person enough to take their advice, then do so with thorough research and preparedness of the situation. Never be afraid to take action to realize your dreams and don't let the criticism and negative opinions get in the way of you pursuing your dreams.

Mood

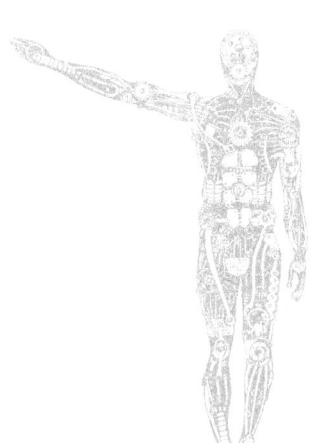

*I don't wait for moods. You accomplish nothing
if you do that. Your mind must know
it has got to get down to work.*

—Pearl S. Buck

*The thing with pretending you're in a
good mood is that sometimes you can.*

—Charles De Lint

I write most of my songs when I'm in a bad mood.

—Trent Reznor

It is important to acknowledge that there are benefits in both the emotions of feeling good and feeling bad when conducting business. It is natural and healthy to feel both types of emotions as they contribute to our well being in their own ways. One interesting piece of information I came across while researching mood and its effects related to business is that there may in fact be benefits even when you are sad or depressed. Therefore, in terms of performing at your highest levels, you may choose to pursue certain goals depending on what mood you are in. We all have a full range of emotions and there are opportune times in which our work should cater to the mood that we are currently in.

Some have even been successful at controlling their mood to match the efforts which must be conducted. They train themselves to do so by techniques such as recalling a bad experience or conjuring something up in their memory that makes them sad. On the other hand, some try to turn their negative feelings into positive emotions, establishing a number of techniques which will quickly change their mindset. The instances in developing this ability effectively are rare and you should try to let your genuine mood dictate your work and not the other way around. In addition, in most situations your mind will recognize that you are faking or manipulating your mood so the benefits may not be realized.

Moods are proven to be contagious in nature. It is important to realize that the effects of your mindset are not limited to yourself but may influence others in your workplace. Therefore, you must consider the results of your actions and how they are perceived by your peers. Caution must be exercised as there are many ways that mood can be perceived such as body language, tone, facial expression, etc. This can have an affect on the environment of the work place if there is a particular perception of mood.

Studies have shown that when managers of a business were in a positive and inspired mood, it influenced the employee's performances, increasing sales and productivity. In contrast, those managers who were in bad moods also infected their coworkers bringing about a negative environment. Some researchers have suggested that the decisions that we choose to make are based on our emotions and that logic is then used to provide an explanation of why this decision was made.

It has also been found that success does not lead to happiness, but instead the other way around. Happy people are more likely to succeed and maintain healthy lives. Happiness and its byproducts actually contribute to putting the individual in a better position to succeed. Factors such as optimism, increased social activity, confidence, motivation and energy are all products of a positive mood, which all lead to greater success in life. According to this information, we can see the importance of our mood and emotions and the affect they may have on performance.

* * *

It comes as a surprise that even when you are in a bad mood, there are advantages to this mindset that you may choose to exploit. Feeling low makes the individual more aware of their environment and less likely to be fooled by some form of deception. This results in less judgmental errors. When you are down, you tend to be more aware that additional misfortune may plague you and add to your misery because you already expect the worst. This increases your defenses and as a result you will be more attentive to your surroundings and ready for upcoming issues. When you are in a good mood you usually will not be worried or concerned with negative occurrences, so the individual does not put up a guard or exercise the same caution.

Studies have concluded that when you are sad, you are more creative. Take the example of artist Van Gough, who was reported as being regularly miserable and depressed, but turned out some of the most famous works in history. Many prominent musicians draw influence from negative emotion when they are dealing with negative circumstances in their lives. Listen to the songs which are about heartbreak or loss, and you can actually feel their emotions when listening to the song. There are a number of additional benefits from feeling down such as having a better memory, being better able to communicate and express thoughts clearer, and devising better strategies toward dealing with demanding situations.

Do not let sadness or a negative moment deem you unproductive, but instead address situations that are better handled when in this particular mood. For example, if you are down you may choose to address career decision choices or read contracts, as this is a time when you need to be more critical and on guard from making mistakes. You may also want to focus on activities which require creativity to complete. Let's say you own a small clothing manufacturing business. As the owner, your position may require you to take on many different roles in the company in situations where an employee quits or you cannot find someone to fulfill a certain position. In these cases if you are in a bad mood, you can confine yourself to creative responsibilities such as designing the clothes, thinking of new ideas for the company, or any other one of the creative processes that need to be addressed.

You may choose to take on the responsibility of the other necessary functions at a later time when you are in a different mood which would cater more to how you are feeling. You can also delegate other responsibilities to another employee which would be in a better mindset to accommodate the situation. This information can also be considered helpful when you are choosing which members of your team will be best suited for a task at hand.

However, there will always be times in which something must be done no matter the mood that you are in. If you don't sometimes address these instances, you will never give yourself an opportunity to develop the necessary skills to work through these types of obstacles. However, the relevancy of considering your mood is important as anything that may give you an advantage toward success should always be considered.

* * *

Overall, there are more benefits to being in a positive mood and you should try to maintain this state of mind as often as possible. Both types of moods are important, and you should not suppress your natural feelings, as they will eventually come out anyway. Sometimes delaying the way you really feel will cause buildup of emotion and may result in intensifying the reactions later on. Perhaps the most relevant advantage of positive mood in regards to business is the increase of productivity. When a person feels happy they are much more motivated and will be more ambitious in pursuit of a goal. The person will also be able to accomplish more and increase their output.

When in a positive mood, they are easier to train and will have an easier time learning new things. They are also more likely to implement this knowledge into their performance. This can lead to a job promotion as it may increase the chances of learning more aspects of a particular field enabling you to take on more types of responsibility. As fewer mistakes are made, there is not such a tendency to come up with excuses, making them more open to fixing and revisiting problem areas. They are less likely to place blame and this accountability may lead to working out deficiencies and improving their business situation. These positive emotions breed a better ability to solve problems and make sound decisions in taking action. Optimism is increased in this state of mind and this will result in more confidence, willingness to take chances, motivation, and having an outlook which is ideal for success.

Others are more likely to want to work with someone who is in a good mood instead of a person who may take out their emotions on others. People are more willing to help you out and work with you if you are happy and may lift their spirits. You may cut off some necessary contributions from others who could have helped put you in a position of success. Networking and interaction between those in the work field is vital in business and there are endless ways that you may benefit from the help of others. An interesting finding in studies concludes that if a person encounters a smiling employee, the customer will actually stay in the store longer and will spend more when leaving the store. Other findings concluded that a happy customer is more willing to spend more money on a particular item than one that is dissatisfied. Customers are more likely to shop and visit more frequently, a store where the environment is friendly and welcoming.

Negative emotions may also affect your health. Energy levels have been known to fluctuate according to mood and those who are positive will have more energy. Stress and negativity have been proven in studies to cause various ailments and health complications. A healthy person is less likely to miss days at work or become unproductive because they are dealing with their condition. Some people, when in a bad mood will even become aggravated with those who are in a good mood. This animosity may show in their actions. Positive mood is more potent and the individual in this mood is more likely to make decisions and take action which will prolong their happiness. The positive reinforcement will continuously be desired, and the person will make all efforts to sustain the condition.

* * *

Mood can be affected from even the slightest factors and changes. There are a number of ways that are not usually considered which may affect your mood. The work environment can greatly affect your mood and performance and you should create a space that is conducive to uplifting your spirit. A clean and organized office promotes productivity. Simply not being able to find something can make you frustrated and put you in a negative mood. Place file cabinets, storage areas, shelves, or any other items that will make it easier for you to function and keep organized.

Items such as pictures, plants, fish tanks or other items can lighten your mood and keep the environment positive. It is worth the investment to create a working space where you will enjoy coming to work. Comfort is also an important consideration and even the chair that you choose to sit in at your desk can make a difference in how you feel. Spending a whole day in a seat that is not comfortable can leave you agitated. If you are at liberty to do so, find an office that has a view that will inspire you. When feeling unmotivated, some people will be able to change their mood positively by changing their work place. If you are a writer, you may choose to go to a coffee shop, beach, different room, etc. which will give you a whole new perspective.

Diet and the food you eat contribute to mood and you should research how certain foods affect the way that you feel. For example, foods containing excitotoxins, aspartame, and monosodium glutamate, may contribute to depression. Blueberries, oranges, spinach, ginseng and others improve concentration and memory. Milk can leave you feeling fatigued or sleepy. The subject of diet is significant and you should further familiarize yourself with how different types of foods can contribute to certain kinds of moods.

Sleep and mood have great affects on each other. Shortage of sleep can cause irritability and stress, while ample amounts of sleep promote well being. The way you feel can affect your sleep and stress can cause conditions such as insomnia. Naps are a great way to boost your energy, productivity and mood. If you have the opportunity to do so, you should implement into you schedule or find time for naps especially when you need the extra boost in your day.

Even colors are said to have an affect on our moods. Reds cause tension but can also increase performance. Blue may cause depression but can also be relaxing. Green has been found to stabilize or promote balance. Yellow is said to revitalize and increase energy. All colors have been found to have some sort of effect on mood as indicated from consistencies found during related studies. In consideration of this information, you may choose to maintain the color of your office by what would cater to the mood desired.

Music can change a person's mood instantly and we react to the lyrics, rhythm, and the memories that a song can remind us of. Listen to different artists, and experiment to see how your mood is affected by the music. Next time you are down, try listening to music that you find inspiring and take note of the results.

Good weather can lift peoples spirits, improve memory, and promote openness to learning new information. When you are down, try to get outside and walk or enjoy the sunlight. It is said that seventy two degrees is the ideal temperature to realize positive benefits.

Exercise and an active lifestyle actually helps put you in a better mood and is said to help with depression. Try to find time to implement a workout or exercise routine into your day, as this not only helps your mood but also promotes good health.

* * *

Considering the fact that mood is contagious in nature, careful consideration must be made to what and who we expose ourselves to. In order to become influenced by the emotions of others we must be attentive to these individuals, so choosing what or what not to focus your attention on is vital. Find the conditions which most affect the way that you feel, and pay close attention to your exposure to these conditions. We can then make the effort to avoid people who bring us down or seem to always be in a bad mood. Also, keep in mind that you must also be careful of the feelings that you are exposing to others, as your emotions may influence them as well. Sometimes, it is even beneficial to manipulate your mood or control it so that you will not negatively influence others in your workplace. This is especially true if you are in a management position or position of authority, as your actions will influence your team and ultimately affect their performance. When you come to work in a bad mood, you do not want to project these feelings to your coworkers, so you may want to refrain from expressing these negative feelings for the overall good of the business. Organize your work environment to promote happiness, productivity, and positive emotion. When choosing people to work with, surround yourself with people who are optimistic, motivated, and are overall positive. Acknowledge the impact that even a small gesture like a smile can make such as increasing sales and keeping your customers coming back.

As you can see by the information provided in this chapter, your mood has a great effect on your professional performance. You should carefully consider your moods in all tasks that you are pursuing and find ways that you can manage them for your professional benefit. Not everyone has the same reactions to various conditions and we must observe how these affect us emotionally. Just remember that feeling sad or depressed does not necessarily deem us unproductive. We can still be very productive choosing to address certain tasks that are best handled during the presence of a particular mood. Most of the times, mood is never even considered as a factor in the workplace. But as we can see by all the information that has been discovered about the influences that mood can dictate on performance, it is important that we use it in the best possible way to dictate our professional well being. Do not neglect the significance of the subject of mood in relation to its effects on business, and use it as an additional tool to improve your practice of the Grind.

Grinding with Others

*Individually, we are one drop.
Together, we are an ocean.*

—Ryunosuke Satoro

My brother is a true animal lover and maintains an aquarium with over a dozen turtles. Part of the aquarium is partitioned off and contains land area for the turtles, while the rest is filled with rock and water. There is a bright halogen heat lamp on the land portion of the aquarium that provides light and heat that the turtles like to bask under. I started noticing that the turtles would pile up on top of each other, probably to get more heat from the lamp. The ones on the bottom did not move but instead seemed like they were willing to serve this purpose as other ones on the top would enjoy more benefits nearer to the heat from the lamps. This is in direct contradiction to the story of crabs in a bucket. The crabs will grab and pull each other down in hopes of getting to the top to escape from the bucket.

Because of this activity none ever get to the top and they all contribute to each others continuing captivity.

The same thing often happens in the work place. Many are more intent on furthering their own careers at the expense of others. They don't value the true worth of team building and networking. If they do network it is only for self gain and the relationship is one sided. As a business owner or manager you must always do your best to stifle this activity. Competition has its purpose when it promotes the best efforts of the individual, but no actions should be taken to undermine others in the same company. Coworkers should work together and gain from the success of the whole company. Everyone must do their part and as a result help each other to the top. In a work environment, even if you are not directly rewarded for accomplishment, you stand to benefit in many ways. The coworkers that you help will be contacts and associates who may return the favor to you one day in their advancements to better positions. The company you work for will experience success, and you as a part of the company will enjoy the benefits. Whether it is a promotion or increase in pay, success as a whole can benefit you in many ways. You are part of a winning team and will enjoy your part of the success. Plus, most activities will require the efforts of a team and your past successes will be recognized by others and leave you in demand for being included on future team efforts.

Part of performing at your highest levels involves your ability to bring out the best in others. Being cutthroat may be beneficial in the short term, but in the long run relationships are invaluable. When working with others, learn by the example of the turtle and avoid the mistakes of the crab.

Teamwork divides the task and doubles the success.
—Author Unknown

A vital means of finding success is surrounding yourself with the right people. It is a benefit to put yourself in the company of like-minded people. These people are the ones who share your same interests, work ethic, goals and characteristics. They will keep you motivated and challenged as they have mutual levels of aspiration. Congregating with them provides a good source for learning from a larger pool of experience. It is important that you know many people who are involved with different areas of your field. They will most likely be the same people you will be surrounded with during your professional life. When the situation arises, some of them will be good prospects to delegate responsibility to as they may have more strength in your areas of deficiency. It will be easier working with them because of your past acquaintance and knowledge of their characteristics. They are also the people you can draw from to put together a team to address a task.

A team is important in many areas of the business environment. When a house gets built, you have various people and company's who take care of different areas such as electricity, plumbing, framing, drywall, roof, and many other responsibilities. Each person has their own area of expertise and contributes their own skill to the project. The way that the members of this construction team perform with one another will determine the quality of the house that is built. With a team, there is a greater contribution of ideas from a variety of individuals from different backgrounds and experience. Problems can be tackled from many different perspectives and there are a variety of solutions that may come about. Team members who may be weaker at certain areas of the business have others to turn to for advice. There is a capacity for accomplishing larger goals that need the contribution of a number of people, that one individual may not be able to handle.

Team building and working with others is a skill in itself and you must figure out the contributions that you may contribute which will best serve the collective interests. Whether it is leading the team or supplementing the direction of others, you must learn to work with others. Even the best basketball player cannot win a championship as an individual and the way that the team is included will show his/her true greatness. The same is often the case in business so master the art of working with others and knowing what tasks require the involvement of others for success.

* * *

Chemistry is a very important ingredient to the team environment. Very much like a relationship, chemistry is a synergy amongst coworkers that enables them to closely relate and fully understand each others' individual characteristics. The better that each individual in the team knows the other's professional makeup, the easier it is to work together. Sometimes this takes years to accomplish and chemistry is built by working experience and going through many situations together. When it is present, members of a team know how to place each other in the ideal circumstances for success. Work becomes cohesive and everyone knows their own particular responsibility as well as the boundaries to avoid that may affect another persons efforts. It involves the ability to communicate with clarity the objectives that are sought after. You should have a good enough rapport with coworkers to be able to mention when they are not performing at their peak levels. It's funny how many hold their tongue because they do not want to offend the other person. In the end, when the goal is not achieved, blame is placed on one another and the relationship is compromised anyway. You should have the type of relationship where people are willing to forego their pride for the betterment of the project. No one should place blame for every mistake but it is important to identify ones that can affect the overall goal and have the potential to lead to a negative result.

With chemistry, members of the team fully understand the desired outcome that they want and the details are maintained by every member of the group. There is a sense of pride amongst the team and their objective is considered a unified cause. There is mutual level of inspiration to accomplish a goal and everyone is willing to put forth the efforts to succeed. Each member keeps the others inspired and it is a positive experience for all that are involved.

It is important to find and stay in touch with people who you share this type of relationship with. It is rare to find these types of alliances and anything that will help you to succeed is important. Whether you own a business and contract work out to affiliates or maintain employment in the company of others; you must seek to build strong relationships with your peers. Cultivate a strong working relationship with others and you will be able to effectively involve them in your vision.

Alone we can do so little; together we can do so much.
—Helen Keller

The art of networking involves the ability to acquaint yourself with others in your profession. It should translate to opening up opportunities to work with people you meet. With these relationships you can share and draw from a pool of resources of a large network of qualified individuals. It further exposes your business reputation and can result in opportunity for additional business. You can keep up with industry trends and follow the direction your profession is headed toward. Making contacts can help you with recommendations, knowledge, consultation, introductions, references, and direct business relations.

In business there is a saying that "it's not what you know, it's who you know." Knowing the right people can get you in positions that otherwise would be very difficult or impossible. Look at the validity of a recommendation or reference from a respected source. This can mean the difference of getting a job or chance at a potential opportunity. Although not a positive reality in business, many often find success because of their connections and not their ability. The business world is filled with people whose involvement was not of their own merit but the acquaintance of the right people. It is a reality so embrace it and gain these benefits where they are available to you.

Always find ways to introduce and familiarize yourself with others. Acquire social skills and render yourself approachable to everyone. The best way to gain these skills is to study those around you who have many acquaintances or deal with many people. Make it a point to meet people with every chance and practice your social skills. Make a memorable first impression, so that you stand out. Seek ways to be distinguishable such as the things you say or a clever business card which draws attention. You never know who you will be dealing with in the future so gain as many useful contacts as possible. Business conventions and events can be a potential place to meet people and discuss your business. There are many social networks and websites which may provide you a means of meeting new people. Associations may exist for your field and joining will give you access to contacts.

Always have a business card available and provide others a variety of ways to communicate with you such as email or website. People like to communicate in a variety of ways so you should make this process convenient for them. Follow up with your new contacts when you are fresh in their minds so you do not get lost in the crowd. Be concise and clearly state what it is you do, most people worth meeting are busy and may not have time for small talk. Practice good business etiquette and look for opportunities to return any favors that may have been granted to you in the past. Relationships thrive when both parties benefit and this will leave others wanting to deal with you in the future. Don't just communicate during times of need but keep in touch on a regular basis. People can sense when you only communicate for reasons of gaining something. Send out cards for the holidays and find any way to keep in touch with others. Introduce people to others and they will most likely help you meet other people also. Do not underestimate the significance of networking, it is an aspect of business that can mean the difference between success or failure.

* * *

Never judge a book by its cover and always give others their proper respect. If not for common courtesy, then the fact that anyone can be in a different position in the future. Today's receptionist can be tomorrow's CEO. This world's nature is one of constant change and you must remember that all great people in business have to start from some point. Being receptive to others, welcomes the opportunities they may provide. When dealing with others keep all relations open and never burn any bridges.

Things are not always what they seem, and you should never assume anything until it is proven in fact. This is a revelation I encountered when I used to sell CDs of my music on the Las Vegas Strip. This was always a good way to open up the marketplace for my music, promote products, and gain feedback by giving contact information such as website and email information for customers to respond. Even if they didn't buy a product, it was a chance to give out a flyer and promote in a forum where there were people from all over the world visiting. Las Vegas is definitely an international attraction with a wide variety of tourists on any given day of the year. To work on my salesmanship I would often try to pick what seemed to me the unlikeliest of customers. I started realizing that many of the people I had prejudged to not buy my music often turned out to be the ones who would make purchases. This told me that you should never predetermine or make any assumptions but instead open your potential to all available parties. Some parents would buy the music for their children. Others thought it would be a good souvenir to bring home to a friend. One of my pitches included saying that you could either gamble your money away at the casinos or spend it on something you could at least walk away with. Others just respected the fact that I was out there taking charge of my destiny by walking the streets and selling my product.

Often, people who are superior in what they do tend not to advertise it. They allow their actions to speak and their reputations to solidify respect. When you deal with anyone, do so with the knowledge that everyone is of value and importance. Also, keep in mind that people are the gateway to further business. Every person who you deal with maintains a scope of communication with others that is limitless. That is simply why there is so much value in recommendation and repeat business. On a negative note, one person's dissatisfaction can also bring you unlimited heartache. There is logic to the advice that in order to get a callback from someone important, build a good relationship with their receptionist. After all this is the person who schedules their priorities and is on the other line every time you call.

Don't limit your opportunities by alienating anyone, but always build a good rapport with everyone around you. I have even met people online who I never met personally, but because I showed a mutual respect, they helped give me information or contacts to others who could provide me benefits. Always value the people that are around you and you just might be able to open up yourself to a new potential opportunity.

A single twig breaks, but the bundle of twigs is strong.
—Tecumseh

There are always situations that come up in business when it will be necessary to work in collaboration with others on joint projects. It may be a situation where you may require the services of another party to complete a task.

Sometimes, in order to get the results that you want, you must make the situation as effortless as possible for others you wish to work with. Even though each party has their own responsibilities to attend to, the other person or company may not be in the best position to do so. What I mean by this is that it may be necessary to help others with their duties so that their participation requires less of a commitment of time.

For example, in my days of running a record label and artist management company, I would often solicit cooperative efforts from other company's to cut down on advertising costs. Sometimes I would share the expense of cross marketing with other entities not in the music business but could benefit off the exposure from my artists. These companies included beverage, skateboarding, clothing, and a variety of others who wanted more exposure in the music community. Because their marketing staff was not necessarily knowledgeable with the music publications I was seeking advertisements in, I would conduct preparation on their behalf. I would obtain advertising rates, compile target audience information, detail artwork specifications, produce advertisement ideas and direction, and many of the other tasks usually required from the company I was dealing with. I presented them with a finished package awaiting approval from the necessary superiors. This cut out the guesswork that might ensue from insufficient knowledge about our cooperative efforts. The ease in which the companies I was working with could proceed, bought many favorable results as I had made their position effortless as possible. I essentially did the work for them. The same can be done in any profession. This practice can also be beneficial in circumstances when you want to stimulate your customers to require your services. For example, it is similar to an accountant who will send a tax packet out to their clients to obtain information on the new years federal taxes. The packet contains a guide to submit information as well as the previous years' information so the client will not have to conduct extensive research. This promotes their clients to act on their responsibility of filing taxes and make the process as painless as possible.

No matter what field you are involved with, seek to make yourself or your company as easy to deal with as possible. This is a huge incentive for others to give you opportunity in this busy world. Go the extra distances it takes to make your clients, customers, or coworkers able to complete their share of any combined efforts. I'm not saying you should waste all your time doing other peoples work, but instead use this as an alternative when there is hesitation from the other party to act or when progress is moving slowly. You have to realize that the prominent people in any field who are most sought out after for their services or contributions, are often very busy. These are the people who you will want to do business with, so you should make the effort to make their contribution to these collaborations as convenient as possible.

Don't Dos of the Grind

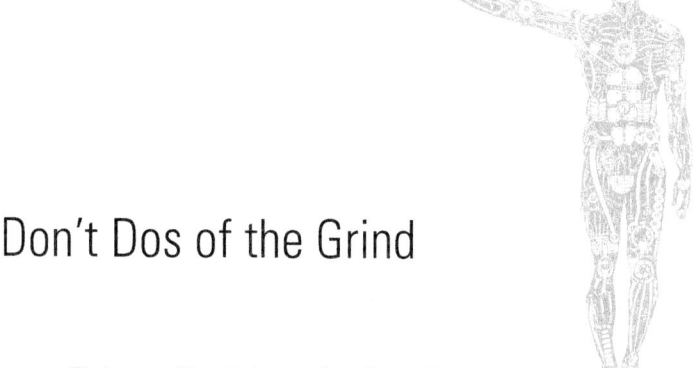

Doing nothing is better than being busy doing nothing.
—Lao Tzu

Sometimes, it's not what you do that matters, but what you don't do that results in a better outcome for a certain situation. Some efforts are better left out of your business practices as they ultimately have a negative effect on the end result of your tasks. The following paragraphs in this chapter, detail practices that you should leave out of your professional regimen to obtain the best results when implementing the Grind. They require discipline to refrain from and just like any other requirements of the Grind, will be easier to uphold with continued practice. Make sure that you place great importance in the practice of patience, as this may have as much significance in your end result as the practices that are necessary requirements of the Grind.

Control your own destiny or someone else will.
—Jack Welch

Do not establish conditions that must be satisfied before you can perform your duties. We sometimes place mandatory requirements as a necessity to get started or to complete a pursuit. The problem is that situations are hardly ever ideal in business and most of the time adversity will show itself unannounced. You must be able to perform without hinging your hopes on ideal conditions. Do not practice this form of procrastination, and be honest with yourself in assessing whether or not you may be making excuses not to start. Most of the time, these delays are just a waste of time so make sure that they are justified for some purpose. Otherwise, plan thoroughly and initiate action so that you do not miss out on any opportunities.

How many times have you or someone you've known come up with a good idea that you tell to others, but never end up acting on it. It seems like we do so to find some form of approval or encouragement from another person as if this will make the idea more sound or increase its potential in any way. This is what happened with David Gold of the 99 Cents Only store, and if it wasn't for a verbal challenge by a friend that was sick and tired of hearing him talk about his idea for a store, it may have never materialized. Gold had got the idea when his wife Sherry owned a liquor store in LA and would run promotions on certain wines selling them for only 99 cents. He noticed how these always sold well at this price, even better than if they were marked at a lower price, and fantasized about opening an entire store that offered all their items at the 99-cent price. For years Gold talked about the idea but never took action to make it a reality, seemingly waiting for some unknown opportune time. The fateful day came when Gold, his wife, and a friend named James Wayner were driving back from the airport. Gold, as he was in the habit of doing, mentioned the 99-cent idea again and Wayne lost his patience telling him that he was sick and tired of hearing him talk about it, and pointed to a store that was for rent asking him why he didn't just grab that one. He actually made Gold pull over and ask about the space, and Gold ended up striking a deal that very day! Gold opened his stores buying mainly closeouts directly from the manufacturers, enabling them to give the customers these low costs. Until then, the "extreme value discounter" stores which the 99 Cent Only stores are in the same category with, were traditionally dark, disorganized, and carried low premium merchandise. Gold innovated the stores to be huge, bright, displayed attractively, and stocked with quality name brands. Unlike their competitors, 60 percent of the merchandise is recognizable brand names like Coke or Hershey. Each store stocks about six thousand items, about 40 percent of which are closeouts. Everyone from all economic classes shop at the store and one point of interest is the Wilshire Boulevard location, a few blocks from Beverly Hills is the highest-grossing store in the chain, proving even the wealthy love a great deal. There are now over 250 locations with sales of over $1.3 billion in 2010.

Procrastination in business happens often, and it seems like people who do so are fishing for something easy to do instead of pursuing a passion that they have for a subject. It seems like they established conditions so that they can have something to blame for failure or not attempting their goals. You may be waiting for an ideal time to initiate action. Just make sure that these delays are made for preparation of the ideal time to act, and not your own predetermined assumptions of the correct time. There is a great difference in preparation and the act of procrastination. Procrastination includes fear, delay, or avoidance of hardship and inconvenience. Procrastination is remaining idle waiting, without any good reasoning, for a time to act. Preparation is in itself action planning and positioning to accomplish a goal. If a condition exists in your life that you feel must be tended to before you can take action, make sure that it is legitimate. Ask yourself if this condition is really a necessity in your progress. If you conclude that this condition may just be an excuse, then focus on finding the real problem area and how you can move forward.

* * *

Don't expect things to happen according to your own ideal time. If things were only this convenient! Sure there are ways to manipulate a situation for intended results, but in the end adversity and fate also have their influence. Many years ago I was helping a friend negotiate a record deal. Several years have passed and I can't remember the specifics of the deal but the following is a summary of the events from my recollection.

We received the recording contract and some of the stipulations were of concern. This had been one of his earlier projects and he wanted to make sure that he did not over commit to any responsibilities. He also wanted to ensure that what was negotiated, translated into the contract that we received. Legal contracts can be a challenge to understand and many times the language can be misinterpreted from those without experience with legalities. As we revised the contract, there were many provisions which needed amendments, omission, editing, and correction. Time began to pass by and both parties of the negotiations were beginning to feel the strain. I can be a little over critical at times and prefer that all matters are attended to before any finalization. I simply never want to make a mistake just because I feel that time is of the essence, especially since it involved my friends' professional well being. We reached a point where there was a standstill, and reluctantly I intended to tell my friend that we were still not in the best position to finalize the deal. There had still been some points of concern and I believed that he would take the staled developments as a negative result. To my surprise he told me something that I keep in mind to this very day whenever a project seems to exceed its intended time of completion. He said, "I've spent a whole lifetime getting to this point, a few more days making sure it was worth the wait isn't going to matter."

What a great way to perceive any of these types of situations which experience delay. Committing or finalizing something prematurely can yield so many negative results. You must remember that if you do so, all the work that was previously done may just be wasted due to impatience. Better that you give it more time and make sure that you are satisfied with the end results. Look at the strategy of car dealerships. The process of buying a car can be a great investment in time. They purposely make you commit a great deal of your time and other resources before ownership so that you will not back out in the end. First they have you test drive the car. Then you and the salesman negotiate the price and various terms. They have you sign that you will take the car at a certain price and terms before they ask the manager for approval. Your credit is checked which may effect your credit rating. You must read over and sign various contracts and paperwork. Most of the time, this process takes many hours. After you drive the car off the lot, they may call you back in to tell you that they could not establish a payment that you had first expected and that the payments must be increased. The reasons often have to do with credit. At this time you have already showed the car to friends, spent hours of time negotiating the sale, obtained insurance, and grown attached to the idea of owning a new car. Many people are so mentally exhausted at this point they just agree to the increased payments instead of returning the vehicle.

Exercising the proper timing is essential in business, and has various implications on the end result of your endeavors. Deciding when to act is a speculative process, and in some circumstances being patient and seeing your investment through may be the best decision to make. Sometimes, knowing when not to act is the best action that you can take. The importance of correct timing transcends to all fields of business and your ability to determine when or when not to take action in your specific profession can directly result in success or failure. Remember, if you are willing to put in the hard work to succeed, you might as well wait for the ideal time to get the best results out of the effort. The biggest waste of time is not taking the time to do something right. Unless you arrive at your intended results, your actions and time spent are in vein. Always plan for the long haul and practice patience so that you can take action when the time is right. Various implications that you can only realize with the passing of time.

* * *

Don't take no for an answer. In business, the gift of making others reconsider and give up their stance on a particular situation is one of the most difficult skills to acquire. However, it is a necessary skill that is required if you are to be competitive in business. It is a skill that takes a great deal of time to perfect. You have to be able to think like the person you are dealing with and eliminate all the reservations they have for not moving forward. Part of being successful in this process is making other people see things from your point of view. It takes finesse to develop the skills to influence others, not in a manipulative way, but in a way that gives them alternatives they don't usually consider. There is a fine line in practicing this skill, and many end up bordering on obnoxious business practices. You never want a person walk away with negative feelings where they felt they were forced to make a decision they really didn't want to make. This may cuts off any future dealings and may hurt your reputation. A truly successful exchange is one where both parties end up satisfied. The truth is that people will never know what they are missing if they never try anything different. Your mission in business is often to give these people a different perspective and make them try things that are new to them. Always look for an angle, or in other words, ways to get through to the people you are doing business with. People can always sense if you have a passion for what you are trying to get across and you should always believe in what you are trying to sell or get someone else to agree with. You have to become immune to accepting the first answer people give you, especially if it is negative. A major aspect of the Grind is persistence and you have to think of ideas to keep the doors of opportunity open.

In his book *Prince of the Magic Kingdom*, author Joe Flower mentions a story where Jeffrey Katzenberg, former Disney executive, was attempting to court Martin Brest for his directorial services. Brest had directed the successful movie *Beverly Hills Cops*, starring Eddie Murphy, and Katzenberg wanted his talents for Disney. He heard that Brest had complained to one of his friends that he gains weight in between his projects so Katzenberg then proceeded to send a bathtub-sized collection of cakes and muffins to his door. Accompanying the tempting gift was a note mentioning that Brest would receive a pile of these weight-inducing goodies everyday until he committed to directing a movie for Disney! Others have said that it would not be unusual for Katzenberg to call a person sixteen times a day to get what he wants. If you did not answer him back, he would then show up at your door. He was all about doing what needed to be done to complete his initiatives, which is apparent in one of his quotes, "What I learned then…is give 110 percent of yourself at everything you do, and no matter what the assignment is that somebody gives you, exceed their expectations just by some little amount."

Remember that one of the mantra's of the Grind is "Whatever It Takes," which is not just an empty phrase, but words to influence the actions you should partake in when in situations when things do not go your way. Always have a plan when you hit a roadblock and do not just accept the first answer you get. Part of being successful is to be able to change a negative outcome, and remain persistent in your efforts to turn the situation around.

* * *

Don't let others influence you by dictating who they want you to be. Take the time to assess who you really are by considering your professional history and the things that you have learned about yourself over the years. Make sure that others' influences or assumptions never change the course of your career goals or cause you to second guess yourself. These outside influences can cause all sorts of self doubt and prevent a person from following their dreams. Don't let others undermine who you are or limit your potential, by labeling you who they would like you to be.

How many times have you heard someone make statements that start off with, "You're the type of person who…," followed by their own assumptions. These types of comments are made by one person to define another, or to box them into a category they feel comfortable with. They are intentionally spoken or said with the aim to control another person's behavior and make them conform to a set of actions that are expected of them. It is a form of "power of suggestion" that is used subconsciously to put the user at ease in social situations. This is usually done because people naturally want to be in control of a situation and know what to expect from other people they regularly come in contact with, so they try to control the interaction by influencing the way another person feels and therefore acts. These situations often take place in the workplace and set precedent as to the views people have of their own business personality. Circumstances such as these and many like them actually influence some to change their true selves and lose parts of their identity. They would rather comply than take the risk of showing the other person a side of themselves that they are not yet confident in. You have to make sure that none of these influences from others will negatively effect or change the course of your goals. Many people define themselves by the way others view them and ignore their true selves. They stay within the boundaries of how they are perceived and end up conforming to the influence. It is a safer state of being as most do not want to leave themselves susceptible to any criticism or failure. They don't have to deal with the risks of establishing their own identity. Whether it is a lack of self confidence, self knowledge, experience, or some other reason, they end up succumbing to the influence of others. We are often exposed to how others see us and become conditioned to believe these opinions. From educational grading systems which tell us how smart we are to being placed in positions at work that determine how capable we are; we are always being categorized. Most of us realize that we have more potential than what these false perceptions determine and it is up to us to change these for ourselves. Bill Gates, Michael Dell, Ralph Lauren, and Richard Branson are all highly successful people who never received a college degree. If it were up to the expectations of professional standards that are set in place, these people should of never achieved these heights of success. If these people allowed others to dictate their future they would likely have a completely different reality.

Never let your thoughts and actions be manipulated against your will by others. You will always receive outside influence as to how you should live your professional life, but it is your choice how this input will affect you. First, you have to realize that every person's definitions of various subjects will vary according to their own individual experiences and how they view them, so their opinion may not be applicable to your unique situation. For example, how they view "hard work" may completely vary from how you view the term. Some may make you feel like you are in some way doing something wrong by working hard and following your dreams aggressively. However, you may feel that you can do much more and may regard hard work a necessity in life. Never let them steer you away from your decided direction and stay on course with the plans that you have established. Your situation is your own and only you can make the decisions that are best for your own interest.

* * *

Do not take things personally when you are conducting business, and always approach obstacles with a level head. In other words, do not let the negative practices which sometime accompany business dissuade you from continuing to pursue your goals. It is the nature of business that those involved will practice competitiveness. At the risk of sounding like an old mob movie, most of the time it is nothing personal and actions are conducted only to further one's business position. Unfortunately, there will always exist shady business dealings and cutthroat activity that goes along with anything that involves monetary gain. It does not necessarily have to be this way but the reality is that these practices still exist and are more prominent as competition increases and economies become weaker.

In 1927, Walt Disney found his first significant breakthrough in the cartoon industry with a series featuring animated character, Oswald the Lucky Rabbit. He was working with a person named Charles Mintz on the new animated series to be put into production for distribution through Universal Pictures. The Oswald the Lucky Rabbit series became an instant success and Disney decided to negotiate a higher fee per short as a result. Instead, Mintz shocked Disney by telling him that he was actually going to reduce Disney's fee per short and that he had stolen his key animators. He had put them under contract and threatened to start his own studio if Disney did not accept the lower fees. He also told Disney that Universal Pictures was the owner of the Oswald trademark, not him, and that he could make the films without Disney's involvement. Disney declined the offer but lost most of his animation staff. Not to be dissuaded, however, Disney began working on a new character and created Mickey Mouse. If it had not been for Mintz's greed, he would not have separated from Universal Pictures, and might not have ever introduced the world to Mickey Mouse, and gone on to build his company into the major success it is today!

It is engrained in business nature for it's participants to strive to get ahead, even if this means the demise of others. You learn very quickly that if you do not help yourself, most of the time no one else will. Inexperience is the stage when you are most vulnerable to mistakes and many of the seasoned members of a profession may use this to their advantage. This is the stage in your career when you must proceed with the most caution and learn as much as you can. Even if two individuals are working for the same company, and supposedly the same cause, there are occasions when one person will try to outdo or undermine the other for personal gain. The key is to be aware of this reality so that you will never be put in a position to suffer from these occurrences.

If you are in a profession that involves contractual obligations, make sure you seek the council of a competent lawyer. Many times, people will try to save money and forego legal requirements only to later be put in a position to lose more than they just paid for the services. Contracts can limit your professional freedom, obligate you to unfavorable terms, give away some of your rights, or place you in other negative situations. For example, a non-compete clause is a provision which restricts you from conducting business in the same field as a competitor for a period of time. You always have to be mindful of what you sign as there can be many repercussions to the commitments you make. Contracts usually consist of legal jargon which can sometimes be very confusing and contain hidden terms, so make sure you seek the services of a competent legal professional.

We have come a long way from when business was conducted with a handshake. Nowadays, we have de-evolved to a society where most disagreements are handled in a court of law. There are many negative aspects of business that exist and you must always be aware of any adversity that may occur. There is nothing wrong with proceeding with a little bit of paranoia in your professional life, as this may provide a barrier of protection that may just maintain your position of prosperity.

> *In order to succeed, your desire for success should be greater than your fear of failure.*
> —Bill Cosby

Do not take failure too seriously, and remember that you can always come back from an unsuccessful attempt. The story of the founder of the Victoria's Secret Empire, Roy Raymond, is a tragic example of what can occur when a person places too much emphasis on failure. There should never be an instance when a few shortcomings should cause a person to give up trying. If you analyze the history of almost every person who has had great success in their life, you will find their stories are littered with failures. These failures are what make the end result worth the effort. If these successes were easily attained then there would be no value in these attempts. These failures are also the lessons that you learn along the way which indicate how you should proceed once you do accomplish your goals. They provide a roadmap of what you should do to keep your position of success and what you should avoid.

Roy Raymond came up with the idea of Victoria's Secret after he encountered an embarrassing experience when trying to buy lingerie for his wife. Like most men, he knew nothing about shopping for women's undergarments. He felt that the store's staff were unsuccessful in making him feel comfortable and were wary about answering his awkward questions. So Raymond set out to create a retail store which would make a man comfortable when purchasing women's lingerie. In 1977 he opened the doors to his first store inside the Stanford Shopping Center after securing a loan of $80,000, half from a bank and half from relatives. The decor of the stores was of Victorian design with wood panel walls. The staff was hired of only friendly and receptive saleswomen to increase the comfortable factor. Instead of bras and panties being hung on racks separately, they were paired together in all sizes and mounted on frames to make the decision simple. He must have done something right as the company was able to earn $500,000 in its first year of operation. He then started a catalogue and began to open more stores. In 1982, after five years of operation, he decided to sell the business to Leslie Wexner, creator of the Limited for $4 million. He had built the Victoria's Secret company into three retail stores and a popular forty-two-page catalogue, grossing $6 million per year. Through the 1980s, The Limited continued to expand Victoria's Secret offering merchandise including shoes, perfumes, and evening wear. By the 1990s, the company became the largest American lingerie retailer with annual sales exceeding $3 billion. A 1998 survey rated it the nation's most recognized brand. However, Raymond did not experience the same type of success with his next venture, My Child's Destiny, a retail store for children, which went bankrupt in 1986. In 1993, Raymond committed suicide by leaping of the Golden Gate Bridge at the age of forty-six. It has been speculated that he was despondent over the failure of both his business and his marriage, and the devastation of selling Victoria's Secret too early at a low price.

Remember that failures do not define your worth. If anything, they are the sign that you are a person not afraid to take action to better your situation. They are an indication of your experience and your attempts toward success. Do not dwell on your failures or live in the past. This is truly a waste of time, and if you doubt this, just think of all the times you have done this in the past and if there were any changes for the better. As hard as it is to get over "what could have been," you have to acknowledge that it is the past. There is nothing you can change now, but you do have the choice to do something that will change your future. These shortcomings are just a small part of your overall story of life. In fact, they should just be considered chapters in a book which you are still writing. You still have every chance to achieve greater achievements and the failures make for great additions to your story of success.

> *He that is good for making excuses is*
> *seldom good for anything else.*
>
> —Benjamin Franklin

Do not focus your attention toward identifying excuses for failures, but instead acknowledge the lessons you may learn from the experience. The saying that "hindsight is 20/20" says that reflection of a failed situation is clearer after the experience. If this is true, than we need to take full advantage of this process. We can prepare for future solutions based on the experience of our past mistakes. An excuse is the act of trying to justify a cause for your failure. Finding reason is reflection of your mistakes in hopes to establish an effective action plan for your next attempt. One is relevant for your past and the other is relevant for your future.

Sam Wyly is a billionaire entrepreneur best known for his arts and crafts chain, Michaels. He has also been accredited for starting or growing a number of companies such as Bonanza Steakhouse, Maverick Capital, Sterling Capital and Sterling Software. He began his career at age twenty-eight, beginning with just $1,000 of his own savings which he used to found University Computing. When he took the company public two years later, it made him a millionaire before age thirty. Wyly showed promise early, joining his high school's football team, despite his inferior size. He was just 5' 7" inches tall and 155 pounds but he didn't let this deter him. Instead this inspired him to improve his speed, endurance, and knowledge of the game. "You've got to be quicker and you've got to be smarter, and you have to understand what the eleven guys on our team are going to do and what the eleven guys on the other team are probably going to do," he said in an interview. In his senior year, he helped lead the team to a state championship earning a football scholarship to Louisiana Tech.

On one occasion, an executive who helped Wyly establish University Computing asked him to guarantee a bank loan for a restaurant. He didn't want to do so as it was always his mother's advice that he should never cosign other people's notes. His sense of loyalty got the best of him and feeling guilty he ended up going against his mother's advice. She turned out to be right and the bank ended up foreclosing, leaving Wyly obligated to pay off the loan and in the position of becoming the new owner of the Bonanza Steakhouse restaurant chain. He was now left to bring the chain back from dire financial straits. Never one to quit, he changed the chain's management and expanded the Bonanza Steakhouse chain from twenty restaurants to six hundred two decades later.

Sometimes, you have to just work with the hand that you are dealt. Making excuses for your mistakes won't help the situation, but instead may slow down the process and create doubt. Next time you make a mistake like Wyly did when he cosigned, don't focus on the negative but try to find the opportunity that may exist in the situation. Instead of dwelling or making excuses he focused on turning around the company and eventually was in a situation where he had a great financial opportunity in his hands.

Do you usually place more blame for your failures on others? Do failures often result from factors outside your control? You must be honest with yourself and see if you are in the habit of making excuses instead of finding solutions for future improvement. This habit is essentially useless in that it is actually the justification of your failure and does nothing in the way of improvement. People who make excuses usually do not think back and contemplate about the true reasons for their failure. In this way they never identify their mistakes and find alternative solutions for the problems they may encounter in the future. Therefore, there is no change to bad practices, poor judgment, or lack of effort. They approach a new venture with no new gained knowledge. I have met so many people in life who can spew off every excuse in the book as to why they have not accomplished what they want out of life. Their failures are a result of hardships from the world around them or outside forces they have to deal with that are unique to their situation. They point the blame toward everyone around them and do little self reflection. The truth of the matter is that the excuses they are able to conclude really don't matter in the end. It still doesn't change the situation they are in. Excuses may justify to ourselves and others the reasons for our failures but they do not change our reality. We are still left with the same outcome and must deal with the consequences.

Instead of focusing on an excuse, figure out the true reasons for the shortcoming. What could you change about what you did that may yield a different outcome? Are there certain skills you must improve to make your results more favorable? How can you resolve the problems that you encountered and what did you do wrong? This action of making excuses becomes a habit and provides shelter to hide behind to avoid accountability. Accountability is the first step to changing this bad habit. When you account for something, you acknowledge that you yourself made an error that needs correcting. You acknowledge that you had a shortcoming and begin to identify the things that you must improve about yourself. Only at this point do you really begin a resolution to the problems and take the necessary action to best prepare yourself for future endeavors. I'm not oblivious to the fact that in business you are sometimes subjected to factors outside your control. I am saying that more effort has to be made so that we are not subjected to these kinds of conditions in the future. You must make attempts to position yourself in these ideal situations to succeed. People will use race, religion, age, weight, background, and almost any other excuse to justify their failures. If these exist then you are in a situation where you just have to work harder. Nothing will change until you realize and accept what it is you have to do to remedy these things.

For every excuse made there have already been people who overcame the very same hardship. Let's examine the accomplishments of Helen Keller. Helen Keller experienced misfortune at the age of two when she became blind and deaf from an undiagnosed illness. She did not allow these iniquities to stifle her success and acquired all necessary skills for herself to succeed and excel at her life ambitions. As a great testament for not dwelling on her weaknesses, she honed in on her abilities as an author and lecturer writing several books and traveling worldwide to train the blind and promote other causes.

> *A business that makes nothing but money is a poor business.*
> —Henry Ford

Do not just perceive success as solely a monetary achievement. Money is not the only indication of success. The truth is that a person who has enough to afford life's basic requirements may be perfectly satisfied. The quality of their life and the presence of friends, family and healthy relationships free from stress and strain leaves them content. A person can choose to devote their lives to helping others through charitable acts and other's well being gives them more gratification than any riches can afford. There are athletes who would prefer to take a salary cut and play on a championship team as the goal of winning is greater than any monetary gain. I have noticed that some of the most successful people do not even regard money as motivation for their efforts.

John Paul DeJoria may be best known to the world as the founder of companies such as Patron Tequila, Paul Mitchell, and the House of Blues. However, his greatest contributions to the world are far from the boardroom. Known as a humanitarian who has given millions to charitable and ecological causes, he lives by his philosophy of "success unshared is failure," and has now been giving back for the last thirty years. For one of the projects, Grow Appalachia, he donated money for gardening tools, seeds, fertilizer, and growing supplies to start one hundred gardens. They teach people in the area how to garden and grow their own food. Those gardens now provide food for ten thousand people of Appalachia to eat this year. He joined "The Giving Pledge" founded by Bill and Melinda Gates and Warren Buffet, which is the largest fundraising drive in history targeted at billionaires, of which sixty-nine have already pledged to give at least 50 percent of their wealth to charity. DeJoria passed up many lucrative offers to buy his prime property in Malibu bordering the national parklands, and instead donated the 410 acres of Tuna Canyon as a wilderness refuge to be enjoyed by "children and adults of the world forever." He is also involved in the business of conflict-free diamonds, which gives back to some of the people that suffered from the conflict areas. People can go online to DeJoria Diamonds, order what they want, check the price, and compare it to other stores to see where they can buy it for cheapest. He has already started a diamond mine in Sierra Leone, and gave part of the diamond mine to the local tribe, doubled their wages, and pledged to take any money that is made to open up more mines, to give to local people. He gives more than monetarily, and has even personally gone down to the Bay of Saint Lawrence to stand in the way of the people who were clubbing the baby harp seals to death in the area. Recently, he aided a tribe of over two thousand Native Americans living in the mountains near the Mexican boarder from extinction sending them food, blankets, seeds, and planting equipment. In fact, the culture at John Paul Mitchell Systems is giving back to others and all their employees participate. They raise money at various events to donate, go down to the beaches of Southern California to clean up, and participate in a number of other charitable events. The example of John Paul DeJoria is one that shows that the rewards of business come in ways that far exceed monetary gain.

Compensation may come in many forms besides financial gain. Furthering a cause that you believe in may be just as fulfilling and provide a reward that no amount of money can buy. When a person reaches a point when they are financially stable, money may no longer provide enough of an incentive to keep motivated through times of great struggle. In these instances, the person must reach inside themselves to realize what else may be important in life which would make it worth it for them to keep persevering through hardships. Every individual should take the time to contemplate thoroughly what is important to them in this lifetime. To some it is to be the best in their respective field. To others it may be to spend as much time with their family as possible. Others may desire to own their own business and control their own destiny. Whatever is important to you should be discovered and set as a goal to attain from the work that you expend. It is important for every person to know what their individual perception of success really is. Money is just one of the rewards of our labor, and if you only have your sights set on making it, you will limit yourself to the other great purposes that life has to offer. The more you discover will enhance your life, the greater the quality of life can be. Realize that success is defined by each individual and the way that you define it, will be the reality that you will be striving for.

Strategies to Keep You On the Grind

If you would not be forgotten as soon as you are dead, either write something worth reading or do something worth writing.

—Benjamin Franklin

This chapter deals with the establishment of strategies which may help in maintaining the requirements of the Grind. The Grind can be extremely tedious and we often lose sight of the focus necessary for success. Sometimes we are in a situation where motivation is needed to continue our efforts. At your own discretion, you may create effective techniques which will keep you driven and inspired. There really is no set format, as long as such techniques are effective for you. Sometimes our success is hinged upon efforts which will take years to realize and our perseverance must occasionally be fueled in order to sustain efforts.

I read an article about Michael Jordan saying that when he is unmotivated or fatigued, he remembers the fact that he was cut from his high school basketball team and pictures the locker room without his name listed. This keeps him on course and fuels his competitiveness. I heard about a study conducted in which a group of employees would keep a picture of the things they wanted pinned up in their working space. Some had a picture of a destination where they wanted to vacation. Others had a picture of a car they wanted to purchase. These served as reminders of the things they were working for. Another study group did not have any pictures posted and all their desires were contained to their thoughts. The group which had the pictures displayed in their workspace performed better because they had a daily reminder of the purpose their efforts was conducted for.

Whatever keeps you driven can be utilized as inspiration to keep you motivated. It doesn't have to be anything orthodox but simply a technique which keeps you motivated through the trying times of your career. We all get complacent and anything that will give us a spark of inspiration can be a great advantage. The following are some strategies which may be utilized to get you back on course in the instances where you feel that you are no longer performing at your best.

Legacy

During one of my visits to church, a pastor offered the church's clergy a scenario to maintain accountability of their daily actions. Upon our death we stand at the gates of heaven in the presence of God. The process of judgment that we have been warned about is amongst us and this is the time that is most relevant for the way we have chosen to live our lives. He examines both our good and bad deeds and evaluates all our past actions throughout our lifetimes. Before admission, he asks what deeds during our life would warrant entry into heaven. What would we say to him? We are faced with a conclusion we may not be ready for. He has been monitoring our whole lives and we must become accountable for all the actions that we conducted in all of our years. In doubt, we long for a second chance to guarantee our entry. If we had another chance at life we would focus a lot more of our attention in ensuring our entry into heaven's gates. All the other things we valued in life that now seem insignificant at this point would not be pursued. We would most likely change many things about the way we lived our life.

The same reflection is a strategy I use to contemplate my efforts on a regular basis. In reflection of our careers, have we done all the things each day needed to realize success? What do you plan to leave behind which would merit prestige or accomplishment in this lifetime? Are you using your time in a way that you are truly satisfied with? Such reflection may be condensed into daily audit to serve as an indication for progress. All of us have hopes and dreams we would like to see transpire in our lives. Make sure you value every passing moment as an opportunity to get you where you would like to be in the future. We only have one chance at this lifetime so why waste such a valuable commodity? Reflect daily on the legacy you would like to leave behind so you will at all times be mindful of your actions.

What we do in our lifetime is what others will remember us by. People in the past are so easily forgotten but our memories survive by the things that we do that stand out as exceptional. Milton Hershey donated all his money to his foundation after his death. He will never be forgotten due to the living legacy of his school, which still survives and benefits many to this very day. Some people say live everyday like you are writing a book and let your experiences fill its pages. Would anyone want to read your book? Another scenario is live your life like your filming a movie and your experiences make up the scenes of the story. Would anyone want to watch this movie? In these types of scenarios, we would be more mindful of all our actions as these will be accountable and viewable by others. When you think of life in these terms every detail is much more significant. Our minds will then take into account the scenes of our life that seem like wasted film and every moment then seem more crucial.

The truth is that real life really is that significant and should be valued for the true gift that it is. Success takes constant accomplishment and any neglect of its requirements is time wasted. Don't put yourself in a position where you look back on your life with any regrets. Take the actions today and make the most of your time on the earth. Make sure that what you leave behind is something that you can be proud of and shows that you lived a fulfilled life, and a legacy worth remembering.

Head Change

Mood and your outlook toward your intended goals are highly significant. Mood can contribute to the outcome of any task and it is always important to approach your work with the proper attitude. All moods have their own particular effect, and I have included more information in the earlier chapters of this book. You should determine which tasks are best pursued according to what you are feeling at the time.

I, like everyone else, have days when it is really a challenge to become motivated or to get in the right frame of mind to conduct business. What I have learned to do is keep a number of outlets in mind that will help me get back on track. I keep a box with some of the memorabilia of my past accomplishments. In there I have magazines featuring articles about my work, awards I have received, pictures with people I respect and have met, contracts, album covers, and many other things that help me remember some of my past accomplishments. Looking at these items gets me motivated and is effective in changing my mood or perspective on a negative situation. I also have places I like to go to get a head change such as a Japanese garden or museum where I can clear my mind. Sometimes all it takes is calling a certain person or taking a drive. You can find any outlet that will stimulate you and help you get focused again. The key is not to overexploit one source and space the timing of usage out so that the retreat will be effective. Anytime you do anything with too much frequency, it begins to lose its effectiveness.

Work can be very strenuous and just as you may desire to exercise extreme effort, you must also find outlets to unwind and balance out your life. Think of things in your life that will change your mood and keep a list of ways in which you can clear your mind. Resort back to the list when all else fails.

Anchoring

Another technique for keeping me at my peak performance is one which I came across taking psychology classes in college. I have modified the process to be relevant to the subject matter of this book but the underline premise is very similar. In my rendition of the process, it involves "anchoring" yourself in a time and place which you had previously performed at your highest abilities. It can also be a time when you accomplished a major goal. Remember and make a mental note of the accomplishment and specifics such as how you felt, your mood, the time and place, any smell, surroundings, any words that were used, tones and sounds, etc. Set a mental anchor at this peak and remember all the specifics associated with this event. At a time in which you feel that you are struggling to accommodate a task, anchor yourself at the previous setting point and bring back the way you felt at a time in which you favored your performance. It is very similar to a song reminding you of a certain situation in life. The song brings back memories of a specific event every time you hear the song.

The technique of anchoring will require practice, but frequency will aid in the effectiveness of this method. With good recollection, this exercise should pull you out of your slump and back to a progressive status. This exercise is helpful when you would like to change your mood or bring about a new mindset. It is no different than the euphoria one may experience after reminiscing of a memorable event in life such as a wedding, first kiss, roller coaster ride, winning an award, etc. Sometimes we must draw upon our past accomplishments to keep us yearning for future satisfaction. Sometimes the reward of feeling this way becomes so distant that we must remind ourselves why we are making such sacrifices. Always keep your past accomplishments in mind because these are what make up your business reputation. The key is to remember them in great detail with as many senses as possible.

Over Your Shoulder

One technique which has been effective in keeping me motivated throughout my work day is to imagine that someone I respect is standing over my shoulder watching me work. For me, this keeps me on point, continuously trying to do all I can to show the person my dedication toward my initiatives. This technique is implemented when I am fatigued or the end of the day is at hand. Ask yourself if you would be doing the same things if there was a person present, who's opinion you valued, closely monitoring your efforts for progress. When I get lazy at times, I quickly visualize that a client or a business competitor is there, which gets me back to work quickly. I would not want them to see me wasting time or giving half an effort toward my work. It is similar to a job interview scenario in which you are trying to impress your interviewer or convince them that you deserve the job. You would prepare and conduct yourself with a greater level of intensity in order to obtain the job. All details would be attended to and all your actions and responses would be calculated. It's also like a first date in which you try your hardest to impress the other person to make a good impression. It's surprising how many people put so much effort into things like this and not their source for income.

In a casino, there are many levels of people watching all activities transpiring. There is so much money present that there are great risks for loss. The casino manager may monitor all the pit bosses, each of whom have their own area of responsibility. The pit bosses watch over all the dealers and make sure there are no discrepancies. Pit bosses and dealers watch over the players. Then, there are the cameras and security personnel who watch over the whole casino to make sure that there is no cheating, theft, or danger on the property. If you have ever been to Las Vegas and walked in one of the larger hotels, you feel like there is always someone watching you. The ceilings are littered with cameras and surveillance equipment. Security guards are everywhere and are very quick to act to any potential disturbances. Most of the time people are on their best behavior and there is rarely any major incidents that transpire.

It seems that we react differently to situations in which there is someone watching or monitoring us as it produces greater self evaluation. This type of scenario can be pictured to maintain high standards of productivity. Realize also that in the end, even if no one is watching you on a regular basis, others will be able to see the final results of your work. It is these results that will be the determination of your reputation to others. In some cases it helps to visualize what assessment would be made if there was a person who was there to evaluate your efforts. What areas would they say that need improvement or better performance? Sometimes our minds are so consumed with our work, that it would help us to step back and look at our performance through the eyes of others.

Make a List of All You've Accomplished Daily

In the efforts of making us aware of our spending habits, one of my teachers made the class write down all the funds that were expended on a daily basis. This list was produced in great detail and everything, no matter how little the cost, was marked for inventory of expenses. After viewing the daily results, one gets the true essence of spending habits. You realize that all small purchases no matter how insignificant will contribute to the sum of your overall spending. These types of expenditures are the ones we ignore the most and the ones which really add up to hurt our budget. A cup of coffee seems irrelevant in the sum total of our spending but over the span of a month can equal significant expenditure.

The same technique can be used to give you inventory of the work that you are able to accommodate in your workday. The list may be categorized noting timeframes and a breakdown of work accomplished. The list can indicate what areas of your profession you focus most on throughout the day. Its results can also show whether you are making the most of your time, show progress from day to day, or used as reference to revisit when mistakes are made. It can give us important data and keep us organized and as efficient as possible. Let's say after viewing your list, it indicates that you are spending too much time on the phone. You may want to begin to format a schedule and methods to keep conversation more concise. Maybe take note of the relevancy of the calls and if they are contributing to any form of progress. Keep conversation focused to the matters at hand and not stray with small talk. You may also have your answering machine or receptionist take messages with reasons for the call. This way you have a chance to consider each matter and come up with a concise way to deal with them before returning the call.

Lists give us an honest reference as to our work habits, our efficiency and our overall progress. Formulate the list in ways that will give you benefit in your own particular situation. At the end of the day review your list and make your determination of whether you made the day worth living. Do you feel that you accomplished and did all that you set out for in that day? Writing things down in the form of a list gives us a true and honest account and leaves nothing to the imagination.

Team Participation

Another technique which can keep you on your grind is enlisting the help of coworkers, a partner, or peers. Sometimes tasks may be so overwhelming its best results can only be attained with the contribution of others. Do not let pride prohibit you from producing the best work possible. When you work with others, the responsibility which you take on is accountable to others. Everyone must pull their own weight and your part of the contribution involves you in a higher cause. This usually keeps most people more efficient and able to better complete tasks. Maybe there are strengths others possess which are greater than yours in a particular area, and you may decide to delegate the responsibility. All members of the team can concentrate on their own areas of strength and the combined efforts will produce the highest quality outcome. The best at their respective fields know themselves well enough to make the best decisions for the entire cause. They use discretion to delegate responsibilities to those who are most fit for accomplishment. This may also be an opportunity to improve your skills by observation of another individual who is stronger in an area which you need to improve on. Working as a team also lightens your workload. It can allow you time to concentrate on other tasks or leave you with more time to dedicate to reviewing your work. Every successful business retains the commodity of talented people who are able to carry out various areas of expertise within the company. It's the teamwork and combined actions which make the company strive. Without the presence of one team member the whole company suffers and is not the same entity it is as a whole. In any sports team, each player has their own position in the team. They each maintain their specific set of skills and contribute in their own ways. This allows them to focus on a specific area of the game, without spending extra resources worrying about their teammates' responsibilities. Together, all their efforts make the team better as a whole and working together helps them toward the common goal.

This situation can be established in the work environment. If you work better in the presence of others, create your work environment as preferred. Sometimes this affords you the chance to bounce ideas off others and gives you more viewpoints. Try to always surround yourself with people who are willing to work hard and have a strong work ethic. Being in the company of these types of people will keep you working at a progressive rate. Also, try to keep in the company of people you can improve yourself with or learn new skills from. This will elevate your talents and give you improvement for future endeavors. Like minded people often have a better chemistry and will work better as a unit to complete any given goals. So be mindful and give careful consideration when choosing a team to help you represent your efforts. Do not forget to utilize the advantages of working with others as another method for keeping motivated.

Fuel for Your Fire

Some people view criticism as strictly a negative subject, a foreshadowing to failure. First, see if the criticism contains any merit before you judge yourself harshly. You have to understand the motivation behind the criticism. Is it present to denote improvement in performance or meant to be constructive? Or is it given by others because of jealousy, hate, or competition? Consider the source and the person who is giving you criticism. Do they have your best interest in mind or do they have anything to gain from your failure? I have always chosen to turn unsubstantiated criticism into positive energy to keep me striving toward my goals. If a person says that I "can't" or "will not," it gives me stronger desire for achievement if it is in line with my true intentions for my personal goals. I work harder knowing that I have an audience which is against me and my efforts are that much more focused on completion. It is an opportunity to prove myself as a worthy recipient for any success. I reflect back on naysayers' words, in times of fatigue, laziness or unmotivation, and this usually gives me a competitive edge. How can another person know the potential that you have within? How can they arrive at a conclusion before any efforts have even been made? So many successful people today have dealt with and overcame criticism because of faith in themselves and their ideas. Think of where they would be today if they had listened to their critics. You have to be thorough in your planning but once you make your decision to commit, stay on course despite what others may say or think. Believe in yourself and your goals and use the negativity of others to gain positive results. If the criticism is warranted, use it positively to improve yourself. Embrace your imperfection, and identify your weak points for improvement. All of us have some weakness and we can use the criticism to help us take inventory of areas we want to stay away from or improve within ourselves.

Fuel Your Competitive Nature

I am not an advocate of comparing yourself to others especially if you don't really know the details of their situation.

However, I do acknowledge that in some instances, competition brings out a person's best. This is especially true in sports and can be present in the work environment also. I've actually met individuals who are more stimulated in situations in which they are facing the rivalry of others in a competitive setting. The reward of winning and outdoing their competitors is what initiates their best efforts. They use this type of drive effectively and turn it into motivation to enhance their performance. Some people are fueled by the need to be better than those around them. Harness this energy and translate it into the betterment of your career. If you choose this outlet, study the people you would like to compete with and their standing in your profession. Always choose adversaries who you consider equal to your skill level or better. There is no benefit to competing with those who you know will not provide any chivalry to bring out your best. Often if we congregate with people who are superior, we are exposed to more we can learn from and we end up matching their standards. Keep the competition healthy and direct your attention on activities that make your employment goals progressive. Competition should never act as a distraction that will take away from your performance. In other words don't get so consumed with the act of competition that it takes you away from the intended goals or makes your work suffer. Competition can bring out the enjoyment in work so long as it is conducted in good spirits. It can make your work fun and allow more interaction at your workplace. This can also be a good outlet to keep the channels of communication open and challenge others to do better. If all members of your team are striving for the best, this will put your company in a better situation for success. Competition in business brings about positive change in the levels of performance. As the curve is raised each improvement then becomes the new standard. Keeping competitive will motivate you to keep current in skill level to others who are in your profession and provide a gauge for you to measure your own progress.

Anticipate the Prize

To some, their efforts are a direct result of what they stand to gain. In these cases, anticipate what it is that you are working for. To remind yourself, envision in great detail the reward that you stand to gain. The more detailed, the better. If it is for a trip to Hawaii, then picture the activities that you will want to engage in once you are on vacation. Contemplate the places you will visit or the sightseeing you will expose yourself to. You can anticipate the different restaurants and foods you will try on your trip. You may even want to put up pictures in your workspace of the places you plan to visit. Doing so reminds you of why it is that you are expending all these efforts for.

Foreseeing the fruition of your work makes it more of a reality for us to pursue. Expectation can be a powerful thing just look at the theories we place around having a bad day. Once we identify that a bad day is occurring, nothing good can seem to come about. Our attitude and expectations dictate our actions, which then influence the almost certain negative outcome. The same can be done positively and we should always be mindful of why we are doing what it is we want to accomplish. When you associate a reward with the completion of certain actions, the worth is seen with more clarity. You are no longer just working for the usual paycheck but you now have a cause in which you are trying to realize. This gives you a better perspective and allows you to keep focused on finishing your tasks so that you can obtain your reward. This also keeps you continuously conscious of the benefits you may obtain from your work and adds to the excitement of accomplishment.

Quotes and Biographies

All of us can probably site different influences which have helped motivate us to pursue our current areas of interest. These individuals have touched us in some way and we draw inspiration from them as they have paved the way by their display of success. When we run into roadblocks in our lives, we can draw upon these examples as motivation for our own situation. When you are facing adversity, just reviewing the obstacles that others have faced and overcome can put us in a different frame of mind. We have that verification that we are not alone and someone else has faced similar problems. By reading and researching their stories, we can form some kind of direction in how we would like to establish our own path. We can get a rough idea of what it will take for success and how we can benefit from not making the same mistakes. These individuals give us a set standard that we can pursue, and we know how hard we must work to make our own situation a reality. Many of us draw inspiration from a number of role models and we can take the best attributes from them to formulate our own blueprints for success. I love to read biographies from people of all different areas of success, and each one is a whole lifetime of experience compressed into one book. This information is invaluable and we can benefit from endless experiences of real life stories. When I feel unmotivated, I will go to the bookstore and pick up books that peak my interest. Even if its not the same field that I am pursuing, their stories give me encouragement and I can take parts of their experiences that can benefit me in my own pursuits.

Another great source of inspiration is quotes from the many notable and accomplished figures throughout history. For some reason, quotes seem to give motivation to the reader. I believe this is so because so many of them can encapsulate some of the thoughts or experiences that we are facing in our lives at a particular time. They express the thoughts that we have in our own lives and give us the motivation to keep going in our own ventures. By reading them we know that we are not alone in these thoughts. One thing that I like to do is write all the quotes that touch me in some way, into a notebook for later review. These can be from any source of inspiration from a great war general to your high school football coach. Reviewing them in a time of need can be a powerful source of motivation.

Bibliography

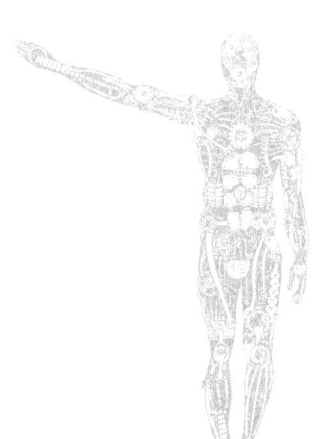

"100 Ways You Can Tap Into More of Your Brain." *OnlineUniversities.com*. OnlineUniversities.com, 26 Aug. 2009. http://www.onlineuniversities.com/blog/2009/08/100-ways-you-can-tap-into-more-of-your-brain/.

"50 Things You Probably Didn't Know about Marilyn Monroe." *Mirror.co.uk*. Mirror.co.uk, 21 Nov. 2011. http://www.mirror.co.uk/3am/celebrity-news/50-things-you-probably-didnt-92960.

"About Leaning Tower of Pisa." *Towerofpisa.info*. Leaning Tower of Pisa, n.d. http://www.towerofpisa.info/.

"About QVC." *QVC.com*. QVC, Inc., n.d. http://www.qvc.com/AboutUsAboutQVC.content.html.

"About Us Dame Anita Roddick." *TheBodyShop.com*. The Body Shop International PLC., n.d. http://www.thebodyshop.com/services/aboutus_anita-roddick.aspx.

"About Us." *99only.com*. 99 Cents Only Stores, n.d. http://99only.com/99about/#about.

"A Class Divided." *Pbs.org*. WGBH Educational Foundation, n.d. http://www.pbs.org/wgbh/pages/frontline/shows/divided/etc/synopsis.html.

Adegoke, Yinka. "Newsmaker: Cook's Vision Center Stage after Jobs's Departure. *Reuters.com*. Thomas Reuters, 25 Aug. 2011. http://www.reuters.com/article/2011/08/25/us-apple-cook-idUSTRE77N8CK20110825.

Adler, Carlye. "The 99¢ Empire HOUSEPLANTS, HAIR GEL, AND THE BEST DEAL ON WINE YOU'LL EVER FIND. HOW ONE ENTREPRENEUR IS REWRITING THE RULES OF RETAIL." *CNN.com*. Cable News Network LP, LLLP. A Time Warner Company., 1 July 2003. http://money.cnn.com/magazines/fsb/fsb_archive/2003/07/01/347322/.

Alcorn, Stacey. "I Want to Be a Failure, Like Walt Disney." *HuffingtonPost.com*. TheHuffingtonPost.com, Inc., 29 Apr. 2013. http://www.huffingtonpost.com/stacey-alcorn/i-want-to-be-a-failure-li_b_3175640.html.

Allen, Jamie. "Samuel Adams Brewer Jim Koch: Beer Career." *CNN.com*. Cable News Network LP, LLLP,

16 Mar. 2001. http://www.cnn.com/2001/CAREER/jobenvy/03/16/koch/.

Allen, Scott. "Ingvar Kamprad: IKEA Founder and One of the World's Richest Men." *About Money.com*. About.com, n.d. http://entrepreneurs.about.com/cs/famousentrepreneur/p/ingvarkamprad.htm.

Alter, Adam L., and Joseph P. Forgas. "On being happy but fearing failure: The effects of mood on self-handicapping strategies." *Journal of Experimental Social Psychology* 43 (2007): 947–954.

"Anita Roddick Biography." *TheBiographyChannel.co.uk*. AETN UK., n.d. http://www.thebiographychannel.co.uk/biographies/anita-roddick.html.

"Anita Roddick Cosmetics with a Conscience." *Entrepreneur.com*. Entrepreneur Media, Inc., 9 Oct. 2008. http://www.entrepreneur.com/article/197688.

"Annual Report 2013." *H&M.com*. H & M Hennes & Mauritz AB, n.d. http://about.hm.com/en/About/Investor-Relations/Financial-Reports/Annual-Reports.html.

"A Positive Mood Allows Your Brain to Think More Creatively." *Pschological Science.com*. Association for

Psychological Science, n.d. http://www.psychologicalscience.org/index.php/news/releases/a-positive-mood-allows-your-brain-to-think-more-creatively.html.

Bangert, Marc, and Eckart O. Altenmüller. "Mapping perception to action in piano practice: a longitudinal DC-EEG study." *BMC neuroscience* 4.1 (2003): 26.

Banner, Lois. "The Magic Red Sweater That Turned 'Norma Jeane, String Bean' into Marilyn Monroe the Sex Symbol." *DailyMail.co.uk*. Associated Newspapers Ltd., 28 July 2012. http://www.dailymail.co.uk/femail/article-2180241/Marilyn-Monroe-The-magic-red-sweater-turned-Norma-Jeane-sex-symbol.html.

Barker, Eric. "What Are the 5 Steps for Changing Bad Habits Into Good Ones?" *Time.com*. Time Inc., 19 Nov. 2014. http://time.com/3593367/change-bad-habits/.

Barr, Naomi. "Roy Raymond: The Tragic Genius at the Heart of Victoria's Secret." *Independent.co.uk*. The Independent, 13 Nov. 2013. http://www.independent.co.uk/news/business/analysis-and-features/roy-raymond-the-tragic-genius-at-the-heart-of-victorias-secret-8935811.html.

"Bass Pro Shops, Inc.: Company Profile, Information, Business Description, History, Background Information on Bass Pro Shops, Inc." *Reference For Business.com*. Advameg Inc., n.d. http://www.referenceforbusiness.com/history2/53/Bass-Pro-Shops-Inc.html.

Baum, J. Robert and Edwin Locke (2004). "The Relationship of Entrepreneurial Traits, Skill, and Motivation to Subsequent Venture Growth." *Journal of Applied Psychology*, 89 (4), 587-598.

Bedos, Nichola S. "Break Bad Habits." *NatureAndHealth.com*. Yaffa Publishing Group, 2 Oct. 2012. http://www.natureandhealth.com.au/news/break-bad-habits.

Begley, Sharon. "The Brain: How The Brain Rewires Itself." *Time.com*. Time.com, Inc., 19 Jan. 2007. http://content.time.com/time/magazine/article/0,9171,1580438,00.html.

Bhasin, Kim. "How Dietrich Mateschitz Ignored The Haters And Created The Top Energy Drink On The Planet." *BusinessInsider.com*. Business Insider Inc., 15 Jan. 2012. http://www.businessinsider.com/how-dietrich-mateschitz-ignored-the-haters-and-created-the-top-energy-drink-on-the-planet-2012-2.

"Biography." History of the World: The 20th Century Ed. Christina J. Moose. *eNotes.com*, Inc. 1999 eNotes.

com. http://www.enotes.com/topics/stephen-king#biography-stephen-king.

Blackmore, Ben. "Taking Over the World." *Fighters Only.* Feb. 2010: 54-62.

Blair, Gwenda. *The Trumps: Three Generations That Built an Empire.* New York: Simon & Schuster, 2000.

Blake, Trevor. "How to Rewire Your Brain for Success." *BigThink.com.* The BigThink Inc., n.d. http://bigthink.com/experts-corner/how-to-rewire-your-brain-for-success.

Block, Alex Ben. "How Jerry Buss Brought Hollywood to the Lakers." *The Hollywood Reporter.com.* The Hollywood Reporter, 18 Feb. 2013. http://www.hollywoodreporter.com/news/how-lakers-owner-jerry-buss-422207.

Blair, Kelsey. "Creative Marketing You Can Do: In-Air Tweet Earns Man Morton Steak On Arrival." *Adweek.com.* Adweek.com, 22 Aug. 2011. http://www.adweek.com/socialtimes/creative-marketing-you-can-do-in-air-tweet-earns-man-morton-steak-on-arrival/76149.

Boice, Danny. "Boxer To Entrepreneur: How Dana White Became The Champ Of Mixed Martial Arts." *Forbes.com.* Forbes, 3 Apr. 2014. http://www.forbes.com/sites/dannyboice/2014/04/03/boxer-to-entrepreneur-how-dana-white-became-the-champ-of-mixed-martial-arts/.

Bono, Joyce E., and Remus Ilies. "Charisma, positive emotions and mood contagion." *The Leadership Quarterly* 17 (2006): 317-334.

Bono, Joyce E., et al. "Workplace emotions: the role of supervision and leadership." *Journal of Applied Psychology* 92.5 (2007): 1357.

Boothby, Suzanne. "How Music Affects Our Moods." *Healthline.com*. Healthline Networks, Inc., 17 May 2013. http://www.healthline.com/health/mental-listening-to-music-lifts-or-reinforces-mood.

"Bowling for Columbine (2002) Quotes." *IMDb*. IMDb.com Inc., n.d. http://www.imdb.com/title/tt0310793/quotes.

Bowling for Columbine. Writ. and Dir. Michael Moore. AV Channel, 2003. DVD.

Branson, Richard. *Business Stripped Bare: Adventures of a Global Entrepreneur*. London: Virgin, 2008.

"Brain Basics: Understanding Sleep." *NIH.gov*. National Institutes of Health, n.d. http://www.ninds.nih.gov/disorders/brain_basics/understanding_sleep.htm.

Braun, Alex. "Making the Label: My Internship with Sean 'Diddy' Combs, Part II." *Internships.com*. Internships LLC, 25 Apr. 2011. http://www.internships.com/eyeoftheintern/applying-2/interviewing/making-label-internship-diddy-part-ii/.

"Breaking Bad Habits Why It's So Hard to Change." *NewsInHealth.com*. National Institute of Health, Jan. 2012. http://newsinhealth.nih.gov/issue/Jan2012/Feature1.

Breene, Sophia. "13 Mental Health Benefits of Exercise." *HuffingtonPost.com*. TheHuffingtonPost.com, 27 Mar. 2013. http://www.huffingtonpost.com/2013/03/27/mental-health-benefits-exercise_n_2956099.html.

Brennan, Carol. "Pam and Taylor, Gela Skaist-Levy." *NotableBiographies.com*. Advameg Inc., n.d. http://www.notablebiographies.com/newsmakers2/2005-Pu-Z/Skaist-Levy-Pam-and-Taylor-Gela.html.

Brenner, Joël Glenn. *The Emperors of Chocolate: Inside the Secret World of Hershey and Mars*. New York: Random House, 1999.

Brooks, Nancy R. "Mrs. Fields Shares a Recipe: To Entrepreneur, Success Tastes Sweet." *LATimes.com*. Los Angeles Times, 4 Sept. 1986. http://articles.latimes.com/1986-09-04/business/fi-14119_1_fields-cookies.

Bryant, Adam. "The Benefit of a Boot Out the Door." *NYTimes.com.* The New York Times Company, 7 Nov. 2009. http://www.nytimes.com/2009/11/08/business/08corner.html?pagewanted=all&_r=0.

Bulygo, Zach. "Tony Hsieh, Zappos, and the Art of Great Company Culture." *KISSmetrics.com.* KISSmetrics, n.d. https://blog.kissmetrics.com/zappos-art-of-culture/.

Busch, Frederick. "Making 'It'" *NYTimes.com.* The New York Times Company, 8 Oct. 2000. http://www.nytimes.com/2000/10/08/books/making-it.html.

Cadwell, Linda Lee. *Bruce Lee: The Man Only I Knew.* New York: Warner, 1976.

"Callaway Golf Company." International Directory of Company Histories. 2002. *Encyclopedia.com.* http://www.encyclopedia.com.

Carlitz, Ruth. "Hot Doughnuts Now: The Krispy Kreme Story." *DukeChronicle.com.* Duke Student Publishing Company, 21 Oct. 2003. http://www.dukechronicle.com/articles/2003/10/22/hot-doughnuts-now-krispy-kreme-story#.VUMMBVeKWuI.

Carr, Austin. "Blockbuster Bankruptcy: A Decade of Decline." *FastCompany.com.* Fast Company Inc. and Mansueto

Ventures LLC, 22 Sept. 2010. http://www.fastcompany.com/1690654/blockbuster-bankruptcy-decade-decline.

Carter, Sherrie Bourg, Psy.D. "Emotions Are Contagious—Choose Your Company Wisely." *PsychologyToday.com*. Sussex Publishers, LLC, 20 Oct. 2012. https://www.psychologytoday.com/blog/high-octane-women/201210/emotions-are-contagious-choose-your-company-wisely.

"CEO Interview: Jeffrey Lubell | True Religion." *Alister & Paine.com*. Alister & Paine Magazine, 16 May 2011. http://alisterpaine.com/2011/05/16/ceo-interview-jeffrey-lubell-true-religion/.

Chafkin, Max. "The Zappos Way of Managing." *Inc.com*. Inc.com, 1 May 2009. http://www.inc.com/magazine/20090501/the-zappos-way-of-managing.html.

Chang, Andrea. "His True Religion Jeans Are a Cult Classic." *Los Angeles Times.com*. Los Angeles Times, 1 Feb. 2009. http://articles.latimes.com/2009/feb/01/business/fi-himi1.

Chesters, Anna. "A Brief History of M.A.C." *TheGuardian.com*. Guardian News and Media Limited, 24 Oct. 2011. http://www.theguardian.com/fashion/fashion-blog/2011/oct/24/brief-history-of-mac.

Churchwell, Sarah Bartlett. *The Many Lives of Marilyn Monroe*. New York: Metropolitan/Henry Holt, 2005.

Clear, James. "The Science of Positive Thinking: How Positive Thoughts Build Your Skills, Boost Your Health, and Improve Your Work." *HuffingtonPost.com*. TheHuffingtonPost.com, Inc., 10 July 2013. http://www.huffingtonpost.com/james-clear/positive-thinking_b_3512202.html.

Clifford, Catherine. "How Sam Adams Is Thriving as a Pony Among Clydesdales." *Entrepreneur.com*. Entrepreneur Media, Inc., 16 July 2014. http://www.entrepreneur.com/article/235627.

Coffey, Brendan. "Every Penny Counts." *Forbes.com*. Forbes.com, LLC, 30 Aug. 2002. http://www.forbes.com/forbes/2002/0930/400068.html.

Compton, William, and Edward Hoffman. *Positive psychology: The science of happiness and flourishing*. Cengage Learning, 2012.

Connor, Tracy. "STILL ALL SHOOK UP OVER ELVIS Presley Rockin' and Sellin' 25 Years after Death.: *NYDailyNews.com*. New York Daily News, 11 Aug. 2002.

http://www.nydailynews.com/archives/news/shook-elvis-presley-rockin-sellin-25-years-death-article-1.502394.

Conte, Christian. "Nordstrom Customer Service Tales Not Just Legend." *Jacksonville Business Journal.com*. Merican City Business Journals, 7 Sept. 2012. http://www.bizjournals.com/jacksonville/blog/retail_radar/2012/09/nordstrom-tales-of-legendary-customer.html?page=all.

Collins, Lauren. "Renzo Rosso: Rags to Riches." *WMagazine.com*. Conde Nast, 22 Aug. 2013. http://www.wmagazine.com/fashion/features/2013/08/renzo-rosso-diesel/.

Cooke, Graham. "No Shortcut to the Top for Naturally Gifted." *AUSport.gov.au*. Australian Sports Commission, n.d. http://www.ausport.gov.au/sportscoachmag/coaching_processes/no_shortcut_to_the_top_for_naturally_gifted.

Cooper, Cord. "COMMUNICATE WITH PEOPLE EFFECTIVELY Snagging Media Attention." *Investor's Business Daily.com*. William O'Neil + Co. Incorporated and MarketSmith, Incorporated., 18 Dec. 2003. http://news.investors.com/management-leaders-and-success/121803-394112-communicate-with-people-effectively-snagging-media-attention.htm.

Covell, Jeffrey. "Michaels Stores, Inc." International Directory of Company Histories. 2005. *Encyclopedia.com*. http://www.encyclopedia.com.

Cuban, Mark. *How to Win at the Sport of Business: If I Can Do It, You Can Do It.* New York: Diversion, 2013.

"Dame Anita Roddick, Body Shop Founder, Dies." *The Telegraph.co.uk*. Telegraph Media Group Limited, 11 Sept. 2007. http://www.telegraph.co.uk/news/obituaries/1562737/Dame-Anita-Roddick-Body-Shop-founder-dies.html.

"Daniel Day-Lewis Biography." *IMDb*. IMDb.com Inc., n.d. http://www.imdb.com/name/nm0000358/bio?ref_=nm_ql_1.

"Daniel Day-Lewis." *Bio*. A&E Television Networks, 2015.

D'Antonio, Michael. *Hershey: Milton S. Hershey's Extraordinary Life of Wealth, Empire, and Utopian Dreams.* New York: Simon & Schuster, 2006.

Darwin, Charles. *The Origin of Species by Means of Natural Selection, or the Preservation of Favored Races in the Struggle for Life.* New York: Modern Library, 1993.

"Debbi Fields." *TopBusinessEntrepreneurs.com*. Famous Entrepreneurs, n.d. http://www.topbusinessentrepreneurs.com/debbi-fields.html.

Dell, Michael, and Catherine Fredman. *Direct from Dell: Strategies That Revolutionized an Industry*. New York: HarperBusiness, 1999.

Dimeglio, Steve. "There Is One Tiger Woods, and Dozens of Hopefuls." *ABCNews.com*. ABC News Internet Ventures, 20 Feb. 2008. http://abcnews.go.com/Sports/story?id=4316089.

Dixon, Rachael G. "Stress and Negativity May Change Size and Function of the Brain." *Patch.com*. Patch Media, 7 Sept. 2012. http://patch.com/california/carlsbad/stress-and-negativity-may-change-size-and-function-of-the-brain.

"DreamWorks Animation CEO Katzenberg Offers Advice." *USAToday.com*. Gannett Satellite Information Network, Inc., 22 Oct. 2012. http://www.usatoday.com/story/tech/2012/10/22/ceo-forum-dreamworks-jeffrey-katzenberg/1646191/.

Duckworth, Angela L., Matthews, Michael D., Kelly, Dennis R., and Peterson, Christopher. *"Grit: Perseverance and Passion for Long-Term Goals."* Journal of Personality and Social Psychology 92.6 (2007): 1087-101.

Duhigg, Charles. "How Habits Work." *CharlesDuhigg.com*. Charles Duhigg, n.d. http://charlesduhigg.com/how-habits-work/.

Duhigg, Charles. *The Power of Habit: Why We Do What We Do in Life and Business*. New York: Random House, 2012.

Dunbar, Polly, and Peter Sheridan. "Why the Man behind £500m Lingerie Empire Jumped off the Golden Gate Bridge: Tragedy of Victoria's Secret Founder Uncovered as First Stores Open in Britain." *DailyMail.co.uk*. Associated Newspapers Ltd., 14 July 2012. http://www.dailymail.co.uk/news/article-2173576/Tragedy-Victorias-Secret-invasion-Britain-Why-man-500m-lingerie-empire-jumped-Golden-Gate-Bridge.html.

Eng, Dinah. "How Cirque Du Soleil Got Started." Editorial. *Fortune* 7 Nov. 2011: n. pag. *Fortune.com*. Time Inc., 8 Oct. 2011. http://archive.fortune.com/2011/10/25/smallbusiness/cirque_du_soleil_guy_laliberte.fortune/index.htm.

Eng, Dinah. "Jim Koch: Samuel Adams's Beer Revolutionary." *Fortune.com*. Time, Inc., 21 Mar. 2013.

http://fortune.com/2013/03/21/jim-koch-samuel-adamss-beer-revolutionary/.

Eng, Dinah. "John Paul DeJoria: Adventures of a Serial Entrepreneur." *Fortune.com*. Time Inc., 25 Apr. 2012. http://archive.fortune.com/2012/04/24/smallbusiness/paul_mitchell_dejoria.fortune/index.htm.

Esaak, Shelley. "The Sistine Chapel Ceiling by Michelangelo." *About.com*. About.com, n.d. http://arthistory.about.com/od/famous_paintings/a/sischap_ceiling.htm.

Evelyn, Kate. "The History of MAC Cosmetics." *EHow.com*. Demand Media Inc., n.d. http://www.ehow.com/about_5055233_history-mac-cosmetics.html.

Fallows, James. "The Steve Jobs of Beer." Editorial. *Atlantic* Nov. 2014: n. pag. *TheAtlantic.com*. The Atlantic Monthly Group. http://www.theatlantic.com/magazine/archive/2014/11/the-steve-jobs-of-beer/380790/.

Fell, Jason. "Mark Cuban: Outwork and Outlearn Your Competition." *Entrepreneur.com*. Entrepreneur Media, Inc., 7 June 2012. http://www.entrepreneur.com/article/223753.

"Fields, Debbi: Overview, Personal Life, Career Details, Social and Economic Impact, Chronology: Debbi Fields

Read More: Fields, Debbi: Overview, Personal Life, Career Details, Social and Economic Impact, Chronology: Debbi Fields." *Encyclopedia.jrank.org*. Net Industries, n.d. http://encyclopedia.jrank.org/articles/pages/6203/Fields-Debbi.html.

Fish, Larry. "The Dynamo Who Founded Qvc After Launching 18 Ventures, Joseph Segel Is Retired. Permanently? Hmmmm..." *Philly.com*. Philadelphia Media Network (Digital) LLC, 7 Mar. 1993. http://articles.philly.com/1993-03-07/business/25951682_1_key-chains-directory-card-sales.

Fisher, Cynthia D. "Happiness at work." *International journal of management reviews* 12.4 (2010): 384-412.

Fishman, Charles. "The King of Kreme." Editorial. *Fast Company* Oct. 1999: n. pag. *FastCompany.com*. Fast Company Magazine, 30 Sept. 1999. http://www.fastcompany.com/37707/king-kreme.

Flower, Joe. *Prince of the Magic Kingdom: Michael Eisner and the Re-making of Disney*. New York, NY: J. Wiley, 1991.

Forgas, Joseph P. "Don't worry, be sad! On the cognitive, motivational, and interpersonal benefits of negative mood." *Current Directions in Psychological Science* 22.3 (2013): 225–232.

"Four Seasons Hotels Inc. Company Profile, Information, Business Description, History, Background Information on Four Seasons Hotels Inc." *Reference For Business.com*. Advameg Inc., n.d. http://www.referenceforbusiness.com/history2/55/Four-Seasons-Hotels-Inc.html.

Frank, Robert. "Billionaire Sara Blakely Says Secret to Success Is Failure." *CNBC.com*. CNBC LLC., 16 Oct. 2013. http://www.cnbc.com/id/101117470.

Freden, Jonas. "Ingvar Kamprad, Founder of IKEA." *Sweden.se*. Swedish Institute, n.d. https://sweden.se/business/ingvar-kamprad-founder-of-ikea/.

Frock, Roger. *Changing How the World Does Business: FedEx's Incredible Journey to Success: The inside Story*. San Francisco, CA: Berrett–Koehler, 2006.

Fussman, Cal. "Dr. Dre: What I've Learned." *Esquire*, 20 July 2013.

"GEICO Corporation: Company Profile, Information, Business Description, History, Background Information on GEICO Corporation." *Reference For Business.com*. Advameg Inc., n.d. http://www.referenceforbusiness.com/history2/46/GEICO-Corporation.html.

"GEICO's Story from the Beginning." *GEICO.com*. GEICO, n.d. https://www.geico.com/about/corporate/history-the-full-story/.

"Genghis Khan." *Bio*. A&E Television Networks, 2015.

George, Nancie. "Surprising Pros and Cons of a Bad Mood." *EverydayHealth.com*. Everyday Health Media, LLC, n.d. http://www.everydayhealth.com/news/surprising-pros-cons-bad-mood/.

Gittleson, Kim. "How Cirque Du Soleil Became a Billion Dollar Business." *BBCNews.com*. BBC, 12 Dec. 2013. http://www.bbc.com/news/business-25311503.

Goodman, Nadia. "How Google's Marissa Mayer Prevents Burnout." *Entrepreneur.com*. Entrepreneur Media Inc., 6 June 2012. http://www.entrepreneur.com/article/241800.

"Gordon." *GordonRamsay.com*. Gordon Ramsay Holdings, n.d. http://www.gordonramsay.com/gordon/.

Goudreau, Jenna. "The Secret to Breaking Bad Habits in the New Year." *Forbes.com*. Forbes, 28 Dec. 2012. http://www.forbes.com/sites/jennagoudreau/2012/12/28/the-secret-to-breaking-bad-habits-in-the-new-year/.

Govindarajan, Vijay, and Srikanth Srinivas. "The Innovation Mindset in Action: Jerry Buss." *HarvardBusinessReview.org*. Harvard Business School Publishing, 9 July 2013. https://hbr.org/2013/07/the-innovation-mindset-in-acti.

Graser, Marc. "Epic Fail: How Blockbuster Could Have Owned Netflix." *Variety.com*. Variety Media, LLC, 12 Nov. 2013. http://variety.com/2013/biz/news/epic-fail-how-blockbuster-could-have-owned-netflix-1200823443/.

Green, David. "Column: Christian Companies Can't Bow to Sinful Mandate." *USAToday.com*. Gannett Company Inc., 12 Sept. 2012. http://usatoday30.usatoday.com/news/opinion/forum/story/2012-09-12/hhs-mandate-birth-control-sue-hobby-lobby/57759226/1.

Green, Emma. "How Much Money Is Hobby Lobby's Morality Worth?" *TheAtlantic.com*. The Atlantic Monthly Group, 11 Feb. 2014. http://www.theatlantic.com/national/archive/2014/02/how-much-money-is-hobby-lobbys-morality-worth/283743/.

Greenburg, Zack O. "The Forbes Five: Hip-Hop's Wealthiest Artists 2014." *Forbes*, 5 May 2014.

Greene, Meg. "Whitman, Meg 1956." International Directory of Business Biographies. 2005. *Encyclopedia.com*. http://www.encyclopedia.com.

Gregoire, Carolyn. "The Daily Habit Of These Outrageously Successful People." *HuffingtonPost.com*. TheHuffingtonPost.com, Inc., 5 July 2013. http://www.huffingtonpost.com/2013/07/05/business-meditation-executives-meditate_n_3528731.html.

Grohol, John M., Psy.D. "Weather Can Change Your Mood." *PsychCentral.com*. Psych Central, n.d. http://psychcentral.com/blog/archives/2008/11/09/weather-can-change-your-mood/.

Gross, Daniel. *Forbes Greatest Business Stories of All Time*. New York: J. Wiley & Sons, 1996.

Grossman, Lev. "Runner-Up: Tim Cook, the Technologist." *Time.com*. Time Inc., 19 Dec. 20012. http://poy.time.com/2012/12/19/runner-up-tim-cook-the-technologist/.

Groth, Aimee. "Marissa Mayer Says She Doesn't Believe In Burnout." *BusinessInsider.com*. Business Insider Inc., 28 Mar. 2012. http://www.businessinsider.com/marissa-mayer-says-she-doesnt-believe-in-burnout-2012-3.

"Group Prejudice: Jane Elliott's Brown Eyes vs. Blue Eyes Experiment." *Study.com*. Study.com, n.d. http://study.com/academy/lesson/group-prejudice-jane-elliotts-brown-eyes-vs-blue-eyes-experiment.html.

Gschwandtner, Lisa. "Success without Limits." *SellingPower.com*. Personal Selling Power Inc., n.d. http://www.sellingpower.com/content/article/?a=7449/success-without-limits.

Guy Laliberté Canadian Performer and Entrepreneur." *Encyclopedia Britannica*. Encyclopedia Britannica Inc., n.d. http://www.britannica.com/EBchecked/topic/1089315/Guy-Laliberte.

Hall, Cheryl. "Chicken Fingers Point Way to Raising Cane's Success." *DallasNews.com*. The Dallas Morning News Inc., 19 May 2012. http://www.dallasnews.com/business/columnists/cheryl-hall/20120519-chicken-fingers-point-way-to-raising-canes-success.ece.

Harrison, J.D. "When We Were Small: Whole Foods." *The Washington Post*, 30 July 2014. http://www.washingtonpost.com/business/on-small-business/when-we-were-small-whole-foods/2014/07/29/5203bd98-1680-11e4-9349-84d4a85be981_story.html.

Harrison, J.D. "When We Were Small: FUBU." *WashingtonPost.com*. The Washington Post, 7 Oct. 2014. http://www.washingtonpost.com/business/on-small-business/when-we-were-small-fubu/2014/10/03/b9280a48-4596-11e4-b437-1a7368204804_story.html.

Hartog, Leo De. *Genghis Khan, Conqueror of the World*. New York: St. Martin's, 1989.

Hartwell-Walker, Marie. "7 Steps to Changing a Bad Habit." *PsychCentral.com*. Psych Central, n.d. http://psychcentral.com/lib/7-steps-to-changing-a-bad-habit/00020119.

Heathfield, Susan M. "The Galatea Effect: The Power of Self-expectations." *About.com*. About.com, n.d. http://humanresources.about.com/od/managementtips/a/mgmt-secret_2.htm.

Hedegaard, Erik. "Gordon Ramsay & the Damage Done." *MensJournal.com*. Men's Journal LLC, Apr. 2013. http://www.mensjournal.com/magazine/gordon-ramsay-the-damage-done-20130306.

Hilburn, Robert. "The Dr.'s Always In." *Article.latimes.com*. *Los Angeles Times*, 23 Sept. 2007. http://articles.latimes.com/2007/sep/23/entertainment/ca-dre23.

"Hip H&M." *Bloomberg Business*. Bloomberg L.P., 10 Nov. 2002. http://www.bloomberg.com/bw/stories/2002-11-10/hip-h-and-m.

"Hobby Lobby Stores Inc. Company Profile, Information, Business Description, History, Background Information on Hobby Lobby Stores Inc." *Reference For Business.com*.

Advameg Inc., n.d. http://www.referenceforbusiness.com/history2/36/Hobby-Lobby-Stores-Inc.html.

"Hongwu." *Encyclopædia Britannica. Encyclopædia Britannica Online.* Encyclopædia Britannica Inc. http://www.britannica.com/EBchecked/topic/276619/Hongwu.

"Hongwu Emperor of China." *New World Encyclopedia,* 20:39 UTC., 18:32 http://www.newworldencyclopedia.org/p/index.phptitle=Hongwu_Emperor_of_China&oldid=979190.

"How Michelangelo Painted the Sistine Chapel." *100falcons.wordpress.com.* Wordpress.com, 5 July 2010. https://100falcons.wordpress.com/2010/07/25/how-michelangelo-painted-the-sistine-chapel/.

"How to Break a Habit in 12 Steps." *Reader'sDigest.com.* The Reader's Digest Association, Inc., n.d. http://www.rd.com/health/wellness/how-to-break-a-habit-in-12-steps/.

"How to Keep Your Brain Fit." *Wall Street Journal.com.* Dow Jones & Company, Inc., n.d. http://guides.wsj.com/health/elder-care/how-to-keep-your-brain-fit/.

Howard, Jacqueline. "Bad Moods Have Important Benefits, Research Suggests." *HuffingtonPost.com.* TheHuffingtonPost.com, Inc., 28 Oct. 2013. http://

www.huffingtonpost.com/2013/10/28/bad-moods-benefits_n_4150083.html.

Hsieh, Tony. *Delivering Happiness: A Path To Profits, Passion, and Purpose*. New York: Grand Central, 2010.

Hsieh, Tony. "Harvard Business Review." Review. *How I Did It: Zappos's CEO on Going to Extremes for Customers* July-Aug. 2010: n. pag. *HarvardBusinessReview.org*. Harvard Business School Publishing. https://hbr.org/2010/07/how-i-did-it-zapposs-ceo-on-going-to-extremes-for-customers.

Hsieh, Tony. "How I Did It: Zappos's CEO on Going to Extremes for Customers." Editorial. *Harvard Business Review* July-Aug. 2010: n. pag. *Harvard Business Review.org*. Harvard Business Publishing, July-Aug. 2010. https://hbr.org/2010/07/how-i-did-it-zapposs-ceo-on-going-to-extremes-for-customers.

Hsieh, Tony. "I Am American Business: Tony Hsieh." *CNBC.com*. CNBC LLC, n.d. http://www.cnbc.com/id/100000559.

"I Am American Business: John Paul DeJoria." *CNBC.com*. CNBC LLC., 23 June 2012. http://www.cnbc.com/id/100000511.

"'I Opened an Account with $20,000 of My Own Money and It Went up to $300,000 in Two Months:' Shia LaBeouf Makes a Killing on Wall Street." *DailyMail.co.uk*. Associated Newspapers Ltd., 25 Sept. 2010. http://www.dailymail.co.uk/home/moslive/article-1314942/Shia-LaBeouf-I-opened-account-20-000-money-went-300-000-months.html.

"Inglourious Basterds Production Notes." *Twcpublicity.com*. The Weinstein Company, n.d. http://www.twcpublicity.com/movie.php?id=87#production.

"J.K. Rowling." *Bio*. A&E Television Networks, 2015.

"Jim Koch." *NotableBiographies.com*. Advameg Inc., n.d. http://www.notablebiographies.com/newsmakers2/2004-Di-Ko/Koch-Jim.html.

John, Daymond, and Daniel Paisner. *Display of Power: How FUBU Changed a World of Fashion, Branding and Lifestyle*. Nashville, TN: Naked Ink, 2007.

"Joseph Segel." *Harvard Business School.edu*. Harvard Business School Publishing, n.d. http://www.hbs.edu/leadership/database/leaders/joseph_m_segel.html.

"Joseph Segel: King of the Startups." *Tumblr.com*. Tumblr, 13 Dec. 2012. http://businessleaders.tumblr.com/post/37821364541/joseph-segel-king-of-the-startups.

"Julia Stewart of IHOP: Making the Partnership Work." *Franchising.com*. Franchising Update Media Group, n.d. http://www.franchising.com/articles/julia_stewart_of_ihop_making_the_partnership_work.html.

Jussim, Lee. "Teacher Expectations." *Education.com*. Education.com, Inc., 31 Dec. 1969. http://www.education.com/reference/article/teacher-expectations/.

K., Nina. "What Does the Brain Need to Function Nutritionally?" *Livestrong.com*. Demand Media Inc., 17 Apr. 2014. http://www.livestrong.com/article/528352-what-does-the-brain-need-to-function-nutritionally/.

Kane, Libby. "One Smart Cookie: The Founder of Mrs. Fields Shares How She Did It." *Learnvest.com*. LearnVest, Inc., 20 Nov. 2012. http://www.learnvest.com/2012/11/one-smart-cookie-the-founder-of-mrs-fields-shares-how-she-did-it/.

Katz, Donald R. *Just Do It: The Nike Spirit in the Corporate World*. New York: Random House, 1994.

Keim, Brandon. "Multitasking Muddles Brains, Even When the Computer Is Off." *Wired.com*. Conde Nast, 24 Aug. 2009. http://www.wired.com/2009/08/multitasking/.

Kenrick, Douglas T., Ph.D. "7 Good Things about Feeling Bad." *PsychologyToday.com*. Sussex Publishers, LLC, 14 June 2013. https://www.psychologytoday.com/blog/sex-murder-and-the-meaning-life/201306/7-good-things-about-feeling-bad.

Khan, Humayun. "How Nordstrom Made Its Brand Synonymous With Customer Service (and How You Can Too)." *Shopify.com*. Shopify.com, 2 Oct. 2014. http://www.shopify.com/blog/15517012-how-nordstrom-made-its-brand-synonymous-with-customer-service-and-how-you-can-too.

King, Danny. "CEO's Corner: Paul Mitchell's DeJoria Talks Philanthropy, Animal Testing, More." *DailyFinance.com*. AOL, Inc., 30 Mar. 2011. http://www.dailyfinance.com/2011/03/30/ceos-corner-paul-mitchells-dejoria-looks-to-share-his-success/.

King, Tom. *The Operator: David Geffen Builds, Buys, and Sells the New Hollywood*. New York: Random House, 2000.

Klosowski, Thorin. "What 'Brain Food' Actually Does for Your Brain." *Lifehacker.com*. The Gawker Media Group, 5 Apr. 2012. http://lifehacker.com/5899379/what-brain-food-actually-does-for-your-brain.

Koch, Jim. "Legacy of Taste." *Time.com*. Time Inc., 21 Sept. 2007. http://content.time.com/time/specials/2007/article/0,28804,1663316_1684619_1715119,00.html.

Krantz, Matt. "Magic Johnson Has Magic Touch in Business, Too." *USA Today.com*. USA Today, 8 Dec. 2008. http://usatoday30.usatoday.com/money/companies/management/entre/2008-12-07-magic-johnson-urban-business_N.htm.

"Krispy Kreme Doughnuts, Inc. Company Profile, Information, Business Description, History, Background Information on Krispy Kreme Doughnuts, Inc." *Reference For Business.com*. Advameg Inc., n.d. http://www.referenceforbusiness.com/history2/68/Krispy-Kreme-Doughnuts-Inc.html.

Kuehner-Hebert, Katie. "How Our Moods Affect Our Money." *Learnvest.com*. Learnvest, 29 Apr. 2010. http://www.learnvest.com/2010/04/how-our-moods-affect-our-money/.

Kumar, Mousumi Saha. "Diesel CEO Renzo Rosso's Journey of Becoming Blue Jean Billionaire." *SuccessStories.co.in*. Success Stories, 23 Apr. 2013. http://www.successstories.co.in/diesel-ceo-renzo-rosso-journey-of-becoming-blue-jean-billionaire/.

Lager, Fred. *Ben & Jerry's, the Inside Scoop: How Two Real Guys Built a Business with Social Conscience and a Sense of Humor.* New York: Crown, 1994.

Lamare, Amy. "While Red Bull Was Giving You Wings, It Was Giving Dietrich Mateschitz An $8 Billion Fortune." *CelebrityNetWorth.com.* Celebrity Net Worth, 29 Dec. 2013. http://www.celebritynetworth.com/articles/entertainment-articles/red-bull-giving-wings-giving-company-founder-dietrich-mateschitz-8-billion-fortune/.

Larsen, James. "Trust and Business Success." *Business Psychology: Latest Findings* (n.d.): n. pag. *Businesspsych.org.* Businesspsych.org. http://www.businesspsych.org/articles/268.html.

"Learn About Todd." *Raisingcanes.com.* Raising Canes, n.d. http://www.raisingcanes.com/learn-about-todd.

LearnVest. "How to Build a Multimillion-Dollar Company: The Story of Mrs. Fields Cookies." *Forbes.com.* Forbes.com, LLC, 20 Nov. 2012. http://www.forbes.com/sites/learnvest/2012/11/20/how-to-build-a-multimillion-dollar-company-the-story-of-mrs-fields-cookies/.

Lee, Bruce. *Tao of Jeet Kune Do.* Burbank, CA: Ohara Publications, 1975.

Lee, Bruce, and M. Uyehara. *Bruce Lee's Fighting Method.* Burbank, CA: Ohara Publications, 1976.

Li, Shan. "Dave Gold Dies at 80; Entrepreneur behind 99 Cents Only Chain." *LATimes.com.* Los Angeles Times, 26 Apr. 2013. http://articles.latimes.com/2013/apr/26/local/la-me-dave-gold-20130427.

Loder, Vanessa. "Why Multi-Tasking Is Worse Than Marijuana For Your IQ." *Forbes.com.* Forbes, 11 June 2014. http://www.forbes.com/sites/vanessaloder/2014/06/11/why-multi-tasking-is-worse-than-marijuana-for-your-iq/.

Lopez, Ana. "Cofounder Brothers Speak To Young Entreprenuers." Editorial. *The Heights* [Boston] 16 Oct. 2008: A3. *Boston College.com.* Boston College. http://newspapers.bc.edu/cgi-bin/bostonsh?a=d&d=bcheights20081016.2.23.

Lyubomirsky, Sonja, Laura King, and Ed Diener. "The Benefits of Frequent Positive Affect: Does Happiness Lead to Success?" *Psychological Bulletin* 131.6 (2005): 803-855.

Lyubomirsky, Sonja, Laura King, and Ed Diener. "The benefits of frequent positive affect: does happiness lead to success?" *Psychological bulletin* 131.6 (2005): 803.

Mabrey, Vicki, and Sarah Rosenberg. "Can Julia Stewart Save Applebee's?" *Abcnews.go.com*. Nightline, 2 Apr. 2008. http://abcnews.go.com/Business/CEOProfiles/story?id=4573076&page=1&singlePage=true.

"MAC Cosmetics - Our History." *MACCosmetics.com*. Estee Lauder Companies, n.d. http://www.maccosmetics.jobs/mac/our-history.html.

Maese, Rick. "UFC President Dana White Aims His Mixed Martial Arts Empire at World Domination." *Thewashingtonpost.com*. The Washington Post, 21 May 2014. http://www.washingtonpost.com/sports/other-sports/ufc-president-dana-white-aims-his-mixed-martial-arts-empire-at-world-domination/2014/05/21/8fd4f78c-df8e-11e3-9442-54189bf1a809_story.html.

Magee, Elaine, MPH, Rd. "How Food Affects Your Moods." *WebMD.com*. WebMD, LLC, 15 Dec. 2009. http://www.webmd.com/food-recipes/how-food-affects-your-moods.

"Managing Emotions in the Workplace: Do Positive and Negative Attitudes Drive Performance?" *Knowledge@Wharton*. The Wharton School, University of Pennsylvania, 18 April, 2007. http://knowledge.wharton.upenn.edu/article/managing-emotions-in-the-workplace-do-positive-and-negative-attitudes-drive-performance/.

"Marissa Mayer." *Bio*. A&E Television Networks, 2015.

Markman, Arthur B. "Bad Habits and Your World." *Dr.Phil.com*. Peteski Productions, Inc., 2007. http://www.drphil.com/articles/article/548.

"Martha Stewart Facts." *YourDictionary.com*. LoveToKnow Corp., n.d. http://biography.yourdictionary.com/martha-stewart.

"Martha Stewart's Incredible Comeback." *Oprah.com*. Harpo Productions Inc., 5 Oct. 2010. http://www.oprah.com/oprahshow/Martha-Stewart-and-Her-Incredible-Comeback.

Martinez, Amy. "Tale of Lost Diamond Adds Glitter to Nordstrom's Customer Service." *The Seattle Times.com*. The Seattle Times Company, 11 May 2011. http://www.seattletimes.com/business/tale-of-lost-diamond-adds-glitter-to-nordstroms-customer-service/.

Matta, Christy. "Does Success Lead to Happiness?" *PsychCentral.com*. Psych Central, n.d. http://psychcentral.com/blog/archives/2012/12/02/does-success-lead-to-happiness/.

Mayberry, Matt. "The Extraordinary Power of Visualizing Success." *Entrepreneur.com*. Entrepreneur Media, Inc., 30 Jan. 2015. http://www.entrepreneur.com/article/242373.

McDonald, Duff. "Red Bull's Billionaire Maniac." *Bloomberg.com*. Bloomberg L.P., 19 May 2011. http://www.bloomberg.com/bw/magazine/content/11_22/b4230064852768.htm.

McDonald, Duff. "Red Bull's Billionaire Maniac Becomes a Media Mogul." *NBCNews.com*. NBC News.com, 22 May 2011. http://www.nbcnews.com/id/43112711/ns/business-us_business/t/red-bulls-billionaire-maniac-becomes-media-mogul/#.VVQU-1exmuI.

"Mindfulness In The Corporate World: How Businesses Are Incorporating The Eastern Practice." *HuffingtonPost.com*. TheHuffingtonPost.com, Inc., 29 Aug. 2012. http://www.huffingtonpost.com/2012/08/29/mindfulness-businesses-corporate-employees-meditation_n_1840690.html.

"Milton Hershey." *Bio*. A&E Television Networks, 2015.

Mischel, W., Shoda, Y. & Rodriguez, M., L. (1989). Delay of gratification in children. *Science, 244* (4907), 933-937.

"Multitasking Doesn't Work." *Scribd.com*. AdibM, 11 Sept. 2010. Web. 23 Apr. 2015. http://www.scribd.com/doc/37255140/Multitasking-Doesn-t-Work#scribd.

Murphy, Jen. "It's Sam Adams Time." *The Wall Street Journal.com*. Dow Jones & Company, Inc., 25 Nov. 2005. http://www.wsj.com/articles/SB113269543287404437.

Nadler, Ruby T., Rahel Rabi, and John Paul Minda. "Better Mood and Better Performance: Learning Rule-Described Categories Is Enhanced by Positive Mood." *Psychological Science* 21.12 (2010): 1770–1776.

Neal, D., Wood, W., & Quinn, J. M. 2006. Habits: A repeat performance. *Current Directions in Psychological Science* 15: 198-202.

Neuhaus, Cable. "Jim Koch Brews Up An Old-Style Beer That Would Have Made His Great-Great-Granddad Proud." *People.com*. Time Inc., 18 Nov. 1985. http://www.people.com/people/archive/article/0,,20092207,00.html.

Niles, Frank. "How to Use Visualization to Achieve Your Goals." *HuffingtonPost.com*. TheHuffingtonPost.com, Inc., 17 June 2011. http://www.huffingtonpost.com/frank-niles-phd/visualization-goals_b_878424.html.

Nisen, Max. "16 People Who Worked Incredibly Hard to Succeed." *BusinessInsider.com*. Business Insider Inc., 5 Sept. 2012. http://www.businessinsider.com/16-people-who-worked-incredibly-hard-to-succeed-2012-9.

Nixon, Robin. "Brain Food: How to Eat Smart." *Livescience.com*. Purch, 7 Jan. 2009. http://www.livescience.com/3186-brain-food-eat-smart.html.

Novellino, Teresa. "99 Was the Magic Number for Entrepreneur Dave Gold." *BizJournals.com*. American City Business Journals, 29 Apr. 2013. http://upstart.bizjournals.com/entrepreneurs/hot-shots/2013/04/29/99-was-dave-golds-magic-number.html.

O'Connor, Clare. "The Mystery Monk Making Billions with 5-Hour Energy." *Forbes.com*. Forbes, 8 Feb. 2012. http://www.forbes.com/sites/clareoconnor/2012/02/08/manoj-bhargava-the-mystery-monk-making-billions-with-5-hour-energy/.

O'Connor, Clare. "Undercover Billionaire: Sara Blakely Joins The Rich List Thanks To Spanx." *Forbes.com*. Forbes, 7 Mar. 2012. http://www.forbes.com/sites/clareoconnor/2012/03/07/undercover-billionaire-sara-blakely-joins-the-rich-list-thanks-to-spanx/.

O'Connor, Clare. "Blue Jean Billionaire: Inside Diesel, Renzo Rosso's $3 Billion Fashion Empire." Editorial. *Forbes* 25 Mar. 2013: n. pag. *Forbes.com*. Forbes, 6 Mar. 2013. http://www.forbes.com/sites/clareoconnor/2013/03/06/blue-jean-billionaire-inside-diesel-renzo-rossos-3-billion-denim-empire/.

O'Donnell, Jayne. "Bass Pro CEO Morris Brings Passion for Fishing to Job." *ABCNews.com*. ABC News Internet Ventures, n.d. http://abcnews.go.com/Business/bass-pro-ceo-morris-brings-passion-fishing-job/story?id=8706964.

Ogunnaike, Lola. "From 'Idol' to Empire: The Success of Ryan Seacrest." *NYTimes.com*. The New York Times Company, 23 May 2006. http://www.nytimes.com/2006/05/23/arts/television/23seac.html?_r=0.

Onderko, Patty. "Meditation: Your Way." *Success.com*. Success Magazine, 18 June 2014. http://www.success.com/article/meditation-your-way.

One Potato Two Potato, prod. "Mangala Express." *Gordon's Great Escape*. Channel 4. New Delhi, 18 Jan. 2010.

Ong, Yudi. "Colonel Sanders and His Fried Chicken." *EntrepreneurInspiration.com*. Entrepreneur-Inspiration.

com, n.d. http://www.entrepreneur-inspiration.com/2011/01/07/colonel-sanders-and-his-fried-chicken/.

Ophir, Eyal, Clifford Nass, and Anthony D. Wagner. "Cognitive Control in Media Multitaskers." *Proceedings of the National Academy of Sciences of the United States of America* 106.37 (2009): 15583–15587. *PMC*.

Ostdick, John H. "Jim Koch Brews Passion into Sam Adams." *Success.com*. Success Magazine, 4 May 2010. http://www.success.com/article/jim-koch-brews-passion-into-sam-adams.

"Our Business Concept." *H&M.com*. H & M Hennes & Mauritz AB, n.d. http://about.hm.com/en/About/facts-about-hm/about-hm/business-concept.html.

"Our Founder." *Wrigley.com*. Wm. Wrigley Jr. Company, n.d. http://www.wrigley.com/global/about-us/ourfounder.aspx.

"Our Story." *VineyardVines.com*. Vineyard Vines, n.d. http://www.vineyardvines.com/good-life-timeline/good-life-timeline.html.

Overturf, Rich. *Thanks Ely!: How Ely Callaway and the Big Bertha Revolutionized Golf.* Victoria, B.C.: Trafford, 2006.

Owens, Shane G., Christine G. Bowman, and Charles A. Dill. "Overcoming Procrastination: The Effect of Implementation Intentions." *Journal of Applied Social Psychology* 38.2 (2008): 366-84.

Paiement, Rebecca. "Then and Now: True Religion Founder, Jeff Lubell." *Apparel Insiders.com*. Apparel Insiders LLC, n.d. http://www.apparelinsiders.com/2011/09/then-and-now-true-religion-founder-jeff-lubell/.

Paul, Annie M. "How To Use the 'Pygmalion' Effect." *Time.com*. Time, Inc., 1 Apr. 2013. http://ideas.time.com/2013/04/01/how-to-use-the-pygmalion-effect/.

Pergament, Danielle. "The Ringleader: M.A.C." *Allure.com*. Conde Nast, n.d. http://www.allure.com/beauty-trends/how-to/2013/the-history-of-mac-cosmetics?currentPage=1.

Platt, Larry. "Magic Johnson Builds an Empire." *The New York Times Magazine*. The New York Times Company, 10 Dec. 2000. http://partners.nytimes.com/library/magazine/home/20001210mag-magicjohnson.html?Src=longreads.

Pomerantz, Dorothy. "The Highest Paid Celebrities." *Forbes.com*. Forbes, 27 Aug. 2012. http://www.forbes.com/pictures/mfl45lhfj/ryan-seacrest-14/.

Posnanski, Joe. "Will Woods Break Nicklaus' Majors Record." *GolfChannel.com*. Golf Channel, 11 Apr. 2013. http://www.golfchannel.com/news/joe-posnanski/will-woods-break-nicklaus-majors-record/.

Pruitt, Sarah. "Celebrating the 75th Anniversary of 'Snow White and the Seven Dwarfs'." *History.com*. A&E Television Networks, LLC., 21 Dec. 2012. http://www.history.com/news/celebrating-the-75th-anniversary-of-snow-white-and-the-seven-dwarfs.

"Psychological warfare." *New World Encyclopedia*, 28 Oct 2013, 15:17 UTC. http://www.newworldencyclopedia.org/p/index.php?title=Psychological_warfare&oldid=975537.

Pychyl, Timothy A. "Procrastination: A Strategy for Change." *PsychologyToday.com*. Sussex Publishers, LLC, 15 Apr. 2008. https://www.psychologytoday.com/blog/dont-delay/200804/procrastination-strategy-change.

"Quality Assurance." *H&M.com*. H & M Hennes & Mauritz AB, n.d. http://sustainability.hm.com/en/sustainability/commitments/provide-fashion-for-conscious-customers/quality-and-safety/quality-assurance.html.

"Quentin Tarantino." *Bio*. A&E Television Networks, 2015.

Parker-Pope, Tara. "Socializing Appears to Delay Memory Problems." *NYTimes.com*. The New York Times Company, 4 June 2008. http://well.blogs.nytimes.com/2008/06/04/socializing-appears-to-delay-memory-problems/?_r=0.

Patel, Arti. "Brain Exercises: How to Stimulate Your Brain And Senses." *HuffingtonPost.com*. TheHuffingtonPost.com, Inc., 15 Oct. 2012. http://www.huffingtonpost.ca/2012/10/15/brain-exercises_n_1966861.html.

Patiky, Mark. "'Be Stupid,' Says Renzo Rosso, Founder and President of Iconic Global Fashion Brand, Diesel." *Forbes.com*. Forbes.com, LLC, 14 Mar. 2013. http://www.forbes.com/sites/businessaviation/2013/03/14/be-stupid-says-renzo-rosso-founder-and-president-of-iconic-global-fashion-brand-diesel/.

Platt, Larry. "Magic Johnson Builds an Empire." *The New York Times Magazine*. The New York Times Company, 10 Dec. 2000. http://partners.nytimes.com/library/magazine/home/20001210mag-magicjohnson.html?Src=longreads.

"QVC Network Inc. Company Profile, Information, Business Description, History, Background Information on QVC Network Inc." *Reference For Business.com*. Advameg Inc., n.d. http://www.referenceforbusiness.com/history2/2/QVC-Network-Inc.html.

Raymond, Chris. "A Peek into the Life of Tim Cook, the Most Private CEO Ever." *Success.com*. Success Magazine, n.d. http://www.success.com/article/a-peek-into-the-life-of-tim-cook-the-most-private-ceo-ever.

"Real Estate Portfolio Waikiki." *Trump.com*. The Trump Organization, n.d. http://www.trump.com/Real_Estate_Portfolio/Honolulu/Trump_Honolulu_Tower/Trump_Honolulu_Tower.asp.

Reilly, Lucas. "How Stephen King's Wife Saved 'Carrie' and Launched His Career." *MentalFloss.com*. Mental Floss Inc., 17 Oct. 2013. http://mentalfloss.com/article/53235/how-stephen-kings-wife-saved-carrie-and-launched-his-career.

Rensin, David. *The Mailroom: Hollywood History from the Bottom up*. New York: Ballantine, 2003.

Rhodes, Nelly. "Victoria's Secret." Contemporary Fashion. 2002. *Encyclopedia.com*. http://encyclopedia.com.

Richards, Jason. "What's Taking Dr. Dre So Long with His New Album?" *Theatlantic.com*. The Atlantic Monthly Group, 1 Sept. 2011. http://www.theatlantic.com/entertainment/archive/2011/09/whats-taking-dr-dre-so-long-with-his-new-album/244390/.

Ridgway, Suzanne. "Profiles of Success: Dave Gold and 99 Cents Stores." *WorkingWorld.com*. WorkingWorld.com, n.d. http://www.workingworld.com/articles/profiles-of-success-dave-gold-and-99-cents-stores.

Ritholtz, Barry. "Kenny G and the Playmate Stock-Pickers." *BloombergView.com*. Bloomberg L.P., 19 Sept. 2014. http://www.bloombergview.com/articles/2014-09-19/kenny-g-and-the-playmate-stock-pickers.

Rivlin, Gary. "When 3rd Place on the Rich List Just Isn't Enough." *NYTimes.com*. The New York Times Company, 17 Jan. 2008. http://www.nytimes.com/2008/01/17/business/17adelson.html?pagewanted=all&_r=0.

Rodriguez, Jayson. "Diplomats Say Working With Dr. Dre Was 'Humbling'." *MTV.com*. Viacom International, 21 Jan 2011. http://www.mtv.com/news/1656452/diplomats-say-working-with-dr-dre-was-humbling/.

Romero, Dennis. "Homelessness, Hair Care and 12,000 Bottles of Tequila." Editorial. *Entrepreneur* July 2009: n. pag. *Entrepreneur.com*. Entrepreneur Media, Inc., 10 June 2009. http://www.entrepreneur.com/article/202258.

Rosenthal, Robert, and Lenore Jacobson. "Pygmalion in the Classroom." *The Urban Review* 3.1 (1968): 16-20.

Ross, Emily, and Angus Holland. *100 Great Businesses and the Minds behind Them*. Naperville, IL: Source, 2006.

"Roy Raymond, 47; Began Victoria's Secret." *NYTimes.com*. The New York Times Company, 2 Sept. 1993. http://www.nytimes.com/1993/09/02/obituaries/roy-raymond-47-began-victoria-s-secret.html.

Rozhon, Tracie. "The Rap on Puffy's Empire." *NYTimes.com*. The New York Times Company, 24 July 2005. http://www.nytimes.com/2005/07/24/business/yourmoney/24puff.html?pagewanted=all&_r=1&.

"Russell Simmons." *Rush Communications*. Rush Communication LLC, n.d. http://www.rushcommunications.com/russell-simmons/.

Ryssdal, Kai. "Zappos CEO on Corporate Culture and 'Happiness'" *MarketPlace.org*. American Public Media, 19 Aug. 2010. http://www.marketplace.org/topics/business/corner-office/zappos-ceo-corporate-culture-and-happiness.

Sainz, Adrian. "How Priscilla Presley Turned Elvis' Graceland Into Big Business 30 Years Ago." *Billboard.com*. Billboard, 13 June 2012. http://www.billboard.com/biz/

articles/news/branding/1093632/how-priscilla-presley-turned-elvis-graceland-into-big-business-30.

Sandoval, Greg. "Blockbuster Laughed at Netflix Partnership Offer." *CNet.com*. CBS Interactive Inc., 9 Dec. 2010. http://www.cnet.com/news/blockbuster-laughed-at-netflix-partnership-offer/.

"Sara's Story." *Spanx.com*. Spanx Inc., n.d. https://www.spanx.com/-cms-spx_saras_story_20130613_150822.

Schawbel, Dan. "Four Career Lessons from Russell Simmons." *Bloomberg Business*. Bloomberg L.P., 1 Mar. 2011. http://www.bloomberg.com/bw/stories/2011-03-01/four-career-lessons-from-russell-simmonsbusinessweek-business-news-stock-market-and-financial-advice.

Schiro, Anne-Marie. "Frank Angelo, 49, Cosmetics Innovator, Dies." *NYTimes.com*. The New York Times Company, 17 Jan. 1997. http://www.nytimes.com/1997/01/17/us/frank-angelo-49-cosmetics-innovator-dies.html.

Schleier, Curt. "Sam Wyly, One Shrewd Billionaire." *Investor's Business Daily.com*. William O'Neil + Co. Incorporated and MarketSmith, Incorporated., 15 Dec. 2008. http://news.

investors.com/management-leaders-and-success/121508-452808-sam-wyly-one-shrewd-billionaire.htm.

Schultz, Howard, and Dori Jones. Yang. *Pour Your Heart into It: How Starbucks Built a Company One Cup at a Time.* New York, NY: Hyperion, 1997.

Segal, David. "Pillow Fights at the Four Seasons." *NYTimes.com.* The New York Times Company, 27 June 2009. http://www.nytimes.com/2009/06/28/business/global/28four.html?pagewanted=all&_r=0.

"Service & Retail." *Forbes.com.* Ed. Matthew Miller and Duncan Greenberg. Forbes.com, LLC, 2 Oct. 2009. http://www.forbes.com/forbes/2009/1019/forbes-400-rich-list-09-mars-toyota-service-and-retail.html.

Sessions, David. "Hobby Lobby Risks Fines to Defy Obamacare." *TheDailyBeast.com.* The Daily Beast Company LLC, 4 Jan. 2013. http://www.thedailybeast.com/articles/2013/01/04/hobby-lobby-risks-fines-to-defy-obamacare.html.

Shah, Dhiram. "The Trump International Hotel & Tower Waikiki Beach Walk Sold Out In A Single Day!" *LuxuryLaunches.com.* LuxuryLaunches.com, 17 Nov. 2006. http://luxurylaunches.com/real_estate/the_trump_international_hotel_tower_waikiki_beach_walk_sold_out_in_a_single_day.php.

Shankman, Peter. "Peter Shankman Tweet Joke Leads To Morton's Surprise Steak Dinner At Newark Airport (TWEETS)." *HuffingtonPost.com*. TheHuffingtonPost.com Inc., 18 Aug. 2011. http://www.huffingtonpost.com/2011/08/18/peter-shankman-mortons-steak-tweet_n_930744.html.

Sharp, Isadore. *Four Seasons: The Story of a Business Philosophy*. New York, NY: Portfolio, 2009.

Shelburne, Ramona. "Jerry Buss: A True Sports Visionary." *ESPN.com*. ESPN, 19 Feb. 2013. http://espn.go.com/los-angeles/nba/story/_/id/8959319/los-angeles-lakers-owner-jerry-buss-had-vision-unlike-other.

Sheppard, Patricia. "Happy 85th Anniversary, Oswald the Lucky Rabbit!" *TheWaltDisneyCompany.com*. The Walt Disney Company, 5 Sept. 2012. https://thewaltdisneycompany.com/blog/happy-85th-anniversary-oswald-lucky-rabbit.

Shin, Laura. "How Yoga and Meditation at Work Are Boosting the Corporate Bottom Line." *Learnvest.com*. Learnvest, 14 Sept. 2012. http://www.learnvest.com/

knowledge-center/how-yoga-and-meditation-at-work-are-boosting-the-corporate-bottom-line/.

Siegel, Joseph. "Using An Imaginary Basketball and Visualization to Succeed in Basketball." *About.com*. About.com, n.d. http://basketball.about.com/od/playingbasketball/ss/basketball-practice-and-visualization-techniques_3.htm.

Siegler, MG. "Snoozing And Losing: A Blockbuster Failure." *TechCrunch.com*. AOL Inc., 6 Apr. 2011. http://techcrunch.com/2011/04/06/make-it-a-blockbuster-night/.

Silverman, Amber. "On Call: Four Seasons' Founder Isadore Sharp Shares Business Philosophy." *LuxuryTravelAdvisor.com*. Questex Media Group, LLC., 3 May 2009. http://www.luxurytraveladvisor.com/supplier-profiles/on-call-four-seasons-founder-isadore-sharp-shares-business-philosophy-699.

Simmons, Russell. *Do You!: 12 Laws to Access the Power in You to Achieve Happiness and Success*. New York: Gotham, 2007.

Simmons, Russell, and Chris Morrow. *Super Rich: A Guide to Having It All*. New York: Gotham, 2011.

"Simon Cowell Net Worth." *Celebritynetworth.com*. Celebrity Net Worth, n.d. http://www.celebritynetworth.com/richest-celebrities/actors/simon-cowell-net-worth/.

Singular, Stephen. *Power to Burn: Michael Ovitz and the New Business of Show Business*. Secaucus, NY: Carol Pub. Group, 1996.

Slater, Robert. *Ovitz: The inside Story of Hollywood's Most Controversial Power Broker*. New York: McGraw Hill, 1997.

"Sleep and Mood." *Harvard.edu*. Harvard Medical School, 15 Dec. 2008. http://healthysleep.med.harvard.edu/need-sleep/whats-in-it-for-you/mood.

Smith, Jacquelyn. "How to Create a Stress-Free Work Environment." *Forbes.com*. Forbes.com, LLC, 18 Nov. 2013. http://www.forbes.com/sites/jacquelynsmith/2013/11/18/how-to-create-a-stress-free-workplace-environment/.

Sollisch, Jim. "Multitasking Makes Us a Little Dumber." *ChicagoTribune.com*. Chicago Tribune, 10 Aug. 2010. http://articles.chicagotribune.com/2010-08-10/opinion/ct-oped-0811-multitask-20100810_1_iqs-study-information-overload.

"Spanx Founder Sara Blakely Dared to Ask, 'Why Not?'" Interview. *Inc.* Mansueto Ventures, n.d. http://www.inc.com/sara-blakely/how-sara-blakley-started-spanx.html.

Stansberry, Glen. "13 Brilliant and Outlandish Marketing Stunts Used by Richard Branson." *American Express.com*. American Express Company, n.d. https://www.americanexpress.com/us/small-business/openforum/articles/14-brilliant-outlandish-stunts-richard-branson-used-market-virgin/.

Stansberry, Glen. "10 Examples of Shockingly Excellent Customer Service." *AmericanExpress.com*. American Express Company, 4 May 2010. https://www.americanexpress.com/us/small-business/openforum/articles/10-examples-of-shockingly-excellent-customer-service-1/.

Stewart, James B. *Disney War*. New York: Simon & Schuster, 2005.

Sullivan, John Jeremiah. "Venus and Serena Against the World." *NYTimes.com*. The New York Times Company, 23 Aug. 2012. http://www.nytimes.com/2012/08/26/magazine/venus-and-serena-against-the-world.html?_r=0.

"S&P Destination Properties: Canadian Real Estate Marketer Sells Over $700 Million US in Record One

Day Condo Sales Launch of Trump Tower Waikiki." *MarketWired.com*. Marketwired L.P., 10 Nov. 2006. http://www.marketwired.com/press-release/s-p-destination-properties-canadian-real-estate-marketer-sells-over-700-million-us-record-621333.htm.

Tabaka, Marla. "Visualize Your Way to Success (Really!)." *Inc.com*. Inc.com, 4 Oct. 2012. http://www.inc.com/marla-tabaka/visualization-can-help-you-succeed.html.

Taber, Linley. "How Juicy Couture's Founders Built a Fashion Empire with $200." *NYpost.com*. NYP Holdings, 25 May 2014. http://nypost.com/2014/05/25/how-the-founders-of-juicy-couture-created-a-fashion-empire-with-just-200/.

Taraborrelli, J. Randy. *The Secret Life of Marilyn Monroe*. New York: Grand Central, 2010.

"The Brothers Behind Vineyard Vines Talk Ties." *BostonCommon-Magazine.com*. Boston Common Magazine, n.d. http://bostoncommon-magazine.com/personalities/articles/the-brothers-behind-vineyard-vines-talk-ties?page=1.

"The History of the Leaning Tower of Pisa." *Leaningtowerofpisa.net*. Leaningtowerofpisa.net, 2010.

http://www.leaningtowerofpisa.net/history-tower-of-pisa.html.

"The Human Brain-Exercise." *Franklin Institute.com*. The Franklin Institute Online, n.d. http://learn.fi.edu/learn/brain/exercise.html.

"The Making of FUBU: An Interview with Daymond John." Interview by Tim Ferriss. *DaymondJohn.com*. Daymond John, n.d. http://daymondjohn.com/news/tim-ferriss-interviews-daymond-john/.

"The Story of Wrigley." *Wrigley.com*. Wm. Wrigley Jr. Company, n.d. http://www.wrigley.com/global/about-us/the-story-of-wrigley.aspx.

"Todd Graves: Founder 'Raising Cane's' Franchise." *Thefundraisingjournal.com*. The Fundraising Journal, Nov. 2009. http://thefundraisingjournal.com/Archive/0911/Individual_Spotlight_Todd_Graves_Raising_Canes.html.

"Tony Hawk Carves a New Niche." Editorial. *Entrepreneur* Oct. 20009: n. pag. *Entrepreneur.com*. Entrepreneur Media Inc., 16 Sept. 2009. http://www.entrepreneur.com/article/203408.

Torekull, Bertil, and Ingvar Kamprad. *Leading by Design: The IKEA Story*. New York: HarperBusiness, 1999.

Tozzi, John. "Gary Vaynerchuk's Startup Advice." *Businessweek.com*. Bloomerg L.P., 18 Sept. 2009. http://www.businessweek.com/smallbiz/content/sep2009/sb20090918_719216.htm.

Trump, Donald, and Tony Schwartz. *Trump: The Art of the Deal*. New York: Random House, 1988.

"Trump International Hotel & Tower Waikiki Beach Walk™ Sells over $700M in One Day Record." *Businesswire.com*. Business Wire, 10 Nov. 2006. http://www.businesswire.com/news/home/20061110005575/en/Trump-International-Hotel-Tower-Waikiki-Beach-Walk#.VVKcD1eKWuI.

Vanderkam, Laura. "Why Visualizing Success Isn't As Farfetched As It Sounds." *FastCompany.com*. Mansueto Ventures, LLC. http://www.fastcompany.com/3040487/why-visualizing-success-its-as-far-fetched-as-it.

Van Edwards, Vanessa. "10 Ways Color Affects Your Mood." *HuffingtonPost.com*. TheHuffingtonPost.com, Inc., 19 Nov. 2012. http://www.huffingtonpost.com/vanessa-van-edwards/color-and-mood_b_2088728.html.

Vinnedge, Mary. "From the Corner Office: David Green of Hobby Lobby." *Success.com*. Success Magazine, 1

Sept. 2010. http://www.success.com/article/from-the-corner-office-david-green-of-hobby-lobby.

"Waking Up on the Wrong Side of the Desk: The Effect of Mood on Work Performance." *Knowledge@Wharton*. The Wharton School, University of Pennsylvania, 26 July, 2006. http://knowledge.wharton.upenn.edu/article/waking-up-on-the-wrong-side-of-the-desk-the-effect-of-mood-on-work-performance/.

Walton, Sam, and John Huey. *Sam Walton, Made in America: My Story*. New York: Doubleday, 1992.

Warner, Brian. "How Cirque Du Soleil Founder Guy Laliberte Went From Homeless Street Performer To Multi Billionaire." *Celebritynetworth.com*. Celebrity Net Worth, 4 Mar. 2013. http://www.celebritynetworth.com/articles/entertainment-articles/how-cirque-du-soleil-founder-guy-laliberte-went-from-homeless-street-performer-to-multi-billionaire/.

Webley, Kayla. "Roy Raymond." *Time.com*. Time, Inc., 2 Apr. 2012. http://content.time.com/time/specials/packages/article/0,28804,2110513_2110512_2110720,00.html.

Weinstein, Bob. "From Beer to Eternity." *Entrepreneur.com*. Entrepreneur Media, Inc., 31 Jan. 1997. http://www.entrepreneur.com/article/13724.

Welch, Liz. "The Way I Work: John Paul DeJoria, John Paul Mitchell Systems." Editorial. *Inc. Magazine* June 2013: n. pag. *Inc.com*. Inc. Magazine. http://www.inc.com/magazine/201306/liz-welch/the-way-i-work-john-paul-dejoria-john-paul-mitchell-systems.html.

"Whole Foods Market History." *Wholefoodsmarket.com*. Whole Foods Market IP. L.P., n.d. http://www.wholefoodsmarket.com/company-info/whole-foods-market-history.

Whitbourne, Susan K. "5 Steps to Breaking Bad Habits." *PsychologyToday.com*. Sussex Publishers, LLC, 23 Aug. 2011. https://www.psychologytoday.com/blog/fulfillment-any-age/201108/5-steps-breaking-bad-habits.

"William Wrigley, Jr." Encyclopedia of World Biography. 2004. *Encyclopedia.com*. http://www.encyclopedia.com.

"William Wrigley, Jr." *Encyclopædia Britannica. Encyclopædia Britannica Online.* Encyclopædia Britannica Inc., 2015. http://www.britannica.com/EBchecked/topic/649624/William-Wrigley-Jr.

Williams, Pat, and Jim Denney. *21 Great Leaders: Learn Their Lessons, Improve Your Influence*. Uhrichsville, OH: Shiloh Run, an Imprint of Barbour, 2015.

Winfrey, Graham. "Search Newsletters Follow Subscribe ICONS OF ENTREPRENEURSHIP How Daymond John of 'Shark Tank' Earned His Fins." *Inc.com*. Inc.com, n.d. http://www.inc.com/graham-winfrey/how-daymond-john-earned-his-fins.html.

Wood, W., Quinn, J., & Kashy, D. (2002). Habits in everyday life: Thought, emotion, and action. Journal of Personality and Social Psychology, 83, 1281-1297.

Woods, Tiger. "Tiger Woods: Health and Fitness." Web log post. *TigerWoods.com*. Tiger Woods, n.d.

Woody, Allen. "Red Bull GmbH Success Story." *SuccessStory.com*. Success Story, n.d. http://successstory.com/companies/red-bull.

Wrathall, Claire. "Room for Expansion; Four Seasons' Grand Plans." *Telegraph.co.uk*. The Telegraph Media Group Limited, 12 Dec. 2014. http://www.telegraph.co.uk/luxury/travel/54860/four-season-hotels-grand-plans-for-expansion.html.

Wu, Annie. "Zhu Yuangzhang: First Emperor of the Ming Dynasty." *China Highlights.com*. CITS Guilin. http://www.chinahighlights.com/travelguide/china-history/zhu-yuanzhang.htm.

Wyly, Sam. *1,000 Dollars and an Idea: Entrepreneur to Billionaire*. New York: Newmarket, 2009.

"Zappos' 10-Hour Long Customer Service Call Sets Record." *HuffingtonPost.com*. TheHuffingtonPost.com, Inc., 21 Dec. 2012. http://www.huffingtonpost.com/2012/12/21/zappos-10-hour-call_n_2345467.html.

Zara, Christopher. *Tortured Artists: From Picasso and Monroe to Warhol and Winehouse, the Twisted Secrets of the World's Most Creative Minds*. Avon: Adams Media, 2012.

Zeleznock, Tom. "7 Entrepreneurs Whose Perseverance Will Inspire You." *Growthink.com*. Growthink Inc., 29 Feb. 2008. http://www.growthink.com/content/7-entrepreneurs-whose-perseverance-will-inspire-you.

Zetlin, Minda. "Listening to Complainers Is Bad for Your Brain." *Inc.com*. Inc.com, 20 Aug. 2012. http://www.inc.com/minda-zetlin/listening-to-complainers-is-bad-for-your-brain.html.

CPSIA information can be obtained
at www.ICGtesting.com
Printed in the USA
LVOW13s1328130117
520887LV00019B/465/P